Room at the Table

Room at the Table

Gluten-Free Recipes, Stories, and
Tips to Share with the People You Love

Lisa Samuel

PHOTOGRAPHY BY MATTHEW LAND

FOR ELIE AND THEO.
This book is my love letter to you.

contents

introduction

I live in the very northwest corner of Washington State, just a short drive from the Canadian border. A gorgeous area of the world, we have sweeping views of the Salish Sea and the San Juan Islands to the west and the snow-capped mountains of the North Cascades to the east. I have found home here, between the mountains and the sea, with my husband, Elie, our son, Theo, and our extended community of family and friends.

As someone who has moved a lot—over twenty-five times and across seven states—I spent much of my young life yearning for community, connection, and meaning. I successfully worked various professional jobs that should have been fulfilling, but instead left me restless and unsatisfied. But I've always found solace in the meditative space of the kitchen—the peeling and slicing, stirring and tasting. It suits me, satisfying the two sides of my brain pulling equally in opposite directions, one for productivity and one for rest. And feeding the people I care about feels gratifying.

When I was growing up, the kitchen was a place of joy and connection. I mostly just watched and asked questions, doing more observing than helping. But I was always a welcome guest, and I tucked the smell and taste of those memories away.

In my Granny's kitchen, I never tired of her stories of young motherhood. She approached living in a farmhouse with three little girls and no running water with the practical spirit born of necessity. She hauled water from the spring to do the dishes and fill the washtub for laundry. With ingenuity, she gathered eggs from the farmyard chickens and used a tin can set in the middle of a cast-iron skillet for a makeshift angel food cake. And she could make a meal stretch to accommodate any friends dropping by for a visit, just adding another cup of water to the chili and spreading the tuna fish sandwiches a little thinner. From Granny, I learned to make the sausage gravy my Pappy savored and how to make Thanksgiving dressing with "lots of celery and sage," always pressed flat for crispy edges. I absorbed Granny's stories and recipes, and I learned food was love.

I also learned food was connection. My parents loved to throw dinner parties, and they would cook for days leading up to the night of the gathering. My mom spent hours twisting homemade rolls into perfect crescents and rhythmically crimping the crust on a trio of pies, while my dad would babysit the roasting lamb—one raised on our farm—basting it until just medium-rare. On the day of, I eagerly set the long mahogany table, placing their wedding silver atop the linen napkin set beside each heirloom china plate. My mom would gather flowers from the garden and weave them into natural arrangements. Candles glowed. Music played. Glasses clinked amongst the buzz of voices and laughter from friends gathered around the table. It felt magical.

Over the years, I slowly started to create a career rooted in the idea of food as a vehicle for both nourishment and connection. I found meaning in growing a business of teaching cooking classes, hosting dinners, and creating beautiful events to offer opportunities for building meaningful relationships and learning. This cookbook is a part of that dream: a desire to share my kitchen with you.

My cooking style now is highly influenced by the diverse heritage in our family and our travels. I grew up in Kentucky, and I still love those classic country dishes of my childhood. My husband, Elie, grew up in Canada, but his mother was born in Jerusalem. When we visit Israel, I am always so inspired by the ingredients, flavors, and traditions, and those foods have become an integral part of my food story. We value travel in our family, and my experiments in the kitchen are often inspired by the food we've eaten on the road.

A few years ago, I adopted a gluten-free lifestyle, which I explain in My Food Story on page 13. Because I didn't want to deprive myself of any of my favorite foods, I started experimenting with gluten-free cooking and baking, earning accolades from family and friends. Developing these recipes—from fried chicken to falafel and biscuits to browned butter cornbread—inspired me to write this cookbook. My goal is to help you make nourishing, delicious meals—that also happen to be gluten-free—for your family and friends.

These days, my kitchen is often a bustling hub of activity. Most weekend mornings, you will find friends in our kitchen and Elie busy making cappuccinos and chatting about his latest coffee roast. Our son, Theo, pulls his stool up to the counter to help me with breakfast, stirring batter for pancakes or carefully slicing peppers for a savory shakshuka. The joyful din of our kitchen on these mornings fills my heart.

Room at the Table is a diary of this kitchen, where I developed my own style and rhythm for gathering friends around the table.

Where I learned how to cook for my son, and how to enjoy bringing him into the kitchen with me. I share the recipes I make for Elie, the ones we enjoy together after Theo is asleep and the house is once again quiet. It also features the favorite meals I make for friends, from a casual weekend brunch to our annual Christmas dinner.

I have learned a rhythm and serenity in the kitchen that comes partly from the confidence of age and partly from earning my 10,000 hours of experience. The recipes and tips in this book are a compilation of the recipes and collected wisdom I've gained over the years. This book is my gift to you, my dear friends, in hopes that I help you find your own ease in the kitchen.

First, almost every recipe includes time-saving or planning tips. For example, I let you know which parts of the recipe can be done ahead of time , how to substitute hard-to-find ingredients, or how to simplify the recipe. Second, I give you ideas on how to make the recipes your own and tailor them to your likes or the needs of your family—for example, ingredient substitutions and plant-based variations.

My hope for *Room at the Table* is that this cookbook will sit on your kitchen counter and become dog-eared and stained with olive oil. I hope it's the book you turn to for the everyday meals you feed your family, and for special recipes you'll make for celebrations. I hope this book inspires you to approach cooking and gathering with joy—to help you offer yourself grace when seating your loved ones around the table. To know that people will remember not what you cook, but how you make them feel. (Although, if they text you to ask for your cauliflower hummus recipe, that's great, too.)

my food story

Brené Brown, a renowned academic expert on vulnerability, says, "Staying vulnerable is a risk we have to take if we want to experience connection." My wish for this book is that it provides both recipes and inspiration—a way to connect through our collective food histories and experiences.

I have been a registered dietitian nutritionist for more than ten years, but I have studied food and nutrition for over 25 years, beginning in college. In that time, I have seen nutrition trends come and go, many of which seemed backed by "good" scientific research at the time. I used to buy into it all—the fads, the diets, the latest nutrition advice I studied in school or from continuing education. But not anymore. The only diet I advocate is one that is plant-rich and mostly based on whole, real foods. But I also believe in eating what you love—what fuels your body and your soul. I believe in developing a nourishing, loving relationship with food. I believe in eating intuitively, honoring my body and its desires. It took me a long time to get here.

When I was eight, for Christmas I received a red leather-bound diary. The first entry, written in my childish print, declared a New Year's resolution to lose weight. My heart aches for that young girl and the messages she must have absorbed so early in life. As I got older, I was fueled by a general disdain for my own body that left me with an obsessive-compulsive desire to be thin—to be "perfect" in my eating and exercise habits, a condition now called orthorexia. I went through phases when I would go to the gym twice a day, morning and night, or do back-to-back step aerobics and kickboxing classes, or feel extreme panic if I didn't get in a run. I compulsively weighed my food, checked nutrition facts, and had a long list of requests at restaurants. Fat was the enemy first, and then, years later, carbs, and then animal products. Stashed away in a box, I still have years' worth of eating and exercise logs where I meticulously wrote down everything I ate and how much I moved each day. I felt shame if my food wasn't "perfect" and often, I just wouldn't eat.

My disordered eating and compulsive exercise took a toll on my health. I stopped having periods. The severe restriction of fat in my diet caused the skin on my hands to crack and bleed. My hair and nails were dry and brittle. I was so tired, all the time. This obsession consumed a lot of my life, affected relationships, and lasted the better part of 30 years.

I realize now that a lot of that quest for perfection came from a general unhappiness with myself, a sense that I wasn't quite good enough just the way I was. I needed to be perfect to feel valued. After going through a traumatic divorce at age 36, I slowly started to change. Issues around food are rarely just about the food—they're a way to have total control over one piece of life. In the time leading up to and after my divorce, I did a lot of inner work to start seeing my own value. I began practicing yoga and meditating, developing a practice around self-compassion. I studied intuitive eating, putting those principles into practice. I grew into myself, so to speak. And I learned to let go—for the most part—of perfection.

For the first time in my life, I was truly happy. My husband, Elie, has a lot to do with my transformation. Knowing he loves me exactly the way I am has helped. Love heals. I created meaningful work I loved. Instead of exercising as a form of purging, I started choosing movement that brought me joy. I learned to eat intuitively, recognizing and listening to hunger and fullness cues, which I had never learned to pay attention to before. The truth is, I had learned how to suppress and ignore them so I wouldn't want to eat. And now, I eat when I'm hungry. I stop when I've had enough. I appreciate my body for all the incredible things it allows me to do.

After Elie, Theo has been my last catalyst for change. In our home, we model a loving relationship with food and our bodies. For Theo, no foods are off-limits. Foods don't have a moral value—they are not good or bad. In our home, all body shapes and sizes are good. Boys are not immune to disordered eating and body dysmorphia, and I want the cycle to stop with me.

Since I accept all foods in my life, you might be wondering: *Why are the recipes in this book gluten-free?*

My journey of healing my relationship with food is complicated by my food sensitivities and intolerances. From the time I was very young, I would get terrible tummy aches when I ate certain foods. For most of my life, I just thought it was normal for food to make you feel sick. I was 35 years old when I attended a seminar on small intestinal bacterial overgrowth (SIBO) in children, and a lightbulb went off. SIBO is a condition in which bacteria migrate from the large intestine to the small intestine (where they are not supposed to live) and feed off certain types of carbohydrates. The gasses produced by the bacteria cause pain, bloating, and other side effects. I got tested, and my SIBO was off the charts. Suddenly, all my pain made sense.

From there, I worked with a series of functional health practitioners to treat the SIBO and determine its cause. I found I had significant heavy metals poisoning which could have caused the SIBO in the first place. I also have a thyroid disorder. Those three conditions all aggravate one another. Since my first diagnosis several years ago, I have done several rounds of treatment for both the heavy metals and the SIBO, and I manage my thyroid with a natural hormone. While I am not totally "healed" yet, my symptoms are significantly better.

I say that the SIBO diagnosis complicates my relationship with food, because—right when I had reintroduced all foods into my diet and was developing a loving relationship with food—I suddenly had to cut out foods again. Part of the SIBO treatment is following a SIBO-specific diet, which can be quite restrictive, and I could feel old obsessions begin to re-emerge. I've had to be very intentional in letting go of restrictions that don't serve me.

Becoming gluten-free is one permanent dietary change stemming from the SIBO diagnosis. For someone who will probably always struggle with maintaining a healthy gut, a gluten-free lifestyle is recommended. After trying a few times to add gluten back in (with painful results), I've fully embraced being gluten-free. Even better, over the last few years, I've learned to make all my favorite recipes gluten-free—the recipes I'm now sharing with you.

The irony in this whole story is how much I have always loved food, how much I have always loved to cook. If you read the Introduction, you'll know the kitchen has always been my solace. Feeding people has always been my joy. I feel so grateful to have come out on the other side of this food story with so much love and grace—and recipes.

There are many specialists who treat disordered eating and body dysmorphia, and if any part of my story sounds familiar to you, I urge you to seek help.

building a pantry

After Theo was born, I tried to become someone who "meal planned," batch cooking to keep our refrigerator and freezer stocked with prepared or cooked foods I could mix and match into easy meals. But for me, it sucked all the joy out of cooking. However, I have learned that by being smart about how I stock my refrigerator, freezer, and pantry, I have options. On days when I can't run to the grocery store, I can create a simple pantry meal with what's on hand. When I have more time, I can supplement my usual larder with fresh or special ingredients. These are the ingredients I keep on hand.

oils and butter

Extra virgin olive oil I buy olive oil in bulk, because it is my everyday oil. I love having a variety of oils for different purposes, including a good-quality but relatively inexpensive organic olive oil for sautéing vegetables, frying eggs, using in baked goods, and for other everyday cooking. For finishing salads, drizzling over vegetables, or serving with bread, I love grassy or spicy artisanal olive oils. I always have a variety to choose from. If you want to know more about olive oil production and how to choose a good oil, the book *Extra Virginity* by Tom Mueller is a great resource.

Avocado oil Any time I need an oil that can withstand higher heat or I want a neutral flavor, I use avocado oil.

Grass-fed butter Cows that are exclusively grass fed are healthier and produce milk (and therefore butter) that is higher in healthy fats. It has a rich, sweeter flavor.

Grass-fed ghee Ghee is clarified unsalted butter with a slightly nutty, caramel flavor. It has a high smoke point, so it is perfect for high-heat cooking. I use it for making pancakes and waffles and for searing meats.

Virgin unrefined coconut oil When I'm making a plant-based recipe, especially baked goods, I often turn to coconut oil.

MCT oil A flavorless oil made from coconuts, MCT oil is rich in medium-chain triglycerides, a form of easily digestible fat. I use MCT oil to thin nut butters.

Avocado oil mayonnaise Most purchased mayonnaise is made from canola oil or other refined oils. Look for one made from avocado oil or extra virgin olive oil (which can be hard to find).

eggs and dairy products

Eggs We're very lucky to have a farmer in our neighborhood who supplies us with beautiful, delicious eggs from happy chickens. If you can, buy eggs from a local farmer or from a farmers' market. Vital Farms eggs are also widely available at most grocery stores across the country.

Almond milk I make a batch of almond milk every four or five days (see page 260 for the recipe). That's what I use for my morning latte and for eating with granola.

Grass-fed whole milk Just as with butter, milk from grass-fed cows is higher in omega-3 fatty acids and other beneficial nutrients. I always cook with and drink whole milk.

Greek yogurt All of my recipes were tested using Straus Organic Whole Plain Greek Yogurt, and it is the brand I prefer. I never buy low-fat dairy products. Studies show full-fat organic and grass-fed dairy products are better for your cardiovascular health. They also taste better.

Cheese I always have a large variety of cheeses stored in my refrigerator—a mix of goat, sheep, and cow's milk cheeses. These are the ones I reach for most often: organic sheep's milk feta, Drunken Goat (semi-firm), Humboldt Fog (soft-ripened goat with a bloomy rind), sharp cheddar (like Beecher's Handmade), Parmigiano-Reggiano, and būf creamery buffalo mozzarella.

acids and condiments

Lemons Most of the time, I grab a lemon to add acid or flavor to my cooking. Whenever I use the juice I also add the zest, so I get all the flavor from those aromatic oils. I joke that I often have a refrigerator drawer full of naked lemons.

Vinegars Raw apple cider vinegar, white wine vinegar, sherry vinegar, and very good balsamic vinegar add flavor to salad dressings and marinades.

Dijon mustard I love a good, spicy Dijon mustard for sandwiches, to add to salad dressings, or use as an ingredient, like in deviled eggs. My favorite brand is Edmond Fallot, which can be found at some specialty stores and online.

Mama Lil's Peppers These peppers are great for when you want to add a spicy, vinegary kick, like in the Pimiento Cheese on page 81.

Olives Theo loves to snack on Castelvetrano olives, and their mild, buttery flavor is widely appealing. It's the type of olive I most use in recipes. I usually also have containers of kalamata olives and oil-cured olives, which have a more intense, bitter flavor.

Jams and marmalades These spreads are great for more than just toast. Add jam to salad dressings, use in place of maple syrup on pancakes, or spread to make a sweet and savory egg sandwich.

Other condiments There are other condiments I keep on hand but don't necessarily call for in the recipes in this book—tamari, coconut aminos, ketchup (Primal Kitchen brand), tamarind paste, capers, kosher dill pickles, other pickled peppers.

salt, spices, and herbs

Sea salt I cook exclusively with sea salt. One, it tastes better to me. Two, sea salt has trace minerals like magnesium that are important for electrolyte balance in the body. Sea salt is widely available at almost all grocery stores and can be purchased in bulk to make it more affordable.

Flaky salt For finishing dishes, I use coarse or flaky salt. Depending on the dish, I'll use Maldon salt, with its crunchy pyramid flakes, or one of the lovely artisanal salts from Jacobsen Salt Co. or San Juan Island Sea Salt, harvested in the United States.

Aleppo-style pepper Aleppo pepper was originally named for the city of Aleppo in Syria. Since the civil war in that country, most of the chiles are sourced from Turkey or other nearby countries, so you'll often see the spice labeled as Aleppo-*style* pepper. I use Aleppo-style pepper for adding a subtly fruity, mild heat to almost every recipe. If you can't find Aleppo-style pepper, substitute red pepper flakes, which will be a little spicier.

Peppercorns I use freshly ground black peppercorns when I want a more pronounced, sharp heat. Different varieties of peppercorns have different flavor profiles, and I often keep a few on hand, like purple peppercorns from Vietnam or Zanzibar black peppercorns. If you love Sichuan peppercorns, try Wild Timur pepper. See the Resource section for sources.

Urfa pepper To add a deep smoky and sweet flavor to braised meats or tomato sauces, I reach for the Urfa pepper, a burgundy-colored chile from Turkey.

Sumac This spice is a beautiful deep red, and is made from ground dried berries of the sumac plant (not the same as poison sumac!). I use sumac to top hummus and tahini, on salads, and anywhere I want a tart, citrusy punch.

Za'atar This spice blend is generally a mix of wild thyme or hyssop, sesame seeds, and sumac. But different blends may include other spices. I always have several jars of za'atar on hand, because different blends have unique flavors.

Saffron A few threads of saffron can add a musky, floral flavor to paella, soups, stews, risotto, and sauces.

Vanilla beans The sweet, rich flavor and aroma of fresh vanilla beans perfumes baked goods and fresh whipped cream differently from vanilla extract. Because vanilla beans are expensive, I save them for special occasions. Buy only what you need for a recipe, because vanilla beans can dry out quickly. After I use the seeds, I drop the vanilla pod into a jar of sugar to infuse the sugar with vanilla.

Other whole spices My spice drawer always contains whole cardamom seeds, cumin seeds, coriander seeds, and fennel seeds. I buy these as whole spices and then toast and grind them myself in small batches. It only takes a minute or two, and the flavor difference is noticeable.

Ground spices For ground spices, I stock allspice, cinnamon, clove, ginger, sweet paprika, and smoked paprika.

Herbs Every week, I purchase parsley and cilantro, which I use frequently. Other herbs, I pick from the garden or buy as I need them.

fruits and vegetables

Onions, shallots, and garlic I keep these stored in a basket in the pantry. If an onion is large, I might only use half for a recipe, then freeze the other half to use to make stock.

Potatoes and sweet potatoes I store potatoes separately from onions, since the gasses given off by onions will cause the potatoes to sprout.

Avocados I buy avocados in bulk, because we go through so many of them. Once they are ripe, I store them in the refrigerator.

Other fruits and vegetables As much as possible, I try to buy fruits and vegetables in season. However, there are some vegetables I purchase year-round, including carrots, celery, kale, and grape tomatoes. If I have those on hand, I can make a meal.

sweeteners and sweets

Honey and maple syrup My preferred sweeteners are local honey and maple syrup, and you'll find that I use those in most recipes. Honey provides a floral note to recipes, and is a little sweeter than maple syrup.

Coconut sugar With a molasses-like flavor, coconut sugar is delicious in baked goods. It's less refined than granulated sugar and raises blood sugar levels more slowly.

Dark brown sugar When baking cookies, adding brown sugar often keeps the cookies moist and chewy. It also has a lovely, rich flavor.

Blackstrap molasses This sweetener has a deep, almost bitter flavor and is delicious in both sweet and savory applications. Blackstrap molasses has trace amounts of calcium and iron.

Pomegranate molasses When I want to add a bright, tangy sweetness to salad dressings or marinades, I reach for pomegranate molasses. The thick, tart syrup also works well as a finishing drizzle over roasted vegetables and meat.

Dark chocolate We have a "chocolate bin" in the pantry stocked with a variety of chocolates for cooking and snacking. For baking, I keep chocolates ranging from 60% to 85% cacao. Guittard and Valrhona are great brands, and most grocery stores will carry at least one of them. For snacking, François Pralus and Chocolat Bonnat are two of my favorite brands.

nuts, seeds, and dried fruit

Nuts and seeds In the pantry, I keep raw almonds, cashews, chia seeds, flaxseed, hazelnuts, hemp seeds. peanuts, pecans, pine nuts, pumpkin seeds, sesame seeds (white and black), sunflower seeds, and walnuts.

Once they are roasted or toasted, I store them in the refrigerator or freezer. Nuts and seeds are so versatile—for snacking, adding crunch to salads or vegetable dishes, adding to granola, grinding into nut butters, and more.

Nigella seeds Sometimes called black cumin seeds, nigella seeds might be a spice you haven't heard of. Find them in South Asian groceries, as they are common in those cuisines. They can often be found in the supplement section of your local grocery store next to the maca and other so-called superfoods. They have medicinal benefits and are thought to help with chronic inflammation. But they are also delicious. They have a bitter flavor, somewhat like cumin. I love them in breads and on salads and as a topping for soup.

Nut butters In general, I make my own nut butters. But we go through so much peanut butter in our house, I keep three or four jars of Santa Cruz Dark Roasted Crunchy Peanut Butter in the pantry.

Tahini As you'll see in this book, I use a lot of tahini in my cooking. All tahinis are not created equal. In fact, most grocery store brands taste bitter and sometimes even rancid. If you can, seek out a tahini made from raw (unroasted) sesame seeds. My favorite brand is Al Arz, the whole sesame version. See the Resources section for ordering information.

Dried fruit I always have dried apricots, currants, dates, and raisins in my pantry, to add to granola or oatmeal, to bring sweetness to a salad, and for charcuterie and snack boards.

canned goods

Canned tomatoes and tomato paste The better-quality tomatoes are canned whole, so I always buy whole canned tomatoes and then crush or blend them myself. I prefer San Marzano tomatoes.

Canned fish and oysters Wild salmon, anchovies, smoked oysters, and sardines are great for a quick snack or lunch, and as an addition to a charcuterie or snack board.

Other canned goods I regularly use full-fat coconut milk (without guar gum), 100% pure pumpkin puree, applesauce, and Thai green and red curry pastes.

rice, pasta, grains, and legumes

Rice I love short-grain rice like Arborio for making risotto and Bomba for making paella. But I also use short-grain rice to make stew-like, creamy soups. When I want a different texture, I mostly use jasmine rice.

Other grains I also keep jars of buckwheat groats, whole millet, whole amaranth, gluten-free oats, polenta, and grits.

Pasta Mostly I make my own gluten-free pasta. But for easy weeknight meals, I keep rice ramen noodles and buckwheat noodles in the pantry and almond flour pasta in the freezer.

Chickpeas For making hummus, I always have a glass jar of dried chickpeas in the pantry.

Crackers I stock a variety of sweet and savory crackers for snacking or charcuterie boards.

broth

Bone broth In case I run out of homemade bone broth, I keep a few containers of chicken bone broth in the freezer. Try a few brands to see which one in your grocery store has the best flavor. I don't bother buying vegetable broth, because it's so quick and easy to make, and I have never found a store-bought brand that tasted good to me.

flours and binders

Almond flour Almond flour adds fat, fiber, and protein to recipes, as well as a delicious flavor, richness, and moisture. It's perfect for baking. You can also use hazelnut flour, which has a more pronounced nuttiness, if you can find it.

Amaranth flour A high-protein grain, amaranth has a nutty, earthy flavor. When I can't find amaranth flour in the store, I make my own by grinding whole amaranth in a high-speed blender. The seeds are so small that it takes only seconds.

Brown rice flour This whole grain flour has a neutral flavor and a texture perfect for homemade pasta. I don't like brown rice flour for cookies, because it can feel gritty. It's best used in recipes that allow the flour to rest and hydrate fully. I use brown rice flour to maintain a sourdough starter. For best results, seek out superfine brown rice flour (see the Resources section).

Buckwheat flour Buckwheat flour is made from grinding buckwheat groats, which are actually not a grain but the seed from a plant related to rhubarb. Most of the buckwheat flour in grocery stores has a dark color and pronounced flavor. I love the flavor of buckwheat, but it can be polarizing, given its earthy profile. If you don't love the flavor, or want a lighter color, you can easily grind your own buckwheat flour from buckwheat groats using a high-speed blender. Buckwheat flour gives chew to breads, so I love adding some to the sourdough flatbread on page 34. And I alternate between buckwheat and brown rice sourdough starters.

Cassava flour This flour is made from the whole cassava root, which is dried and ground. I primarily use cassava flour to make tortillas (see the variation on page 43).

Chickpea flour Made from dried chickpeas, chickpea flour is often used in Middle Eastern and Indian cooking. Most often, I use it to make farinata (see the recipe on page 38). But it can also be used as a thickener or binder, or to make papadums and pakoras.

Ground flaxseed Also called flaxseed meal, ground flaxseed is high in fiber and protein. When mixed with water, it forms a gel, making an excellent binder for baked goods. You can use ground flaxseed and water as an egg replacement. To make 1 flax "egg," stir together 1 tablespoon flaxseed meal with 3 tablespoons water. Keep flaxseed meal in the refrigerator or freezer, as it can quickly go rancid.

Masa harina Masa harina is a specially prepared corn flour used for making tortillas, tamales, arepas, and other corn recipes. I always look for organic or non-GMO sources. See the Resources section for my favorite brand of heirloom masa, which makes the most delicious tortillas.

Millet flour A staple grain in Asia and Africa, millet is a cereal grass seed with a sweet, corn-like flavor. I often add whole millet to bread, and the flour works well in pancakes, waffles, and cakes.

Oat flour This flour is made from grinding whole or rolled oats. Oat flour can produce a soft texture and stretch when added to bread doughs. It is excellent in quick breads and cookies.

Potato starch Made from dried potatoes, potato starch helps give structure and tenderness to gluten-free baked goods. Like tapioca starch, it helps give a crisp texture, especially to fried foods. In the homemade pasta recipe on page 45, potato starch gives the pasta its chew and spring. If you avoid potatoes, you can substitute arrowroot powder or tapioca starch for potato starch.

Psyllium husk powder When mixed with water, this high-fiber powder forms a gel that acts as a binder in gluten-free baking. It gives elasticity and stretch to sourdough or yeast breads, and enough structure to rise. If you can only find whole psyllium husks at your grocery store, blend them to a fine powder in a high-speed blender. See the Resources section for ordering psyllium husk powder online. Note that availability often changes.

Sorghum flour Another whole grain flour with a sweet, malty flavor, sorghum flour is high in protein and fiber, and helps bind baked goods. Like brown rice flour, sorghum flour can be gritty if not fully hydrated.

Tapioca starch Tapioca starch is a gluten-free binder made from the starchy root of the cassava. It helps baked goods rise and provides stretch for breads. It also helps foods crisp, so it's great when you want a crunchy or crispy texture, like in the fried chicken on page 56.

Teff flour Another high-protein and high-fiber flour with a malty, earthy flavor, teff is probably best known as the flour for injera, the fermented flatbread from Ethiopia. Teff is a more dense flour, so it's best mixed with other gluten-free flours as a blend.

Xanthan gum Xanthan gum acts as a binder in gluten-free recipes, helping the dough stick together and not become crumbly. Because xanthan gum is a more highly processed ingredient, I use it sparingly, only where it's essential to the texture.

kitchen tools

Have you ever stayed in an Airbnb with a poorly equipped kitchen and struggled to make the same meals you easily make at home? I have had this experience often enough that I travel with a chef's knife and Microplane in my suitcase. Having good kitchen tools actually makes cooking easier. By "good," I don't necessarily mean expensive, although some of the items on this list are investments.

Chef's knife One of the best gifts you can give yourself is a good, sharp chef's knife that fits your hand comfortably. It's best to buy a knife in person, so you can learn about different knives and find one that fits your hand and budget—and learn how to keep it sharp. But if you don't have a store near you, I share my favorite one in the Resources section.

Cast-iron skillet Please put away all your nonstick skillets and buy one 12-inch cast-iron skillet. This one skillet can fry an egg, sear meat, and make pancakes with perfectly lacy edges. Cast iron is very affordable, and you can often pick up skillets in secondhand shops.

Carbon steel pan If you want to invest a little more, purchase a carbon steel pan. Like cast iron, they are nonstick, but you can cook acidic foods in them. I share my favorite sources in the Resources section.

Dutch oven I couldn't cook without my enameled Dutch ovens, essential for making soup, braising meats and so much more. If you are only going to buy one size, the 5 ½-quart is the one I use most often. I use the 12-quart for making large batches of chicken and vegetable stocks. While you can invest in Le Creuset or Staub, Lodge also makes affordable enameled Dutch ovens.

Sheet pans I have a stack of heavy rimmed sheet pans that have turned black from years of use. I line them with parchment paper and use them for roasting vegetables, making cookies, and more. Using parchment paper makes for easy cleanup. I use unbleached parchment paper, which does not contain chlorine.

Microplane grater I use my Microplane every day, mostly for grating lemon zest, but also for parmesan cheese.

Dough whisk Instead of making pizza or bread dough in the stand mixer using a dough hook, I prefer to mix it by hand using a dough whisk. I find it easier and faster.

Thin, flexible metal spatulas These make flipping eggs and pancakes so much easier. You can easily find them on Amazon.

Wooden spoons Beside my stovetop is a crock filled with wooden spoons. Some I use every day and some have sentimental value. My favorites are the ones with a flat edge.

KitchenAid stand mixer Under the category of "investment" is a KitchenAid stand mixer. I don't just use it for baking cookies. I use the meat grinder attachment, the attachments for rolling and cutting pasta, and a Mockmill attachment for grinding grain. My KitchenAid stand mixer is probably 35-plus years old.

 Look for this symbol. It highlights recipes that need advance planning.

Vitamix blender While a high-speed Vitamix is expensive, it will also last a very long time. Ours is 10 years old. I use it every day to make nut butters, salad dressings, smoothies, sauces, and soups.

Kitchen scale I don't generally use a kitchen scale for baked goods like cakes and cookies. Especially when baking with Theo, I find measuring cups easier to use and accurate enough. However, I do use a kitchen scale for making bread, or if I'm using tapioca or potato starch, since those starches are easy to compress.

Dry and liquid measuring cups I have several sets of dry measuring cups and multiple glass liquid measuring cups (1-, 2- and 4-cup measures). For dry ingredients, I stir the flour in the container, dip and sweep off the excess.

CHAPTER ONE

BREADS, TORTILLAS, & PASTA

daily bread

2 cups (473 grams) water, heated to 110 degrees F

2 teaspoons honey

2¼ teaspoons (7 grams/1 packet) active dry yeast

¼ cup (55 grams) apple cider vinegar

3 tablespoons (26 grams) psyllium husk powder

2 tablespoons (20 grams) ground flaxseed

1 cup (136 grams) tapioca starch

1 cup (140 grams) sorghum flour, plus more for dusting

½ cup (75 grams) millet flour

½ cup plus 2 tablespoons (60 grams) gluten-free oat flour

⅓ cup (46 grams) amaranth flour

¼ cup (45 grams) whole grain teff

2 tablespoons (30 grams) whole millet

2 teaspoons (12 grams) sea salt

You don't need to be an expert bread baker to make a beautiful, delicious loaf of bread. When I first started experimenting with gluten-free baking, I turned to cookbooks like *Cannelle et Vanille* by Aran Goyoaga, *River Cottage Gluten Free* by Naomi Devlin, and *America's Test Kitchen's How Can It Be Gluten Free* for inspiration and to learn the science and techniques for gluten-free baking. This loaf is the result of a lot of experimentation, and it has become our daily bread. Without gluten to provide structure and strength to the dough, gluten-free breads require binders to create a tall bread with a lovely lattice of air pockets. In this boule, I use a combination of psyllium husk powder, ground flaxseed, and tapioca starch, which results in a large loaf and open crumb. Adding apple cider vinegar helps the bread rise, tenderizes the dough, and gives a slight tang reminiscent of sourdough. This bread is equally delicious spread with butter and orange marmalade as it is toasted and topped with smashed avocado and a perfectly fried egg. · MAKES 1 LOAF

1 Place a cast-iron Dutch oven in the oven. Preheat the oven to 475 degrees F.

2 Place the water, honey, and yeast in a 1-quart glass measuring cup or medium bowl. Whisk together and let proof for about 10 minutes, until the yeast forms a foamy layer on the surface of the water. Whisk in the vinegar, psyllium husk powder, and ground flaxseed. Let it sit for 5 minutes to gel.

3 Put the tapioca starch, flours, teff, millet and salt in a large bowl. Whisk to combine. Add the yeast gel mixture. Using a dough whisk or wooden spoon, stir until the dough starts to come together. It will seem like the gel will not absorb all the flour, but it will. Once the dough is mostly combined, turn it out onto the counter and knead until all the flour has been absorbed and the dough is smooth. Shape the dough into a ball.

RECIPE CONTINUES

TROUBLESHOOTING

If the inside of the bread separates from the crust, a couple of different things might have happened.

One, the dough was too hydrated, meaning it has a high ratio of water to flour. Be sure to knead in all the flour.

Two, the dough was over-proofed. Keep the proofing time to only 30 minutes or less at room temperature. If the kitchen is hot (75 degrees or more), reduce the proofing time to 20 or 25 minutes.

MAKE IT YOUR OWN

You can make this bread with any combination of gluten-free flours. I love the flavor and texture of a wide variety of grains, but the bread will work as long as the total weight of the flour remains the same, at about 320 grams. For example, you could use 320 grams of all sorghum flour or superfine brown rice flour.

SUBSTITUTIONS

If you can't find whole teff, substitute whole amaranth or whole millet, or even gluten-free oatmeal or sunflower seeds. If you have a hard time finding amaranth flour, buy whole amaranth and grind it into flour using a high speed blender.

4 Dust a proofing basket with sorghum flour and place the dough in it. (If you don't have a proofing basket, line a medium bowl with a clean kitchen towel and dust the towel with flour.) Cover the dough with a clean kitchen towel and let it proof in a warm place for 30 minutes. The dough will not fully double.

5 Remove the Dutch oven from the oven. Carefully turn the dough out of the proofing basket and place it in the center of the Dutch oven. Score the top with a sharp knife or lame.

6 Cover the Dutch oven with its lid and place it back in the oven. Bake for 30 minutes.

7 Remove the lid, reduce the temperature to 425 degrees F, and continue to bake for another 30 minutes, until the crust is brown and feels firm when tapped.

8 Transfer the boule to a wire rack and let cool completely. Don't be tempted by the appeal of warm bread! Cutting the bread too soon will result in a gummy interior. Store the bread in a bread box or brown paper bag for up to 3 or 4 days. Alternatively, slice the bread and freeze in an airtight container; it will keep for up to 3 months.

flaky southern-style biscuits

8 tablespoons
(1 stick/115 grams)
unsalted butter

½ cup millet flour
(63 grams), plus more
for dusting

½ cup (68 grams)
tapioca starch

⅓ cup (56 grams)
potato starch

⅓ cup (46 grams)
sorghum flour

2¼ teaspoons baking
powder

¼ teaspoon baking soda

1 teaspoon sea salt

¼ teaspoon xanthan gum

½ cup (115 grams) whole
milk Greek yogurt

Up to ½ cup (120 grams)
whole milk, plus more for
brushing

Flaky salt, for sprinkling

MAKE AHEAD

These biscuits are best eaten
the day they are made. To get
a head start, I often make the
flour mixture the night before,
or even several days in advance.
You can also grate the butter,
add it to the flour and then put
it in the refrigerator until you're
ready to mix. I've done that
several hours before baking,
with great results.

One of my earliest memories is of my great-grandmother Granny Dixon baking biscuits. I can still picture her, hair tied in a bun at the nape of her neck, wearing a housedress, with a pink printed apron tied at her waist. The kitchen table is covered with a blue and white tablecloth and the table is set, including the small green juice glasses that now sit in my own cupboard. She didn't need a recipe. Her hands sifted, stirred and cut cold butter by the memory of a thousand biscuits. I think she would be proud of these. · MAKES 8 BISCUITS

1 Place the butter in the freezer for at least 30 minutes, until frozen. Preheat the oven to 500 degrees F.

2 In a large bowl, whisk together the rice flour, tapioca starch, potato starch, sorghum flour, baking powder, baking soda, salt, and xanthan gum.

3 Remove the butter from the freezer and grate it on the largest holes of a box grater directly into the dry ingredients. Toss everything together lightly with your hands. Stir the yogurt into the flour-butter mixture. Add half of the milk and stir together until the milk is absorbed. Slowly drizzle in the rest of the milk while stirring, adding just enough to bring the dough together without it being dry. You might not need all the milk.

4 Turn out the dough onto a flour-dusted surface and form it into a rectangle about ½ inch thick. Lift one end of the dough using a bench scraper and fold it over to the middle of the dough. Lift the other end of the dough and fold it over the dough, just like folding a letter in thirds. Using your hands, flatten the dough back down to ½ inch thick. Repeat this folding and flattening two more times.

RECIPE CONTINUES

A COUPLE OF TIPS

This recipe was inspired by the one in Aran Goyoaga's beautiful book *Cannelle et Vanille*, adapted to be reminiscent of the best laminated biscuits from my childhood.

1. The frozen butter method for making biscuits is one I learned years ago, before I became gluten-free, in my quest to make a perfect biscuit. Grating in frozen butter easily distributes the fat and keeps the flour and butter very cold—the key to flaky biscuits. Use the largest holes of the box grater, because you don't want the butter pieces to be *too* small. As the butter melts, it creates steam that helps the biscuits rise.

2. I have always used a combination of Greek yogurt and milk in my biscuits. The yogurt replaces traditional buttermilk, providing acidity and also extra fat. I find that combination makes for a flaky, tender biscuit.

3. I learned the folding method from my friend, Mataio. Folding the biscuit dough creates those distinct, pull-apart layers that make biscuits so irresistible. It might take you a few tries to get the technique down, but don't be afraid! You'll get it.

5 Using the sharp edge of the bench scraper, cut the dough in half lengthwise, being sure to press straight down and straight back up (instead of dragging the scraper sideways through the dough). Then cut the dough crosswise, making 8 biscuits of equal size. (Lifting the bench scraper straight up when you cut will ensure that the biscuits will rise evenly in the oven.)

6 Transfer the biscuits to an ungreased baking sheet and brush the tops with whole milk. Sprinkle with flaky salt.

7 Place the baking sheet in the oven and immediately reduce the temperature to 450 degrees F. Bake for 15 to 18 minutes, until the biscuits are deeply golden brown. Let them cool slightly before transferring from the pan to a serving bowl lined with a clean kitchen towel or napkin. Serve warm.

nut and seed bread

¾ cup raw, unblanched almonds

½ cup raw pecans

½ cup blanched hazelnuts

½ cup raw pumpkin seeds

½ cup raw sunflower seeds

½ cup raw sesame seeds

½ cup poppy seeds

½ cup flax seeds

½ cup chia seeds

½ cup extra virgin olive oil

6 large eggs

2 teaspoons sea salt

MAKE AHEAD

This bread freezes well, tightly wrapped. I usually cut it in half and store it in a reusable food storage bag in the freezer. Thaw in the refrigerator.

MAKE IT YOUR OWN

As long as the total volume of nuts and seeds is kept constant, you can vary the type of nuts and seeds that you add to the bread. I prefer more seeds and fewer nuts, but feel free to play around. You can also experiment with adding lemon or orange zest, spices, or fresh herbs.

This nutrient-rich bread is incredibly versatile. And so easy! It contains only nuts, seeds, olive oil, eggs, and salt. Think of it as you would a dense German bread. It's delicious spread with avocado, or layered with crème fraîche and smoked salmon, or topped with a thin layer of fig jam and a sliver of Délice de Bourgogne cheese. Add it to snack plates or charcuterie boards. And since it is so high in protein, it makes a great snack for hikes or tucked into your carry-on bag for travel days. · MAKES ONE LOAF, ABOUT 24 SLICES

1 Line an 8½ by 4½-inch loaf pan with parchment paper. To help hold down the parchment paper, use all-metal binder clips on the sides of the loaf pan.

2 Place the almonds, pecans, and hazelnuts in a food processor. Pulse until coarsely chopped. Pour the chopped nuts into a large bowl. Add the pumpkin seeds, sunflower seeds, sesame seeds, poppy seeds, flaxseed, and chia seeds.

3 Whisk together the oil, eggs, and salt in a medium bowl until blended. Pour the egg mixture into the nut and seed mixture and stir until combined. Pour the batter into the prepared loaf pan. Place the pan in the oven, then turn on the oven to 350 degrees F. Bake for 60 minutes, until the top of the bread feels firm and the edges are brown.

4 Let the bread cool completely in the pan. Lift it out of the pan using the edges of the parchment paper. Store the bread in an airtight container in the refrigerator for up to 5 days.

sourdough flatbread

1¼ cups (270 grams) filtered water, at room temperature

1 tablespoon (12 grams) psyllium husk powder

2 tablespoons (20 grams) ground flaxseed

1 teaspoon (6 grams) sea salt

½ cup (125 grams) Gluten-Free Sourdough Starter (page 278)

1 cup plus 2 tablespoons (157 grams) superfine brown rice flour

⅓ cup (56 grams) potato starch

2 tablespoons (17 grams) tapioca starch

1 tablespoon extra virgin olive oil, plus more for the pan

MAKE AHEAD
The dough can be made up to 24 hours before baking and kept in the refrigerator. In fact, a long, slow ferment in the refrigerator gives it a better sourdough flavor.

This flatbread is inspired by the laffa we eat in Israel, a soft, pliable bread traditionally cooked on the wall of a wood-fired oven. Often it's doused in olive oil and sprinkled with za'atar. I make this bread at least once a week, to serve with dips and spreads, as part of a charcuterie or snack board, to eat with soup, or to dip in shakshuka. I would go so far as to say the recipe is foolproof—even if your starter isn't active, if you under- or overproof the dough, if you leave the bread just a little too long in the oven, it's a forgiving recipe. •
MAKES ONE 10- OR 12-INCH FLATBREAD

1 Pour the water into a large bowl. Add the psyllium husk powder, ground flaxseed, and salt and whisk well, making sure there are no lumps. The mixture will quickly start to gel.

2 Add the starter, flour, potato starch, tapioca starch, and oil and mix until the ingredients come together into a shaggy dough. (A dough whisk works well for this.)

3 Turn out the dough onto a clean surface and knead a few times, just until it comes together into a ball. Place the dough back in the bowl and cover with a clean kitchen towel. Let rise at room temperature for about 4 hours, or in the refrigerator for up to 24 hours. When it is ready, the dough will have puffed up but not doubled in size.

4 Preheat the oven to 500 degrees F.

5 Drizzle a couple of tablespoons of oil evenly in a 10- or 12-inch cast-iron or carbon steel skillet. Place the dough in the middle of the pan and use your fingers to press it to about a 1-inch thickness or until it covers the skillet. Make a raised edge of taller crust at the edges. If your fingers stick to the dough, wet them with a little water.

6 Bake for 20 to 25 minutes, until the dough has puffed up and is evenly browned. For a more charred crust, place the skillet under the broiler for 1 minute. Watch carefully, as the flatbread can burn quickly.

7 Remove the flatbread from the oven and drizzle with more oil. For the best results, let the flatbread cool before cutting into slices; if you cut it too soon, the crumb will be gummy.

MAKE IT YOUR OWN

Change the flavor and texture of the flatbread by varying the type of sourdough starter. Using a buckwheat sourdough starter will create a darker, heartier bread than if you use a brown rice starter.

I often vary the flour, depending on what I'm serving the bread with. Using all brown rice flour gives a bread with a mild taste, most like white bread. For a heartier bread, experiment with using a combination of sorghum, amaranth, teff, and buckwheat flours. As long as the total weight of the flour remains the same (157 grams), you can be creative.

Drizzle the flatbread with olive oil, then toss different spices or toasted seeds on top. Try za'atar (pictured), sumac, dried oregano, sesame seeds, or nigella seeds.

browned butter cornbread

2 cups stone-ground yellow or white cornmeal

1 teaspoon sea salt

½ teaspoon baking powder

½ teaspoon baking soda

1 large egg

¾ cup whole milk Greek yogurt*

¾ cup whole milk*

6 tablespoons (¾ stick) unsalted butter

*If you substitute low-fat yogurt or milk, the cornbread will be dry. It really needs the extra fat to retain moisture.

My memory of cornbread is shaped by my two grandmothers. My Granny's, fried in Crisco in a perfectly seasoned cast-iron skillet. And my Grandmother's, slightly sour from buttermilk and white cornmeal. At either house, my Dad would eat the leftover cornbread for dessert, crumbling it into a tall glass of milk and eating it with a spoon. These sensory memories are integral to my early childhood and have forever shaped my love of cornbread. One of the secrets to great cornbread is a hot cast-iron skillet. Preheating the skillet in the oven allows the cornbread crust to begin to cook immediately, giving those crispy fried edges. · MAKES ONE 9-INCH ROUND LOAF; SERVES 6

1 Whisk together the cornmeal, salt, baking powder, and baking soda in a large bowl. In another medium bowl, whisk together the egg, yogurt, and milk. Add the wet ingredients to the dry ingredients and whisk well, until completely smooth. Let the batter sit for 30 minutes to allow the cornmeal to absorb the liquid.

2 While the batter is resting, place a 9-inch cast-iron skillet in the oven and preheat the oven to 450 degrees F.

3 After the skillet has heated for 30 minutes and is very hot, remove the skillet from the oven. Place the butter in the skillet. Watch the butter carefully as it foams and then starts to turn brown and smell nutty. Add the browned butter to the batter. Whisk the batter well. Pour and scrape the batter into the cast-iron skillet. The batter will immediately sizzle around the edges and begin to fry.

4 Place the skillet back in the oven and bake for 20 to 25 minutes, until the cornbread is deeply golden brown on top. Let the cornbread cool slightly. Cut into wedges and serve. This cornbread is best the day it is made. However, leftovers can be stored, tightly wrapped, for a day or two.

chickpea flatbread

A.K.A. FARINATA OR SOCCA

1 cup chickpea flour

½ teaspoon sea salt

⅛ teaspoon Aleppo-style pepper

1¼ cups warm water

2 to 3 tablespoons extra virgin olive oil

MAKE AHEAD

The flatbread can be made up to a day ahead. It won't have the crispy edges, but it is still delicious. To store, wrap the flatbread tightly with plastic wrap or place in a reusable storage bag. Store at room temperature for a day or two.

This chickpea flatbread is known as farinata in Italy and socca in France. It is incredibly simple, making it an easy pre-meal snack to serve to guests. Sometimes I like it served with something creamy, like crème fraîche, fresh ricotta, or burrata. It's great as an accompaniment to soups or stews. And sometimes I like to flavor the flatbread itself, with things like fennel and Castelvetrano olives. You can either add the ingredients to the batter before you put the flatbread in the oven, or garnish with toppings after it comes out of the oven. Any way, it's delicious. Leftovers also make a good snack. · MAKES ONE 10- OR 12-INCH FLATBREAD

1 In a large bowl, whisk together the flour, salt, and pepper. Whisk in the water. Let sit, covered, at room temperature, for at least 4 hours. The long soaking time is required for the chickpea flour to absorb water. If you want to let it sit overnight, cover the bowl and place it in the refrigerator. Bring to room temperature before baking.

2 Place a 10- or 12-inch cast-iron or carbon steel skillet in the oven. Preheat the oven to 450 degrees F.

3 Carefully remove the skillet from the oven. Pour in enough oil to coat the bottom. Pour and spread the batter in the skillet Place the skillet back in the oven and bake for 10 to 15 minutes, until the flatbread is firm and the edges are set and beginning to brown. If you want, place it under the broiler for extra browning. Cut into wedges and serve warm or at room temperature.

ONION-GOAT CHEESE · Add ½ cup of caramelized onions to the batter. After baking, top with crumbled goat cheese and thyme.

FENNEL AND OLIVE · After baking, top with a salad of thinly sliced fennel and fennel fronds, sliced pitted Castelvetrano olives, Aleppo-style pepper and a drizzle of olive oil. Serve with labneh (recipe on page 274), if desired.

WILD MUSHROOM AND SAGE · Add ½ cup of sautéed wild mushrooms to the batter. After baking, top with fried sage leaves.

nigella seed cheddar wafers

1 cup grated sharp cheddar cheese (3 to 4 ounces)

4 tablespoons (½ stick) unsalted butter, at room temperature

¾ cup superfine brown rice flour

½ teaspoon sea salt

⅛ to ¼ teaspoon cayenne pepper

About 2 tablespoons nigella seeds

I adapted this recipe from a recipe for traditional benne seed (sesame) wafers in *The Foothills Cuisine of Blackberry Farm* by Sam Beall. These crackers are addictive. They're perfect with the pimiento cheese in this cookbook (page 81), but they're also good straight on their own with a glass of crisp white wine. The cayenne gives them a nice spice—adjust the amount according to your tolerance for heat. I love the flavor of nigella seeds, but you can substitute white or black sesame seeds. · MAKES ABOUT 2 DOZEN WAFERS

1 Put the cheddar and butter in the bowl of a stand mixer fitted with the paddle attachment. Beat together on medium speed until smooth and creamy. Add the flour, salt, and cayenne to taste, and mix on low speed until a thick dough starts to form. It will still be crumbly at this part. Don't be afraid.

2 Pour the dough from the bowl onto a large piece of parchment paper. Gently knead until it comes together. Form the dough into a disk and cover with another piece of parchment paper. Using a rolling pin, roll it out to about ⅛ inch thick. Place the parchment paper–covered dough on a baking sheet and refrigerate for at least 4 hours.

3 Preheat the oven to 375 degrees F. Line a baking sheet with parchment paper.

4 Use a 1½-inch-diameter cookie cutter to stamp out the wafers. If you don't have a round cookie cutter, you can use a juice glass. Reroll the scraps and continue to cut wafers, using all the dough.

5 Arrange the wafers on the baking sheet, making sure they don't touch. (They will spread a little bit.) Prick the center of each wafer several times with the tines of a fork. Sprinkle the tops with nigella seeds, pressing lightly so they stick to the dough.

6 Bake until the wafers puff slightly and are starting to brown around the edges, about 12 minutes. Let cool on the baking sheet before serving. Store the wafers in an airtight container for 3 or 4 days.

corn tortillas

1 cup organic or non-GMO masa harina

¼ teaspoon sea salt

¾ to 1 cup warm water

MAKE AHEAD

Tortillas for tacos are best eaten right after they are cooked, while they are warm. However, if you are making enchiladas, you can make the tortillas earlier in the day, or even use leftover tortillas from the night before. Wrap the tortillas tightly in plastic wrap or place in a reusable storage bag and store at room temperature for a day or two.

Homemade tortillas are so much better than store bought. And once you get the hang of making them, they are so fast and easy. We make tortillas a few times a week in our house. Theo loves to help—the rolling and pressing are great activities for kids. I have adopted the philosophy that anything can be a taco—braised meats, roasted vegetables, fried halloumi cheese. If it's wrapped in a fresh tortilla and topped with something spicy, something bright, and something crunchy, it's going to be delicious. · MAKES 10 TO 12 TORTILLAS

1 Place the masa harina in a medium bowl, add the salt, and stir. Add ¾ cup water, stirring it in with a spoon. Knead the dough together until it is smooth and the consistency of Play-Doh. If it feels too dry and crumbly, and won't hold together, knead in a little more water. It should be smooth and pliable, but not sticky. Cover the masa tightly with plastic wrap until you're ready to cook.

2 Place a cast-iron or carbon steel skillet over medium-high heat. Roll all the masa into Ping Pong ball–sized balls while the skillet is heating. (You should get 10 to 12 balls.) Line a plate with a clean cloth napkin or kitchen towel. Line the tortilla press with a large piece of plastic wrap or parchment paper that covers both the top and bottom of the press.

3 Place one ball of masa on the press and close it to flatten the dough to about 1⁄16 inch thick. Place the tortilla in the skillet and cook for about a minute on each side, until the tortilla has begun to puff and is browning in spots. Remove the tortilla to the prepared plate and cover with the napkin to capture the steam. Continue pressing and cooking the rest of the tortillas. The tortillas will stay steamy and pliable for over an hour if you keep them wrapped, but they are best if you serve them immediately.

CASSAVA TORTILLAS •

You can make tortillas with cassava flour using the exact same technique as corn tortillas and the same measurements. Just substitute cassava flour for the masa harina. Cassava tortillas puff beautifully and are soft and pliable. I often serve them with chili, or with a mezze platter when I don't have time to make flatbread.

TURMERIC TORTILLAS •

Add 2 teaspoons to 1 tablespoon ground turmeric (depending on how much you like its flavor) to the masa (or cassava flour) along with the salt. The tortillas will be subtly orange in color and have a beautiful, earthy flavor.

VEGETABLE TORTILLAS •

You can also vary the flavor of tortillas using up to ¼ cup vegetable puree in place of that much water. Spinach and butternut squash work well.

homemade gluten-free pasta

1½ cups (210 grams) superfine brown rice flour, plus more for kneading and dusting

½ cup (90 grams) potato starch

1 tablespoon xanthan gum

1½ teaspoons sea salt

5 large eggs

2 tablespoons extra virgin olive oil

INGREDIENT TIPS

I make pasta with whole eggs instead of just egg yolks because the protein in the white gives the pasta more chew and makes it easier to work with.

The addition of olive oil gives the dough flavor and also makes it easier to roll.

While I try to limit starches and ingredients like xanthan gum as much as possible, they are essential in gluten-free pasta to give it structure.

If you've never made your own pasta, don't worry! It's actually incredibly easy and comes together quickly. Without gluten, you don't have to knead the dough as long as traditional pasta. You do need a pasta roller, which can be an attachment to a stand mixer or a stand-alone hand crank machine. If you don't have a pasta machine, you can just roll the dough very thin with a rolling pin for a more rustic pasta. This works best for short shapes, like the strozzapreti. Making gluten-free pasta at home is so satisfying--it's low effort, high reward. I hope you try it. • MAKES ABOUT 1 ½ POUNDS DOUGH, ENOUGH FOR 6 TO 8 SERVINGS

1 In a large bowl, whisk together the flour, potato starch, xanthan gum, and salt. Using your hands, make a well in the middle of the dry ingredients. Pour in the eggs and oil. Using a fork, whisk together the eggs and oil, slowly incorporating the flour around the edges of the well into the eggs. Continue to whisk until all the eggs and oil have been mixed in and formed a dough. You may have some leftover flour in the bowl.

2 Turn out the dough onto the counter, including any leftover flour in the bowl. Knead until it feels smooth, about 5 minutes. If the dough feels sticky, add more flour, a little at a time. (It depends on how big your eggs are and the humidity in the air. I usually add up to another ¼ cup flour while kneading.) The dough should feel fairly stiff. When you press it with your finger, it should bounce back, slowly. Wrap the dough in plastic wrap and let it rest at room temperature for 30 minutes.

3 While the dough is resting, set up a pasta rolling machine. Adjust the machine to the widest setting. Line two baking sheets with parchment paper and dust the parchment with flour. Dust the counter with a little flour.

4 Using a knife or bench scraper, cut the dough into 8 equal pieces. Work with one piece of dough at a time, keeping the rest of the dough covered. Using a rolling pin, roll 1 piece of dough into a rectangular shape, flat enough so it will go through the widest setting on your pasta machine. Run the

RECIPE CONTINUES

MAKE AHEAD

Homemade pasta freezes beautifully, for up to 3 months. Wrap unrolled pasta dough in plastic wrap, then put it in an airtight container. Thaw the dough in the refrigerator overnight before rolling and cutting. To freeze rolled and cut pasta, place the baking sheet with the cut pasta in the freezer until frozen. Transfer the pasta to an airtight container. Cook the pasta from frozen.

MAKE IT YOUR OWN

You can make flavored pasta by adding dried herbs or spices (like freshly ground black pepper), or color the pasta using blanched basil, steamed spinach, sun-dried tomato puree, or other vegetables. Add 2 to 4 tablespoons of pureed herbs or vegetables to the eggs and whisk well until smooth.

You can also laminate pasta sheets by pressing herbs or edible flours between two sheets of pasta and rolling them together.

dough through the machine, then lay the rolled dough on the parchment paper or on the counter and fold it in thirds like a letter. Run the dough back through the machine, still on the widest setting with an uneven edge facing down. Repeat the letter fold, then run the dough through the machine again. You may need to repeat this two or three times, until the pasta sheet is very smooth. If the pasta is sticking, dust it with more flour.

5 Adjust the machine to the next narrowest setting and run the pasta sheet through. Continue to adjust the machine and roll the pasta thinner and thinner, until it gets almost translucent. (For my machine, I go to number 4 or 5. After that, the pasta starts to tear.)

6 Lay the sheet of pasta on the second flour-dusted sheet pan. Repeat the same process with the remaining dough. Place a piece of parchment paper on top of each sheet of pasta to keep them from sticking together.

7 At this point, you can cut or form the pasta into any shape you desire.

- Keep the pasta in sheets to make lasagna.

- Use the pasta cutter on the machine to cut into linguine or tagliatelle. As you cut each sheet, wind the pasta strands into a nest and place on the flour-dusted baking sheet. Leave the pasta nests on the baking sheet, uncovered, until you're ready to cook.

- Cut the pasta crosswise into 1-inch-wide strips and twist each strip to make strozzapreti (photo on page 133), which is perfect for baked pastas.

8 Fresh pasta cooks quickly, in just 3 to 4 minutes. Bring a large pot of well-salted water to a boil and add the pasta, stirring to make sure it doesn't stick together. While it is still al dente, remove it from the water and add it to whatever sauce you are serving, stirring to coat the pasta. Allow it to finish cooking in the sauce and absorb those flavors. If you need to thin your pasta sauce, add a little of the cooking water.

COOKING WITH KIDS

From the time Theo could stand, I shared the kitchen with him. Over the years, this has become our special time together.

We started simply, with dumping ingredients. When he was 12 to 18 months old, I would sit him on the counter next to the Vitamix blender to help me make almond milk or smoothies. He dumped in the almonds, tore the dates in half and pulled out the pits, added salt. We'd cover our ears and laugh at the loud roar of the blender.

By the time he was two, I would pull a stool up to the counter and give him a bowl of flour to play with. He scooped flour from one bowl to the next for an hour or more, making train tracks or roads for invisible cars. He got used to scooping and measuring, leveling the cups with his plump little index finger.

At this same age, he started asking to do more. He unwrapped butter, spooned peanut butter into the measuring cup, stirred batters, and scooped cookie dough (haphazardly) onto sheet pans. We started counting. Four cookies up. One, two, three, four. Three cookies across. One, two, three.

For the most part, I followed his lead. As he asked to do more, I let him. I tried not to make anything off-limits, but did closely supervise any tasks around the stove or sharp knives.

Around age three, he wanted to start cracking eggs. At first, he would crack the egg on the counter and hand it to me to break it into the bowl. With encouragement, he learned he could tuck his thumbs into the shell to pull it apart, letting the egg fall into the bowl. He was proud of himself.

When he asked to use a knife, I tried one of those knife sets for kids. I found them more dangerous, because they aren't sharp enough. Instead, a serrated steak knife became a great option. We started with apples. I showed him how to cut one side to create a flat surface that wouldn't roll around. We practiced making a bear claw, to keep his fingers tucked away from the blade of the knife. Soon he could slice an apple—always with supervision.

From there, he wanted to start cooking on the stove. We practiced keeping arms and hands away from the burner and the sides of the pan while he dropped pancake batter in the center. He practiced sliding a thin metal spatula under the pancake, lifting and flipping it to the other side.

At age six, Theo is very comfortable in the kitchen. To me, that's the only secret of cooking with kids: Let them in and let their natural curiosity guide you. For me, it's been a powerful way to bond with my son, doing something we both enjoy.

I know not everyone enjoys cooking with kids. Maybe you have three young children and inviting them into the kitchen would create chaos. Or maybe you have older children with no interest in cooking. I don't believe in parent shaming, and there's absolutely no judgment here if cooking with your kiddos feels stressful. If you want a silent kitchen to yourself, I get it. Sometimes I want that, too.

CHAPTER TWO

BREAKFAST FOODS
FOR ANY TIME OF DAY

sourdough pancakes

Heaping ¾ cup (240 grams) cold Gluten-Free Sourdough Starter (page 278)

½ cup sorghum flour

½ cup millet flour

1 cup almond flour

¼ cup ground flaxseed (optional)

1 cup whole milk Greek yogurt

1 cup whole milk

1 tablespoon honey

3 tablespoons unsalted butter, melted

4 large eggs

1 teaspoon baking soda

1 teaspoon sea salt

Ghee, for cooking

for serving (optional)

Compote of Any Berry (page 275)

Maple Syrup

Peanut butter

Honey

Jam or marmalade

Fried eggs

It's a bold statement, but I think these are perfect pancakes. First, they are nutritious. Whole gluten-free grains and flax-seed provide fiber. Almond flour, milk, Greek yogurt and a good amount of eggs provide protein. But most importantly, they are delicious--fluffy and tender with a distinct sour-dough tang. Don't be tempted to skimp on the ghee. Frying the pancakes in ghee creates lacy edges that make these pancakes irresistible. The even heat of a cast iron skillet is another secret ingredient to great pancakes, ensuring a crisp, golden crust. We make a batch once a week, storing leftovers in the freezer for easy weekday breakfasts. PHOTOGRAPH ON PAGES 50-51 · MAKES ABOUT 12 PANCAKES

1 Make the batter the night before you are going to cook the pancakes, or even 2 days before. In a large bowl, whisk together the sourdough starter, sorghum, millet, and almond flours, flaxseed (if using), yogurt, milk and honey. Cover the bowl and place in the refrigerator for at least 8 hours, or up to 48 hours.

2 When you are ready to make the pancakes, preheat the oven to 175 degrees F.

3 Remove the bowl from the refrigerator. Whisk in the butter, then the eggs. Add the baking soda and salt and whisk well. The batter should start to bubble and puff.

4 Heat a 10- or 12-inch cast-iron or carbon steel skillet over medium-low heat. Add a little ghee and swirl the pan to coat the bottom. Add a heaping ⅓ cup of the pancake batter to the middle of the pan. Let the pancake cook on one side until the edges are brown and crispy and bubbles appear in the center of the pancake. Flip the pancake and cook on the other side until browned and cooked through. (If you press your finger on the center of the pancake, it should feel springy and not at all wet in the middle.)

5 Place the pancake on a plate and put in the preheated oven to keep warm. Repeat with all the remaining batter, adding more ghee to the pan as needed.

6 Serve these pancakes with the Compote of Any Berry (page 275) or simply with maple syrup. Make a peanut butter and honey version by spreading a hot pancake with peanut butter and drizzling with honey. For a sweet and savory version, I love to spread mine with orange marmalade and top with a fried egg and flaky salt.

SOURDOUGH WAFFLES · You can use this same sourdough pancake recipe to make sourdough waffles. Reduce the milk to ½ cup. (For waffles, you want a thicker batter.) To make a crispier waffle (and we all want crispy waffles) increase the honey to 2 tablespoons and the melted butter to 5 tablespoons. The added fat and sugar will create a crisp crust. To bake the waffles, coat a waffle iron with a little spray ghee or coconut oil and add ⅓ cup batter. Cook according to the manufacturer's instructions until browned and crispy. Keep the waffles warm in the oven until they're all cooked.

SUBSTITUTIONS

I love these pancakes using a buckwheat sourdough starter, but Elie prefers the milder taste of the brown rice starter.

As long as the total amount of flour adds up to about 1 cup (plus 1 cup of almond flour), you can experiment with different flours, adding buckwheat or teff or using all millet or all sorghum flour. I find the addition of ground flaxseed makes for a better texture, but you can leave it out if you don't love the flavor.

MAKE AHEAD

Our freezer is always stocked with stacks of pancakes. Let the pancakes cool completely, then layer them with parchment paper in between. Place the stack of pancakes in a reusable food storage bag and freeze. Warm them in the toaster to serve.

IF YOU FORGET TO MAKE THE BATTER THE NIGHT BEFORE

Don't worry! The pancakes will be a little thinner and won't have as pronounced of a sourdough flavor, but they will still be tender and delicious. I make them this way all the time.

cornmeal waffles

1 cup millet flour

1 cup fine cornmeal

1 cup almond flour

2 teaspoons baking powder

1 teaspoon baking soda

1 teaspoon sea salt

1½ cups whole milk
Greek yogurt

1 cup whole milk

4 tablespoons (½ stick)
unsalted butter, melted

4 large eggs

Spray ghee or coconut oil,
for greasing the waffle iron

COOKING TIP
Placing the cooked waffles on a wire rack in a warm oven will keep them crispy until serving. Try to keep them in a single layer; stacking them on top of each other will cause them to steam.

MAKE AHEAD
Just like the pancakes, these waffles keep well in the freezer. Let the waffles cool completely, then layer them with parchment paper in between. Place the stack of waffles in a reusable food storage bag and freeze. Warm them in the toaster to serve.

The crunch and flavor of the cornmeal makes these savory waffles a perfect accompaniment to the Hot Fried Chicken on page 56. But they are equally delicious topped with crispy bacon and fried eggs. If you like your waffles on the sweeter side, see the variation. · MAKES ABOUT A DOZEN 7-INCH WAFFLES

1 In a large bowl, whisk together the millet flour, cornmeal, almond flour, baking powder, baking soda, and salt. In a medium bowl, whisk together the yogurt, milk, butter, and eggs. Stir the wet ingredients into the dry ingredients. Whisk well until completely smooth. Let the batter sit for at least 30 minutes and up to 2 hours to allow the cornmeal to absorb the liquid and soften.

2 While the batter is resting, preheat a waffle iron according to the manufacturer's instructions. Preheat the oven to 175 degrees F. Line two rimmed baking sheets with wire racks and place them in the oven.

3 Grease the waffle iron. Pour in ⅓ cup batter. Close the iron and cook until quite browned, according to the manufacturer's instructions. Transfer the waffle to a wire rack in the oven. Repeat with the remaining batter, placing the waffles on the racks in a single layer. Serve warm.

THEO'S MILLET WAFFLES · Theo prefers his waffles a little sweeter. I replace the cornmeal with millet flour and add 2 tablespoons honey to the wet ingredients. It's a perfect waffle for butter and maple syrup. You can also make them into waffle sandwiches by spreading peanut butter and jam between two waffles. It's a great lunchbox treat.

hot fried chicken and waffles

WITH HONEY-CHILI BUTTER

marinated chicken

2 cups whole milk
Greek yogurt

2 cups whole milk

Grated zest and juice of
1 lemon

2 bay leaves

10 sprigs fresh thyme

1 teaspoon dried oregano

½ teaspoon freshly ground
black pepper

¼ teaspoon red pepper
flakes

¼ teaspoon cayenne pepper

1 tablespoon sea salt

6 boneless, skinless chicken
thighs (about 2½ pounds)

breading

1¼ cups superfine brown
rice flour

⅓ cup potato starch

2 tablespoons tapioca
starch

2 tablespoons baking
powder

½ teaspoon freshly ground
black pepper

1 teaspoon sweet paprika

1 teaspoon sea salt

½ teaspoon cayenne
pepper

Grated zest of 1 lemon

INGREDIENTS CONTINUES

Chicken and waffles is one of those incongruous dishes that doesn't sound like it should be good, but is really quite addicting. Elie usually requests chicken and waffles for his birthday dinner. This version is a cross between traditional chicken and waffles and Nashville's hot chicken (another favorite). It's sweet and savory and spicy, all at once. To brighten up the meal, serve the chicken and waffles with Cabbage and Fennel Salad (page 112). · SERVES 6

1 In a large bowl, whisk together the yogurt, milk, lemon juice and zest, bay leaves, thyme, dried oregano, black pepper, pepper flakes, and sea salt. Add the chicken thighs and stir, making sure the chicken is covered by the marinade. Cover and refrigerate overnight.

2 At least 30 minutes before you'll be breading the chicken, remove it from the refrigerator and let come to room temperature. Place paper towels or a clean kitchen towel on the counter, and place a large wire rack on top.

3 To make the breading, whisk together the flour, potato starch, tapioca starch, baking powder, black pepper, paprika, sea salt, cayenne, and lemon zest in a large bowl. Using tongs, remove a chicken thigh from the marinade and let any excess marinade drip off. Place the chicken in the breading and turn to coat, pressing the breading onto all surfaces of the chicken with a clean hand. Transfer the chicken to the wire rack. Repeat with the remaining pieces of chicken. Let the chicken rest on the rack for about an hour, giving it time for the coating to adhere.

4 Attach a deep-frying thermometer to the side of a Dutch oven (preferably enameled cast iron). Pour in the oil and bring it to 350 degrees F over medium heat. Line a large platter with paper towels.

RECIPE CONTINUES

for cooking and serving

2 quarts avocado oil

Flaky salt

6 Cornmeal Waffles
(page 55), warm

Honey-Chili Butter
(page 265), melted

COOKING TIPS

If you forget to marinate the chicken overnight, it's okay. Just let it soak in the marinade for as long as possible. The flavor of the marinade won't have a chance to perfume the chicken, but it will still be tender and crispy.

Over the years, I've learned a few tricks for great fried chicken.

First, marinate the chicken overnight to let the meat absorb flavor and keep the meat succulent.

Second, let the chicken rest for at least an hour after breading and before frying, to give the crust a chance to adhere to the chicken.

Third, I have found that frying the chicken in an enameled cast-iron pot maintains even heat, cooking the chicken through without danger of burning.

Lastly, partially cover the pan with a lid to keep the heat consistent but still allow steam to escape. You'll end up with perfect fried chicken, each time.

5 When the oil is hot, use clean tongs to place 3 pieces of the chicken in the oil. Partially cover the pot with a lid and set a timer for 6 minutes. After 6 minutes, remove the lid. Using tongs, flip the chicken to the other side. Partially cover the pot again and set the timer for 5 minutes. After 5 minutes, check the temperature of the largest piece of chicken using an instant-read thermometer. The chicken is done when it is golden brown and reaches 165 degrees F. Remove the chicken from the oil and place on the platter. While the chicken is still hot, sprinkle it with flaky salt. Repeat with the remaining chicken.

6 To serve, place a waffle on each plate and top with a piece of chicken. Drizzle honey-chili butter over the chicken and waffle and serve.

oatmeal sundae

1 cup water

⅛ teaspoon sea salt

½ cup gluten-free Old-fashioned rolled oats

½ cup fresh or frozen blueberries

½ cup fresh or frozen raspberries

1 to 2 tablespoons ground flaxseed

1 to 2 tablespoons unsweetened coconut flakes, toasted

1 to 2 tablespoons Golden Almond Butter (page 262)

1 to 2 teaspoons honey (optional)

1 teaspoon bee pollen (optional)

COOKING TIP

For an oatmeal with texture, only stir the oatmeal once, when you add it to the water. Don't stir again until you stir in the berries at the end.

MAKE IT YOUR OWN

To make a green oatmeal, mix 1 serving of your favorite green powder into the water.

For a rich and creamy oatmeal, stir a little ghee or butter into the oatmeal and top with a drizzle of half-and-half and extra berries.

Other ideas for toppings include cocoa nibs, chopped almonds or pecans, Greek yogurt, maple syrup, gogi berries, chopped dates, and currants.

I think oatmeal has a reputation as a boring breakfast. But it doesn't have to be. We call our morning oatmeal 'sundaes,' because it's all about the toppings. Blueberries and raspberries provide natural sweetness in addition to a good dose of antioxidants and fiber. Ground flaxseed has additional fiber and plant-based omega-3s. The coconut flakes are delicious and provide crunch, and the almond butter boosts the protein. I love the slightly sweet, earthy flavor of the bee pollen, but it's optional. Sometimes I also stir adaptogens, like ashwagandha or cordyceps, into the oatmeal. (I like Hyperion Herbs brand.) If you like, drizzle the top with a little honey. It's a beautiful, nourishing, and filling breakfast. PHOTOGRAPH ON PAGE 15 · SERVES 1

1 Combine the water and salt in a small pot. Place over high heat and bring to a boil. Add the oats and immediately reduce the heat to low. Stir once. Cook for 5 minutes or until all the water has been absorbed.

2 Add the blueberries and raspberries, but do not stir. Place a lid on the pot and let sit for 5 minutes.

3 Remove the lid and stir the berries into the oatmeal. Transfer the cooked oatmeal to a bowl. Top with the ground flaxseed, coconut flakes, and almond butter. Garnish with honey and/or bee pollen, if desired.

huevos divorciados

1 small onion (about
5 ounces), cut in large
pieces

2 cups cherry or grape
tomatoes, or 2 large
tomatoes, cored

4 or 5 tomatillos, husked

2 jalapeños chiles, seeded
if desired

4 cloves garlic, peeled

Sea salt

Extra virgin olive oil or
avocado oil

1 bunch fresh cilantro

Grated zest and juice of
2 limes

8 large eggs

8 Corn Tortillas (page 42)

6 ounces sharp cheddar
cheese, shredded
(about 1½ cups)

8 pieces bacon, cooked
until crispy

Sliced avocado (optional)

Several years before Theo was born, Elie and I were vacationing in Puerto Vallarta, staying on the top floor of a small inn in the historic district, the bedroom doors opening to a rooftop garden. Our hosts generously brought breakfast to the garden each morning, usually huevos divorciados or 'divorced eggs.' The name of the dish comes from the separated eggs, each with its own sauce. We ate the eggs and homemade tortillas drowned in spicy twin red and green salsas while overlooking the rooftops that stretched to the sea. While the melted cheese and bacon aren't traditional, we are big fans of both.
SERVES 4

1 Preheat the oven to 425 degrees F.

2 In one baking dish, combine the onion, tomatoes, 1 of the jalapeños, 2 of the garlic cloves, and ¼ teaspoon salt. Drizzle with 2 tablespoons oil.

3 In another baking dish, combine the tomatillos, the other jalapeño, and the remaining garlic. Season with ¼ teaspoon salt and drizzle with 2 tablespoons oil.

4 Place both baking dishes in the oven and roast for 30 to 40 minutes, until the vegetables have started to lose their juices and are caramelizing.

5 Remove both baking dishes from the oven. (Leave the oven on.) Transfer the tomatillos and garlic to a high-speed blender. Add a big handful of the cilantro sprigs. Add the lime zest and juice. Blend on medium speed until all of the ingredients are finely chopped and the texture resembles a fine salsa. Taste for seasoning and adjust if necessary. Pour the green salsa into a jar or bowl.

6 Transfer the roasted tomato mixture to the blender (no need to wash the blender) and add the remaining cilantro. Blend as above, then pour into a second jar or bowl.

RECIPE CONTINUES

7 Line a baking sheet with parchment paper. Place the tortillas on the baking sheet and divide the cheese between the tortillas. Bake just until the corn tortillas are warm and the cheese is melted, about 5 minutes. Keep warm.

8 Heat a large skillet over medium heat. Pour in just enough oil to cover the bottom. Add 4 of the eggs. Cook, basting the sides and tops of the eggs with oil, until the whites are set but the yolks are still runny. Remove to a plate and season with salt. Repeat with the remaining eggs.

9 To serve, place 2 tortillas, slightly overlapping, on each plate. Top each pair of tortillas with 2 pieces bacon and 2 fried eggs. Spoon green salsa on top of 1 egg and spoon red salsa on top of the other. Add sliced avocado, if desired.

shakshuka

¼ cup extra virgin olive oil

1 large onion, thinly sliced

2 cloves garlic, thinly sliced

¼ teaspoon sea salt, plus more if needed

1 red bell pepper, seeded and sliced

1 small fresh chile (like a jalapeño), stemmed, seeded, and cut in small dice, or a pinch of red pepper flakes

1 tablespoon My Spice Blend (page 262)

One 28-ounce can whole San Marzano tomatoes

1 cup water, plus more if needed

6 large eggs

3 ounces feta, crumbled (about ¾ cup)

Fresh cilantro sprigs, for garnish

Fresh cayenne pepper or other spicy pepper, sliced, for garnish (optional)

Toasted Pumpkin Seeds (page 260), for garnish

Sourdough Flatbread (page 34) or sliced Daily Bread (page 27), for serving

MAKE AHEAD

The sauce for the shakshuka can be made a day or two ahead and reheated gently over low heat. Alternatively, freeze the sauce in an airtight container for up to 3 months. Thaw in the refrigerator overnight before reheating. Cook the eggs in the sauce right before serving.

When Elie and I first started dating in 2010, he gave me an Israeli cookbook and I made my first shakshuka. Back then, shakshuka hadn't yet reached its current level of fame, gracing the pages of magazines and making its way onto restaurant menus around the world. There's a reason it has become so popular. It's comforting and delicious. This rich tomato stew, perfumed with the flavor of toasted cumin, coriander, cardamom, and fennel, serves as a bed for eggs softly simmered in the sauce until the yolks are just set. When I make shakshuka, I love to start by slowly cooking the onions until they are almost caramelized, creating a deep, slightly sweet base to the dish. This is my basic recipe, but see the ideas on the next page for making it your own. Served with homemade bread, this makes a lovely one-pan meal for brunch or dinner. · SERVES 3 OR 4 AS A MAIN COURSE, OR 6 AS PART OF A BREAKFAST SPREAD

1 Heat a large heavy-bottomed skillet (not cast iron) over medium heat. (The larger the surface area of the skillet, the better.) Pour in the oil. Add the onion, garlic, and salt, Cook, stirring often, until the onions are almost caramelized, about 20 minutes.

2 Add the bell pepper and chile and cook until they begin to soften, about 3 or 4 minutes.

3 Stir in the spice blend and cook for another minute.

4 Crush the tomatoes with your hands, breaking them into large pieces. Add tomatoes with their juice and the water to the vegetables. Bring to a boil, then reduce to a simmer. Cook for at least 30 minutes and preferably an hour, stirring occasionally, until the sauce is thick and flavorful. If too much liquid has evaporated—the sauce should be the consistency of pasta sauce—add a little water to thin. Taste for seasoning and add salt if necessary.

RECIPE CONTINUES

COOKING TIP

It can be tricky to get the eggs just right, with the whites cooked but the yolks still runny. With practice, you can do it! It's a matter of keeping the heat low and keeping a lid partially on to cook the eggs from below and above. But if your egg yolks cook until they are hard, it's okay. I have eaten many a shakshuka at an Israeli restaurant with hard-cooked yolks.

If you're nervous about overcooking the eggs in the sauce, you can poach or fry them separately and top the sauce with them when serving. It's a little more labor.

MAKE IT YOUR OWN

Shakshuka is a blank canvas for your imagination. I love adding roasted cubed eggplant. You can make it heartier by adding cooked chickpeas, spicy chorizo or Italian sausage. All of these can be added at the same time as the tomatoes. Make a lamb version by adding ½ pound ground lamb with the onions, spicing it with a little harissa. Often, I stir in a handful of spinach or baby kale right before adding the eggs.

5 Reduce the heat to medium-low. Using the back of a large serving spoon, make six wells in the sauce to hold the eggs. Crack an egg and carefully place it in one of the wells. Repeat with remaining eggs. Using a fork, spread the whites into the sauce, being careful not to break the yolks. Partially cover the pan with a lid, allowing steam to escape. Cook until the whites are firm but the yolks are still custardy in the middle, about 8 to 10 minutes.

6 Serve the shakshuka in the skillet, garnished with feta, cilantro, sliced fresh pepper, and pumpkin seeds. Serve hot, with the bread for scooping up all that sauce.

green shakshuka

2 leeks, halved lengthwise and thinly sliced

Extra virgin olive oil

Sea salt

1 head fennel, trimmed, cored, and thinly sliced

2 cloves garlic, thinly sliced

Pinch of Aleppo-style pepper or red pepper flakes

1 small bunch kale, stemmed and chopped (about 2 cups)

1 small bunch Swiss chard, stemmed and chopped (about 2 cups)

½ bunch fresh parsley

1 ounce Parmigiano-Reggiano cheese, finely grated (about ¼ cup)

6 large eggs

3 ounces feta cheese, crumbled (about ¾ cup)

Toasted Pumpkin Seeds (page 260), for garnish

Sourdough Flatbread (page 34) or sliced Daily Bread (page 27), for serving

COOKING TIP
See page 64 for tips on cooking the eggs.

Green shakshuka reminds me of traditional French baked eggs Florentine, but with a Middle Eastern twist. Slowly sautéed leeks and wilted greens are blended to create a luscious sauce in which to poach the eggs. It's topped with salty and creamy crumbled feta, and toasted pumpkin seeds for crunch. Just like with the tomato-based shakshuka on page 63, serve this with bread for sopping up the custardy egg and sauce. SERVES 3 OR 4 AS A MAIN COURSE, OR 6 AS PART OF A BREAKFAST SPREAD

1 Heat a large, deep skillet over medium-low heat. Pour in 2 tablespoons oil. Stir in the leeks and ¼ teaspoon salt. Cook, stirring often, for 5 to 7 minutes, until the leeks are very soft. Add the fennel, garlic, and pepper and cook for another 3 to 5 minutes, until the fennel is soft.

2 Add another tablespoon or two of oil. Add the kale and Swiss chard and another ¼ teaspoon salt. Cook, stirring often, until the greens have wilted, about 5 minutes. You may need to add a couple of tablespoons of water if the pan becomes dry.

3 Spoon half of the leek-and-greens mixture into a blender. Add the parsley. Blend until smooth, adding a couple of tablespoons of water if necessary to keep it moving. Pour the puree back into the skillet with the remaining leeks and greens and stir them together. If the mixture seems dry, stir in a couple of tablespoons of water. Stir in the parmesan.

4 Using the back of a large serving spoon, make six wells in the leek and greens mixture. Crack an egg and carefully place it in one of the wells. Repeat with remaining eggs. Using a fork, spread the whites into the sauce, being careful not to break the yolks. Partially cover the pan with a lid, allowing steam to escape. Cook until the egg whites are firm but the yolks are custardy in the middle, 8 to 10 minutes.

5 Serve the shakshuka in the skillet, garnished with the feta and pumpkin seeds. Serve hot, with bread.

israeli breakfast

FRIED EGGS, HERB SALAD, YOGURT WITH OLIVE OIL, AND OLIVES

2 large eggs

Extra virgin olive oil

Flaky salt

Aleppo-style pepper

½ cup coarsely chopped fresh herbs (such as cilantro, parsley, mint, and/or dill)

Pinch of grated lemon zest

Pinch of sumac

⅓ - ½ cup whole milk Greek yogurt

Freshly ground black pepper

Olives

Sourdough Flatbread (page 34)

Close to the Shuk HaCarmel (Carmel Market) in Tel Aviv, there used to be a small bohemian-style café called Sheleg. Before heading to the beach in the morning, we would crowd into the small tables for breakfast, ordering lattes and freshly squeezed orange and pomegranate juice. I didn't even need to look at the menu. I ordered this simple breakfast every time: olive oil–fried eggs topped with sumac and served with bitter olives, a bright herb salad, and a shot of Greek yogurt topped with olive oil and black pepper. Simple, savory and satisfying. SERVES 1

1 Heat a medium skillet over medium heat. Add enough oil to cover the bottom, about 3 tablespoons. Carefully add the eggs and season with flaky salt and Aleppo-style pepper. Let the eggs cook for 1 to 2 minutes, until the edges start to brown. Tilting the skillet slightly, spoon up some of the hot oil and baste the top of the whites, just until the whites are set. Avoid basting the yolk, so it stays bright orange and runny. Transfer the eggs to a plate.

2 Place the herbs in a small bowl. Top with lemon zest, sumac, and a drizzle of olive oil. Place on the plate next to the eggs.

3 Fill a small glass with the yogurt. Drizzle about a teaspoon of oil over the top and sprinkle with black pepper. Place on the plate with the eggs and herbs. Serve with olives and flatbread.

creamy scrambled eggs,

RADISH SPROUTS, AVOCADO, FETA, AND SUMAC

12 large eggs

¼ cup whole milk

¼ teaspoon sea salt

⅛ teaspoon freshly ground black pepper

6 ounces sharp cheddar cheese, grated (about 1½ cups)

4 tablespoons (½ stick) unsalted butter

½ cup radish sprouts

2 avocados, pitted, peeled, and sliced

6 ounces feta, crumbled (about 1½ cups)

⅛ to ¼ teaspoon sumac

When I'm making brunch for a lot of people, I don't want to stand at the stove frying eggs to order. Instead, I make a big pan of softly scrambled cheesy eggs. I cook them slowly over low heat, and remove them from heat before I think they are done, to keep them luscious and creamy. Topped with sprouts and feta and served with sliced avocado, this is a beautiful dish to accompany the sourdough pancakes (page 52) or biscuits (page 29). · SERVES 6

1 Break the eggs into a large bowl. Add the milk, salt, and pepper and whisk well, until combined. Add the cheddar and whisk again.

2 Heat a large skillet over medium-low heat. Add the butter and let it melt and start to foam. Add the eggs and let them set for a minute. Scrape a spatula across the eggs slowly. Continue to move the spatula slowly across the eggs, creating large, creamy curds.

3 Before you think the eggs are quite done (when they're still shiny and look wet, about 5 to 8 minutes), remove the pan from the heat and pour the eggs onto a warm serving platter. Nestle the avocado slices on the side and sprinkle with the radish sprouts, feta, and sumac. Serve immediately.

DAIRY-FREE CREAMY SCRAMBLED EGGS · Cook the eggs in 2 to 3 tablespoons extra virgin olive oil instead of butter and omit the cheddar cheese. Instead of topping the eggs with feta, use 2 tablespoons Toasted Pumpkin Seeds (page 260) or 1 teaspoon nigella seeds.

country ham biscuit sandwiches

8 Flaky Southern-Style
Biscuits (page 29)

Cherry jam

8 ounces thinly sliced
cooked country ham or
prosciutto

8 ounces sliced sharp
cheddar cheese

Dijon mustard

SERVING TIP

When I host Christmas parties,
I turn the idea of this biscuit
sandwich into an unexpected
comfort food buffet. I put out
big platters of biscuits, country
ham, a variety of cheeses,
mustard, and jams. It's an
opportunity for everyone to
make their own sandwich or
snack as they please. With a big,
crisp salad, a variety of desserts,
and champagne, it's all you
need.

If you've never had country ham, it's like the prosciutto of the
South. Salty and subtly smoky, it's meaty and flavorful. I order
country ham from Newsom's Country Ham in Kentucky—a half
is all you'll need. However, it is a splurge, so you can substitute
prosciutto or regular baked ham. Country ham and biscuits
are a classic combination, but here I've layered them with
cherry jam, melted cheese and spicy Dijon. It's so good.
MAKES 8 SANDWICHES

1 Preheat the oven to 375 degrees F. Line a baking sheet with
parchment paper.

2 Cut the biscuits in half. Lay the bottom halves on the parchment paper, cut side up. Spread cherry jam on each and top
with ham and cheese. Place the top halves on the baking sheet
separately, so they also warm in the oven.

3 Bake for 8 to 10 minutes, until the cheese is melted and
bubbling. Remove the baking sheet from the oven. Spread
mustard on the cut sides of the top half of the biscuits and
place on top of the bottom half. Serve warm.

WHAT CAN YOU DO WITH COUNTRY HAM?

Fry thin slices of ham and serve
with Creamy Scrambled Eggs
(page 71).

Thinly slice ham and serve with
Fresh Corn Polenta (page 161)
and Marinated Tomato and
Cucumber Salad (page 107).

Use as a topping for Deviled
Eggs (page 82).

Use the country ham to flavor
the Collard Greens (page 146),
adding the ham after sautéing
the onions. Because the ham
is so salty, omit the salt in the
recipe.

SETTING THE TABLE

My great-grandmother, Granny Dixon, was a regal woman, always with her snow white hair pinned in a low bun at the nape of her neck. Her immaculate, stylish home in Appalachia was a pastel confection of rooms painted light pink, minty green and robin's egg blue. The china cabinet in her dining room displayed a set of pink and gold Haviland china, with gleaming Rose Point silver tucked into the drawers. A talented seamstress, her embroidered table linens were precisely stacked between crisp, transparent sheets of tissue paper. Every detail of her home was thoughtful, filled with moments of curated beauty.

Sitting at Granny's table in her bright, cheerful kitchen, even for a simple breakfast of fried eggs and biscuits, felt special. A vase of pink peonies, freshly cut from her garden, sat in the center. Green footed juice glasses sat by each plate, ready for orange juice. Pink napkins, ironed into a triangle, were tucked beside each blue and white Homer Laughlin plate. Every detail felt thoughtful, her way of saying, "I am glad you are here."

My mom, Carolyn, has this same gift. When you walk into her home for a meal, you immediately feel special. Mom embodies gracious hospitality. She deeply considers the personalities and preferences of her guests as she chooses the place settings, arranges the flowers, prepares the food. She carefully presses each napkin, polishes every glass. She loves the process of creating every detail, and it shows. There's a special magic in that kind of preparation, that thoughtfulness, that makes a gathering sparkle. These gestures are not superfluous; they connect us.

Thoughtfully setting the table creates an opportunity for us to honor the ritual of sitting down together, a moment to pause and revel in these moments of beauty and connection.

What is the secret of setting a table? Authenticity. Don't worry about creating something worthy of social media. Be you. If it's your style, make it fancy. Pull out the heirloom china and silver. Create an intricate centerpiece. Light the candelabra. If you and your guests are more understated, keep it simple. Use your everyday plates or mismatched vintage finds and un-ironed linen napkins—or paper napkins. I always include fresh flowers or greenery clipped from the garden and a few low candles. I prefer to leave lots of room for platters of food and the elbows of guests leaned forward in conversation.

For me, taking time to create a beautiful setting for a shared meal feels like meditation. As I center each plate and line up the silverware, I am thinking about creating a thoughtful space that makes guests feel special and seen, one that invites shared stories and true connection.

CHAPTER THREE

SNACKS & STARTERS

marinated feta

WITH FRESH OREGANO AND SUMAC

One 7-ounce block sheep and goat's milk feta cheese, drained of its brine

2 tablespoons extra virgin olive oil, plus more for garnish

Grated zest of 1 lemon

1 teaspoon finely chopped fresh oregano leaves

⅛ teaspoon sumac, plus more for garnish

When I'm having friends over for dinner, I keep the appetizer simple, generally a beautiful charcuterie board dressed up with something homemade, like the Fresh Chile Harissa on page 273 or this marinated feta. A simple dressing of olive oil, lemon zest, fresh oregano, and sumac elevates feta into something special. Serve it with Sourdough Flatbread (page 34) and more olive oil. PHOTOGRAPH ON PAGE 80 · SERVES 4 TO 6

Using your hands, break the feta into rough 1-inch pieces and place them in a medium bowl. Add the oil, lemon zest, oregano, and sumac and toss together to combine. Transfer to a serving bowl and top with additional sumac and another drizzle of olive oil. The marinated feta can be made up to 8 hours in advance. Tightly cover and place in the refrigerator. Remove the cheese from the refrigerator and allow to come to room temperature before serving.

roasted carrot–harissa dip

1 pound carrots (about
5 large carrots)

4 tablespoons extra virgin
olive oil

¼ teaspoon sea salt, plus
more if needed

¼ cup raw tahini

2 tablespoons Fresh Chile
Harissa (page 273), plus
more for drizzling

If I can't sleep at night, sometimes I pass the time by inventing new recipes in my head. When I thought about this recipe, I could imagine exactly how it would taste—slightly smoky from the roasted carrots and spicy from the harissa, with a creamy texture from the tahini. When I made it, I didn't change a thing from the invented recipe. I love it when that happens. This bright orange dip adds beautiful color and bold flavor to a mezze platter or cheese and charcuterie board. Plus, it's dairy free. PHOTOGRAPH ON PAGE 81 · MAKES 1 TO 1½ CUPS

1 Preheat the oven to 375 degrees F. Line a rimmed baking sheet with parchment paper.

2 Cut the carrots into large pieces (no need to peel) and place on the baking sheet. Drizzle the carrots with 2 tablespoons of the oil and sprinkle with the salt. Toss to coat. Roast for 25 to 30 minutes, until the carrots are very soft and starting to brown.

3 Transfer the carrots to a food processor. Add the tahini and harissa and blend until smooth. Add water, a couple of table-spoons at a time, until you get to the desired consistency. Taste and adjust the seasoning, if necessary.

4 Spoon the carrot dip into a shallow bowl. Using the back of a spoon, create a bed for the olive oil. Pour the remaining 2 tablespoons oil over the carrot dip. This will keep in the refrigerator for several days, tightly covered.

tangy pimiento cheese

1 pound sharp cheddar cheese, grated (about 4 cups)

⅓ cup Homemade Mayonnaise (page 274) or purchased mayonnaise

½ cup Mama Lil's Sweet Hot Peppers

2 tablespoons juice from the Mama Lil's peppers, or apple cider vinegar

1½ teaspoons Dijon mustard

⅛ teaspoon red pepper flakes

½ teaspoon sea salt

Freshly ground black pepper

Pimiento cheese reminds me of my childhood. After school, I'd get off the bus at my friends' house and we'd head inside to make snacks before choreographing another dance routine to "You're the One That I Want" or practicing back walkovers in the backyard. More often than not, we'd grab the tub of creamy, orange pimiento cheese from the refrigerator and slather it between two slices of soft white bread. In my memory, it was so good. This pimiento cheese is a fancier version of the one from my childhood. Traditional pimiento cheese uses jarred pimiento peppers, but I like the tangy spiciness of Mama Lil's peppers. If you can't find Mama Lil's, use a tablespoon of the Fresh Chile Harissa (page 273). ·
MAKES ABOUT 3 CUPS

Place the cheese, mayonnaise, peppers and pepper juice, mustard, pepper flakes, salt, and 1/8 teaspoon black pepper in a food processor. Pulse to combine, until the texture is the texture and consistency of cottage cheese. Taste and adjust the seasonings, if necessary. Transfer to a bowl, cover, and chill at least 30 minutes before serving. The pimento cheese will keep, tightly covered, in the refrigerator for up to a week.

WHAT CAN YOU DO WITH PIMIENTO CHEESE?

Serve with the Nigella Seed Cheddar Wafers (page 41) as a snack or appetizer.

Make a grilled pimiento cheese sandwich.

Slather pimiento cheese on toasted bread and top with a fried egg.

Top a grass-fed beef burger with pimiento cheese.

Make pimiento macaroni and cheese.

Stir into Creamy Polenta or Grits (page 176).

deviled eggs

Ice water

12 large eggs

½ cup Homemade
Mayonnaise (page 274)

2 tablespoons Dijon
mustard

1 tablespoon apple cider
vinegar

½ teaspoon sea salt

⅛ teaspoon freshly ground
black pepper

⅛ teaspoon Aleppo-style
pepper or a pinch of
cayenne pepper

optional toppings

Finely chopped fresh
parsley or tarragon leaves

Fresh dill sprigs

Fresh basil flowers

Finely chopped cooked
bacon

Sliced smoked salmon

Salmon roe or caviar

PICKLED DEVILED EGGS •
If you would like some of the
deviled eggs to be bright
purple in color, pickle them
in beet juice: Drain the brine
from a jar of pickled beets
into a bowl. Add whole
peeled hard-boiled eggs.
Cover and refrigerate for
12 to 24 hours, turning the
eggs occasionally, until
colored as desired. Remove
the eggs from the brine and
dry them with a paper towel.
Use the pickled eggs to
make deviled eggs.

I'm always thrilled when I see deviled eggs at a party. They evoke such nostalgia. I can't remember a childhood barbeque, church supper or Easter lunch without a tray or two of deviled eggs. Leave them plain or be creative with the toppings, adding fresh herbs, smoked salmon, crispy bacon, or caviar or less expensive salmon roe. I usually pickle half of the eggs, because the bright purple color is so pretty. Using homemade mayonnaise to whip with the egg yolks makes these eggs special. But if you don't want to make mayonnaise, an avocado oil mayonnaise is a good substitute. • MAKES 24 DEVILED EGGS

1 Fill a large bowl with ice water. Fill a large pot with an inch or two of water. Place a steamer basket in the pot. Turn the heat to high and bring the water to a boil, then reduce the heat to medium. Using long-handled tongs, carefully place the eggs in one layer in the steamer basket. Cover the pot. Cook the eggs for exactly 12 minutes. Using a slotted spoon, remove the eggs to the ice water. Alternatively, use the egg function on your Instant Pot. (Steaming or using the Instant Pot ensures easy-to-peel eggs.)

2 As soon as the eggs are cool, peel them. Cut the eggs in half lengthwise. Place the yolks in the bowl of a stand mixer. Arrange the whites on a deviled egg platter or large serving platter.

3 Fit the mixer with the whisk attachment. Add the mayonnaise, mustard, vinegar, salt, black pepper, and Aleppo-style pepper to the eggs. Whip on high speed until very smooth. If you want to remove any lumps from the egg yolk filling, transfer it to a fine-mesh sieve and use a spatula to press it through the sieve into a bowl. (Honestly, though, I don't usually do this step.)

4 Using a small cookie scoop, fill each egg white half with the yolk filling. Alternatively, fit a piping bag with a ½-inch plain tip, transfer the filling to the bag, and pipe it into the egg halves.

5 Cover the eggs loosely with plastic wrap and refrigerate until chilled. Before serving, garnish as desired.

tahini sauce

1 cup raw tahini

Grated zest of 1 lemon

About ¼ cup fresh lemon juice

¼ to ½ teaspoon sea salt

About ½ cup cold water

SERVING TIPS

All these tahini sauces look beautiful served in shallow bowls. Take the back of spoon and make a swoop or swirl through the top of the sauce, leaving an indentation. Garnish as desired with a drizzle of olive oil and a sprinkling of sumac, za'atar, or Toasted Pumpkin Seeds or Toasted Sunflower Seeds (page 260).

Serve any of the tahini sauces with raw or roasted vegetables, crackers, or flatbread. Or just eat with a spoon.

If you haven't eaten tahini sauce before, it's a rich, creamy spread with a flavor reminiscent of sesame seeds, but not at all the same. Plain tahini sauce, blended simply with lemon, is the version I make most often. But for a bight green, verdant version, make an herby tahini or a slightly bitter (in a good way!) kale tahini. I almost guarantee you will want to eat this with a spoon. It's equally good as a dip for roasted vegetables as it is spooned onto falafel or as part of a mezze platter. You can use it as the base for salad dressing or hummus. The only trick to good tahini sauce is good tahini. Look for tahini made from unroasted sesame seeds, from Israel or Lebanon. Check your local Mediterranean market or purchase it online. My favorite brand is Al Arz. · MAKES ABOUT 1 ½ CUPS

Put the tahini in a medium bowl. Whisk in the lemon zest and juice, and ¼ teaspoon sea salt, making a thick paste. It will turn a strange color and consistency and you'll think you've ruined it. Whisk in water until the tahini becomes the consistency of a thick sauce. (I generally use about ½ cup, but you can add less or more to get the consistency you want.) Taste for the right balance of lemon and salt and adjust as desired. Tahini sauce will keep in the refrigerator for 1 week, tightly covered.

HERBY GREEN TAHINI SAUCE · Make the tahini sauce by combining everything in a food processor. Add ½ cup fresh parsley leaves or a mix of parsley and cilantro. Blend until smooth.

KALE TAHINI SAUCE · Make the tahini sauce by combining everything in a food processor. Add 4 large kale leaves (stemmed), ¼ teaspoon sumac, and ⅛ teaspoon Aleppo-style pepper. Blend until smooth.

olive oil–avocado dip

2 or 3 large ripe avocados

Grated zest of 1 lemon

3 to 5 tablespoons of lemon juice

¼ to ½ teaspoon sea salt

⅛ to ¼ teaspoon Aleppo-style pepper (depending on how much you like spicy)

3 tablespoons extra virgin olive oil

¼ cup loosely packed fresh cilantro leaves, chopped

Toasted Pumpkin Seeds (page 260), for garnish

Flaky salt, for garnish

MAKE AHEAD

The avocado dip can be made up to a day ahead. Press a piece of plastic wrap securely onto the top of the avocado, so that no air can reach the dip. (Oxygen is what causes the avocado to brown.) When you're ready to serve, remove it from the refrigerator, stir, and add the garnishes.

MAKE IT YOUR OWN

You can certainly make this with lime juice instead of lemon juice. You can also vary the herb for different flavors. In the winter, I like to top it with pomegranate seeds and serve it as part of a charcuterie and cheese board.

I know this recipe sounds very simple—and it is—but it's always a crowd pleaser. People are so used to adding onions and garlic to their avocado, this clean-tasting version can be a revelation. I make this several times a week—for avocado toast, for tacos, or to serve with Sourdough Flatbread (page 34) or cut vegetables as a simple snack before dinner. Theo loves it, so it's often on his dinner plate. · SERVES 4 TO 6

1 Halve the avocados and remove the pits. Working with one avocado half at a time, use a small knife to score the flesh diagonally one way and then the other way, all the way to the skin (but not through it). (You're creating dice that will make smashing easier.) Repeat with the remaining halves.

2 Using a spoon, scoop the avocado flesh into a medium bowl. Add all the lemon zest and some lemon juice, starting with 3 tablespoons. Add ¼ teaspoon sea salt, ⅛ teaspoon pepper, and 2 tablespoons of the oil. Using a fork, smash the avocado until fairly smooth. Taste and adjust for salt, lemon juice, and spice. (You'll probably need 4 or 5 tablespoons, but taste to be sure. I like mine quite lemony.) Stir in the cilantro.

3 Transfer the avocado mixture to a serving bowl. Drizzle the remaining tablespoon oil over the top and garnish with pumpkin seeds, more Aleppo-style pepper and flaky salt.

If you visit the Old City of Jerusalem, walk through the entrance to the Muslim quarter and follow the sloped path through the spice vendors and past the shops selling trinkets and kitchenware, until you get to the end. Turn left, and there, on your right, you will find a tiny restaurant—a proverbial hole in the wall—with a few plastic tables and chairs. All they serve is hummus. When you order, the shallow bowl of still-warm hummus comes ladled with cooked chickpeas and doused with a big swirl of rich olive oil. Along with the hummus you'll get a bowl of pickles, wedges of raw onions, and piles of fluffy, tender pita. As you tear off a wedge of pita and drag it through the hummus, you'll leave a trail of olive oil behind. And it will be the best hummus you've ever tasted.

hummus worth making from scratch

2 cups dried chickpeas

1 teaspoon baking soda

1 cup raw tahini, plus more if needed

3 to 6 tablespoons fresh lemon juice

1 teaspoon sea salt, plus more if needed

Ice water (optional)

Extra virgin olive oil

⅛ to ¼ teaspoon sumac, for garnish

Soft pita or sourdough flatbread (page 34), for serving

WHAT CAN YOU DO WITH LEFTOVER CHICKPEAS?

If you have any chickpeas left over, use them within 5 days or freeze them in their cooking liquid.

Add 1 cup cooked chickpeas to Shakshuka (page 63).

Add 1 or 2 cups to the Turmeric Chicken and Rice (page 127). Add after the rice is cooked, to prevent the chickpeas from overcooking.

For a plant-based picnic salad, add 1 or 2 cups of cold chickpeas to the Chopped Tomato Salad (page 111).

Sauté onions, garlic and red peppers and then add cooked chickpeas and a tablespoon or two of Fresh Chile Harissa (page 273). Use as a plant-based taco filling.

Creamy homemade hummus is a completely different food from the stiff dips sold in plastic containers. Hummus should be silky and smooth and not too thick, so you can easily scoop it with a piece of bread or pita. The trick to this hummus is lots of tahini. And while cooking the chickpeas takes some planning ahead and stove time, it's completely hands-off and very rewarding. · MAKES 4 TO 5 CUPS

1 The night before you plan on cooking them, put the chickpeas in a large bowl with the baking soda. Cover them with cold water, at least 4 inches above the top of the chickpeas. Leave to soak overnight at room temperature.

2 When you're ready to cook them, drain the chickpeas. Place them in a large pot and cover with fresh water to 2 inches above the chickpeas. Bring to a boil, then reduce to a simmer. Skim off any foam and all the skins that float to the surface. Cook until the chickpeas are very tender, between 1 and 3 hours, adding water if necessary to keep them covered. (The cooking time will depend on the age of your chickpeas.)

3 Let the chickpeas cool to room temperature in the cooking liquid, then refrigerate for at least 2 hours, until very cold.

4 Using a slotted spoon or sieve, scoop out 3 cups of the chickpeas and place them in a high-speed blender. (You can make the hummus in a food processor, but it won't get quite as smooth. A high-speed blender will give you the silkiest texture.) Add the tahini, 3 tablespoons of the lemon juice, and 1 teaspoon salt. Process until very smooth. The hummus should be the consistency of Greek yogurt. If it's too thick, add a little ice water or some of the cooking liquid and blend again. Taste and adjust the tahini, lemon juice, and/or salt to taste. I usually add about 3 more tablespoons of lemon juice.

5 To serve, scoop the hummus into a shallow bowl. Use a spoon to swirl a sort of riverbed through the hummus. In the indention in the hummus, add some of the whole cooked chickpeas and a big drizzle of olive oil. Sprinkle the sumac on top. Serve with pita. The hummus will keep, tightly covered, in the refrigerator for up to 4 days.

cauliflower hummus

1 medium head cauliflower (about 1½ pounds, 4 to 5 cups florets)

1 tablespoon extra virgin olive oil, plus more for garnish

Sea salt

⅛ teaspoon Aleppo-style pepper or red pepper flakes

½ cup raw tahini

Grated zest and juice of 1 lemon (about 2 tablespoons lemon juice), plus more juice if needed

⅓ cup water, plus more if needed

About ⅛ teaspoon sumac, for garnish

MAKE AHEAD

The cauliflower hummus can be made up to 8 hours ahead of serving. Cover and refrigerate. It's best at room temperature, so pull it out of the refrigerator an hour before serving. Garnish right before serving.

MAKE IT YOUR OWN

If you're a garlic lover, go ahead and add a smashed garlic clove to the tahini. It will give the hummus a spicy kick. Feel free to experiment, adding ground cumin, or making a green cauliflower hummus by adding in a big handful of fresh herbs like parsley and cilantro (up to 1 cup).

If you make only one recipe from this cookbook, make this cauliflower hummus. It makes use of the mercurial properties of cauliflower—that ability to transform into something greater than itself. Cooking the cauliflower until tender and then blending it with rich tahini results in a creamy, smooth version of hummus quite different from the chickpea variety. · MAKES ABOUT 2 TO 3 CUPS; SERVES 4 TO 6

1 Preheat the oven to 425 degrees F. Line a baking sheet with parchment paper.

2 Place about 1½ cups of the cauliflower florets on the baking sheet. Drizzle with the oil, then sprinkle with ⅛ teaspoon salt and the pepper. Use your hands to evenly distribute the olive oil, salt, and pepper on the cauliflower. Roast the cauliflower for 20 to 25 minutes, until deeply browned and crispy. Set aside to cool.

3 While the cauliflower is roasting, place about 1 inch of water in a medium-sized pot. Bring to a simmer and add ½ teaspoon salt. Add the remaining cauliflower florets and simmer uncovered for about 10 minutes, stirring occasionally, until the cauliflower is very tender and most of the water has been evaporated.

4 Combine the tahini, ⅓ cup water, and the lemon zest and juice in a high-speed blender. Blend on high speed for 30 seconds to a minute, until well mixed. (The mixture should be quite thick.)

5 When the cauliflower is tender, remove it from the cooking water with a slotted spoon or sieve and add it to the tahini sauce in the blender. Blend on high speed until very smooth and creamy. If the hummus seems too thick, add a little more water, a tablespoon at a time. Taste and add salt or more lemon if needed. The hummus should be lemony and bright, but not make you pucker. If it tastes flat, add more salt.

6 To serve, pour the hummus into a shallow bowl. Smooth the top with a spoon, then swirl the back of the spoon through the top of the hummus to make an indentation. Pour a little olive oil on top and garnish with a sprinkling of sumac and the roasted cauliflower florets.

TIME SAVER

While I love the roasted cauliflower as a garnish, it's not imperative. You could garnish the hummus with Toasted Pumpkin Seeds or Sunflower Seeds (page 260), a sprinkling of Aleppo-style pepper or just simple sumac and olive oil.

OF NOTE FOR SPECIAL DIETS

This cauliflower hummus is a perfect dip to serve to loved ones who avoid legumes and can't eat traditional hummus.

For people who are sensitive to sesame, you can use walnut butter or finely ground walnuts instead of tahini. I've also tried it with toasted sunflower seed butter, which is delicious. Garnish the top with extra sunflower seeds.

lemony eggplant

2 large eggplants

¼ teaspoon sea salt

⅛ to ¼ teaspoon Aleppo-style pepper

Grated zest and juice of 1 lemon

4 tablespoons extra virgin olive oil, plus more if needed

¼ to ½ teaspoon za'atar, sumac or Aleppo-style pepper, for garnish

MAKE AHEAD

You can roast the eggplant up to a day ahead. Scoop out the eggplant flesh and store, tightly covered, in the refrigerator until you're ready to use it.

This bright eggplant dip is so versatile—as a part of a mezze platter, as a delicious bed for the slow-roasted lamb on page 212 or olive oil–poached halibut on page 225, or just scooped up with the sourdough flatbread on page 34. Be sure to pierce the eggplant with a knife or fork a few times, so that it doesn't explode while it's cooking. (I learned that the hard way: I once had an eggplant explode all over me just as friends were walking through the door.) · MAKES ABOUT 2 CUPS

1 Preheat the oven to 500 degrees F.

2 Place the eggplants on a rimmed baking sheet and pierce them a few times with the tip of a knife or a fork. Roast the eggplants, turning them occasionally with tongs, until they are charred and completely collapsed, 30 to 40 minutes.

3 Transfer the eggplants to a colander placed in the sink or over a bowl to drain. Let sit for about 10 minutes, until the eggplants are cool enough to handle.

4 Scoop the eggplant flesh out of the skins and drop it into a high-speed blender. Add the salt, ⅛ teaspoon Aleppo-style pepper, the lemon zest and juice, and 2 tablespoons of the oil. Blend on high speed until very smooth. Taste and adjust the seasoning, if necessary. If the eggplant tastes too bright and acidic, add a little more olive oil.

5 If you're serving this as a dip, pour the eggplant puree into a shallow bowl. Using a spoon, make a swoop through the eggplant to create a swirly bed for the olive oil. Pour the remaining 2 tablespoons of oil over the eggplant and sprinkle with the za'atar. This is best eaten the day it is made, although it will keep in the refrigerator, tightly covered, for a couple of days.

BABA GANOUSH · You can easily turn this spread into baba ganoush by adding about ¼ cup raw tahini when blending the eggplant. Adjust the lemon and salt as needed.

herby, crispy falafel

1 cup dried chickpeas

1½ teaspoons of My Spice Blend (page 262)

1 small onion (about 5 ounces)

1 clove garlic, peeled

About 1 cup loosely packed fresh parsley leaves and stems

About 1 cup loosely packed fresh cilantro leaves and stems

¼ teaspoon Aleppo-style pepper or a small pinch of red pepper flakes or cayenne pepper

½ teaspoon baking powder

1¼ teaspoon sea salt

Grated zest of 2 lemons

2 tablespoons water

1½ tablespoons rice flour

About 3 cups extra virgin olive oil or avocado oil (see Cooking Tip)

About ¼ cup raw sesame seeds, for coating

MAKE AHEAD

You can make the falafel mixture up to 24 hours in advance. The falafel are best eaten the same day they are fried.

COOKING TIP

I'm not afraid to fry in extra virgin olive oil. We're only heating this oil to 350 degrees F, which is below the smoke point of olive oil. It tastes better and is healthier than using a seed oil or vegetable oil. You can also use avocado oil.

This is my version of falafel, inspired by the one from Yotam Ottolenghi's *Jerusalem*. If you aren't used to frying foods, this is a good recipe to start with. It's quite easy and the process of rolling and frying the falafel is surprisingly quick. Plus, the reward is high—a large bowl of delectable, crispy balls of falafel. Adding a large amount of finely chopped herbs and lemon zest to falafel creates a bright and verdant center, balancing the richness of the fried exterior. The sesame seed coating toasts as they fry, providing both texture and that lovely, nutty flavor. The whole process is much easier and less messy than you think it will be. I hope you try it. • MAKES 15 TO 20 FALAFEL

1 The day before you are going to make the falafel, place the chickpeas in a bowl and cover them with cold water by a couple of inches. Soak at room temperature for at least 12 hours, but 24 hours is even better.

2 Coarsely chop the onion and place it in a food processor with the garlic. Blend until very finely chopped. Add the herbs and process again until the herbs are finely chopped. Drain the chickpeas and add them to the onion mixture. Pulse until the chickpeas are also very finely chopped. (It's the right consistency when it holds together when you press it between your fingers.) Add the pepper, spice mix, baking powder, salt, lemon zest, water, and flour. Pulse a few times, just to combine. Pour the mixture into a large bowl, cover, and refrigerate for at least an hour or up to overnight.

3 Fill a deep skillet (like a cast-iron pan) or Dutch oven with enough oil to come up 2 to 3 inches on the side. Heat the oil to 350 degrees F. If you don't have a deep-frying thermometer, test one falafel. The oil should vigorously bubble when the falafel is added to the pan, and the falafel should cook through completely in 4 minutes without burning.

4 Set a wire rack over a rimmed baking sheet and place it in the oven. Preheat the oven to 175 degrees F.

5 Spread the sesame seeds on a small plate. Using a small ice cream scoop or tablespoon measure, scoop out 1 tablespoon of the falafel mixture, about the size of a large date. Press with your hands to form a ball. Roll the ball through the sesame

seeds to coat, then set it aside on a large plate. Roll only as many as you'll be able to fit in the skillet without crowding. Fry the falafel a few at a time for 4 minutes, until deeply browned, cooked through, and dry on the inside. Depending on the depth of the oil, you may need to turn the falafel. Once cooked, transfer the falafel with a slotted spoon or tongs to the wire rack in the oven, to keep warm. Repeat with the remaining mixture, being sure not to crowd the pan. Serve hot or at room temperature.

SERVING TIPS

Serve the falafel as a snack with Tahini Sauce (page 85).

To make a pita, stuff falafel into a pita and top with Chopped Tomato Salad (page 111), Tahini Sauce (page 85), and Zhug (page 271).

Serve falafel as one part of a larger Israeli dinner or mezze platter (see page 98).

sizzling halloumi

WITH TOMATOES, LEMON, AND CHILE

1½ cups Olive Oil–Roasted Tomatoes (page 268)

Extra virgin olive oil

8 to 9 ounces halloumi, sliced ⅓ inch thick

1 tablespoon finely chopped fresh parsley

1 jalapeno or serrano chile, thinly sliced

Sourdough Flatbread (page 34)

Zhug (page 271), optional

Olives, optional

In the hills of the Galilee, near Yodfat, there is a goat farm called Goats with the Wind, an oasis of tree-shaded gazebos furnished with low wooden tables and deeply pigmented Persian rugs. When we arrive, we remove our shoes and sit cross-legged on the rug, listening to the peaceful sounds of goats bleating in the distance and the warm breeze rustling the trees. Dalia and her husband prepare lunch, including a variety of soft and aged goat cheeses made on the farm. The halloumi comes sizzling in a pool of olive oil with tomatoes, spicy chiles, and fresh herbs, with homemade bread served alongside. This recipe is inspired by that dish. If you aren't familiar with halloumi, it's a firm cheese typically made from goat or sheep's milk. It has a squeaky texture when you bite into it and holds its shape when cooked. It's delicious fried in olive oil or grilled. · SERVES 4 AS AN APPETIZER

1 Heat the tomatoes in a large skillet (not cast iron), and keep warm over low heat.

2 Heat a second large skillet over medium heat. Add enough olive oil to cover the bottom in a thin layer. Add the halloumi in a single layer. Let the halloumi cook for 2 to 3 minutes on one side, until browned. Using tongs, turn the halloumi to the other side and brown, another 2 to 3 minutes. Don't walk away, as the halloumi can turn from browned to burnt quickly.

3 Arrange the cooked halloumi on top of the tomatoes. Sprinkle with the parsley and sliced chile. Serve with flatbread, zhug and olives on the side.

WHAT CAN YOU DO WITH HALLOUMI?

Theo loves to eat fried halloumi as a snack, or for dinner.

Serve on top of a grain bowl, with roasted vegetables and either Zhug (page 271) or Fresh Chile Harissa (page 273).

Make halloumi tacos.

Top avocado toast with thin slices of seared halloumi.

Coat halloumi like fried chicken (see page 56) and serve with baked potato fries for a vegetarian version of fish and chips.

MAKING A MEAL OF SNACKS AND SIDES

Elie's mom grew up in the Old City of Jerusalem, where her family has lived for at least seven generations. When we were still dating, Elie took me to Israel for the first time, and we have returned almost every year since. I fell deeply in love with the country and its unique cuisine. Because Israel is a melting pot of different cultures and diverse influences, the food is richly vibrant and varied. Ingredients, spices, and traditions all coalesce in this small country.

But Israelis, no matter their heritage, have all adopted a bountiful way of dining—small dishes overflowing the table, offering a little something for everyone. Breads for savory dips and spreads sit beside a variety of cheeses marinated with olive oil and sumac, bright salads to eat alongside roasted meats, and an abundance of charred vegetables glistening with olive oil and finished with za'atar, all meant to be shared.

My first experience with this eating style came right after arriving at Ben Gurion Airport in Tel Aviv for the first time, bleary-eyed and weary from hours of travel. Elie's cousins enthusiastically met us at the airport, ushering us to the car and straight to Doda Malka's house ("doda" means aunt in Hebrew), where a full table awaited. It's the same every visit: always pita, hummus, tahini, and zhug, kebabs, potatoes crushed with fresh herbs, perhaps some falafel and a chopped tomato salad. Simple, satisfying, and nourishing.

In homes and restaurants across Israel, this pattern repeats. At a traditional Palestinian restaurant in the old city of Jaffa, dozens of small bowls arrive as soon as you're seated, all to be sopped up with blistered laffa. At the raucous fine-dining experience of Machneyuda in Jerusalem, the dishes from the playful menu arrive from a kitchen filled with music, the chefs chopping and stirring to the beat. All of this is food meant to be shared, elbows on the table, relished together.

This is now my favorite way to eat—making a meal of snacks, dips, spreads, and side dishes. This kind of menu invites a warm, casual approach to eating. Lots of dishes can be made ahead of time and everything is good at room temperature. It's a menu that lends itself to snacks and sips of wine in the kitchen as the table is slowly filled to overflowing. I especially love serving this kind of a menu at gatherings, because it ensures something for everyone.

There are no rules for a mezze meal—just a combination of colorful dishes that complement each other. I like to include something substantial, like falafel or sizzling halloumi. I make one fresh salad, like one of the tomato salads or kale salad. Bread, like sourdough flatbread, is essential for scooping up hummus or kale tahini sauce, slathering with labneh, or topping with feta marinated with fresh oregano and sumac. A variety of condiments, like zhug, fresh chile harissa, and olives allows everyone to make the meal as flavorful and spicy as they like. This is one example of a mezze meal. (Pictured, from top to bottom: tahini sauce, labneh, kale tahini, cauliflower hummus, fresh chile harissa, zhug, chopped tomato salad, falafel, olives.)

Mezze means to relish,
to savor the time at the table,
lingering over small plates,
snacks and side dishes in
community with others. As hands
reach across the table, it invites
communion, the sharing of both
food and stories.

CHAPTER FOUR

SALADS

little gem and herb salad

WITH CREAMY AVOCADO DRESSING

1 large avocado, halved, pitted, peeled, and chopped

Grated zest and juice of 2 lemons

2 to 4 tablespoons extra virgin olive oil

6 to 8 basil leaves

¼ cup loosely packed fresh parsley leaves

¼ teaspoon sea salt

⅛ teaspoon freshly ground black pepper, plus more for garnish

4 heads Little Gem lettuce or hearts of romaine, separated into leaves

¼ cup finely chopped fresh parsley

1 tablespoon finely chopped fresh dill

MAKE IT YOUR OWN

While I love simple salads, I know others like a lot more going on in their salad. Here are a few ideas.

Add toasted, chopped hazelnuts and crumbled feta cheese.

Turn this into a cobb-style salad with crumbled bacon, blue cheese and chopped hard-boiled eggs. Add extra avocado, cubed.

Top with fried tofu, extra cubed avocado and a large sprinkling of toasted sunflower seeds.

Beginning with the first warm days of spring, our Saturday morning routine includes a family bike ride to our community farmers' market. The market in spring always feels like a celebration, as the first asparagus and greens begin to appear. Discovering ruffled heads of Little Gem lettuce is always a delight, inspiring this salad. While avocados are obviously not local to the Pacific Northwest, I love how this creamy dressing coats the leaves, holding the shower of fresh herbs. · SERVES 4

1 Add the avocado, lemon zest and juice, 2 tablespoons of the oil, the basil, parsley leaves, salt, and pepper in a high-speed blender. Blend until smooth. Taste and add more olive oil if the dressing is too bright and acidic. Adjust salt and pepper, if needed.

2 Place the lettuce leaves in a large bowl. Add about ¼ cup of the dressing and toss to coat the lettuce; add a little more dressing if needed. The salad should be lightly dressed, with just enough dressing to coat the leaves. Top with the chopped parsley, dill, and more pepper. Store any remaining dressing in an airtight container in the refrigerator for up to 5 days.

frisée, radicchio, and fennel salad

WITH LEMON AND OLIVE OIL

1 small head radicchio
(about 6 to 8 ounces),
leaves torn or sliced in
2-inch pieces

1 head frisée, core removed
and leaves torn or very
coarsely chopped

1 head fennel, trimmed,
cored, and thinly sliced (by
hand or with a mandoline)

¼ cup finely chopped
fresh parsley leaves

5 large basil leaves,
finely chopped

¼ cup grated Parmigiano-
Reggiano

1 lemon, plus more fresh
juice if needed

3 to 4 tablespoons extra
virgin olive oil

¼ teaspoon flaky salt
(like Maldon)

Freshly ground black
pepper

Nine times out of ten, this is the salad I make as an accompaniment to dinner. The bitter greens are bracing and refreshing. I can make it ahead and it won't wilt. All I need to do is toss the leaves in lemon juice and add a few big swirls of good olive oil right before serving. It's especially good when paired with a rich dish like pasta or steak. I tear the radicchio and frisée in fairly large pieces, so it becomes a knife and fork salad. · SERVES 6

1 Place the radicchio, frisée, and fennel in a large bowl. Add the parsley, basil and Parmigiano-Reggiano and toss everything together.

2 Using a Microplane, grate the lemon zest over the salad. Halve the lemon and squeeze the juice over the salad, then evenly pour on 3 tablespoons of the oil. Add the salt and a few grinds of black pepper. Toss everything together and taste, adding more lemon juice, oil, salt, or pepper, as desired. It should be fairly tart and refreshing.

MAKE IT YOUR OWN

Vary the herbs, depending on what you have on hand. Any soft herb—mint, tarragon, or cilantro—would be a delicious addition. I also love adding crunch with chopped hazelnuts or pistachios or toasted buckwheat. Top with a poached egg for a breakfast salad or light lunch.

marinated tomato and cucumber salad

3 large, ripe heirloom tomatoes

3 small cucumbers, peeled

3 tablespoons apple cider vinegar

3 tablespoons extra virgin olive oil

¼ teaspoon sea salt, or to taste

Freshly ground black pepper

5 or 6 basil leaves, torn

Flaky salt, for serving

A FEW TIPS

Don't refrigerate this salad, as chilling the tomatoes will make them mealy.

If you can't find heirloom tomatoes, pick the ripest tomatoes you can find. Often, Roma tomatoes can be the most flavorful.

You can vary the flavor of this salad substantially by changing the type of vinegar and herbs. Try white wine vinegar with tarragon or chervil, sherry vinegar with parsley, or balsamic vinegar with chives.

If you like the flavor of raw onion, layer a small white onion, very thinly sliced, between the tomatoes and cucumbers. You can also marinate the onions in the apple cider vinegar for at least 20 minutes and up to an hour, to lessen the bite.

My Dad grew up in Pikeville, Kentucky, in the heart of Appalachia. Our family reunions each summer took place on the Fourth of July, perfect timing for juicy ripe tomatoes and flavorful cucumbers from the garden. I'm quite sure the tomato and cucumber salad at those reunions was made with white vinegar and vegetable oil and doused with sugar, so this recipe isn't completely true to tradition. But it's a perfect salad to accompany something rich like fried chicken. It's also great for picnics, since it just gets better as it sits. · SERVES 6

1 Slice the tomatoes in ⅓-inch-thick slices. Thinly slice the cucumbers.

2 Layer the tomatoes and cucumbers on a large platter, overlapping the slices. Drizzle them with the vinegar and oil. Sprinkle the salad with the sea salt and pepper to taste. Garnish with the basil and flaky salt.

3 Let the salad sit at room temperature until you're ready to serve, up to 2 hours.

my favorite kale salad

1 large or 2 small bunches lacinato (Tuscan) kale* (about 1½ to 2 pounds)

Sea salt

1 head fennel, trimmed, quartered, and cored

2 ounces ricotta salata or Parmigiano-Reggiano, shaved, or crumbled dry feta

Grated zest of 1 lemon

3 to 5 tablespoons fresh lemon juice (juice of 1 to 1½ lemons)

3 to 5 tablespoons extra virgin olive oil

Pinch of red pepper flakes or Aleppo-style pepper

¼ cup Toasted Pumpkin Seeds (page 260)

¼ cup Toasted Buckwheat (page 261)

Flaky salt

*If you can't find lacinato kale, substitute curly kale. The texture won't be quite the same, but it will still be good.

DRESSING TIP

Start with the smaller amount of lemon juice and olive oil and then taste. You can always add more, but you can't take it away. It should be bright but not make you pucker. If it's too sour, add a little more olive oil until the balance is just right.

When Elie and I first started dating, we spent a lot of time in Los Angeles exploring the city's incredible food scene. Gjelina has now become an LA icon, but in 2010 it was still relatively new. My first taste of Gjelina's kale salad was a revelation—I can still remember the first taste. Silky kale, salty ricotta salata, and a fine shower of crunchy breadcrumbs. I created a similar one to have at home. Instead of bread-crumbs, I top the salad with toasted buckwheat, which adds crunch and a deep, earthy flavor against the brightness of the lemon. This is the perfect salad to pack for a picnic or share at a potluck, because it just gets better as it sits. · SERVES 4 TO 6

1 Remove the stems from the kale, then tear the leaves into large pieces. Place the kale in a large mixing bowl. Sprinkle a big pinch of sea salt over the kale (a heaping ⅛ teaspoon), then massage the kale (sort of crushing it aggressively with your hands) until the leaves turn a dark, shiny green and feel almost silky. Taste and add more salt, if needed. It should taste seasoned but not salty.

2 Thinly slice the fennel on a mandoline or with a knife and add to the salad. Shave the ricotta salata using a vegetable peeler, making large curls of cheese. Add those to the salad. Sprinkle with the lemon zest.

3 Add 3 tablespoons each lemon juice and oil, and the pepper flakes. Toss it all together. Taste and adjust salt, lemon juice, and/or oil as desired. Top with the pumpkin seeds, buckwheat and a sprinkling of flaky salt and serve.

4 This salad will keep, well covered, in the refrigerator for up to 5 days. It's a great brown-bag or picnic salad, since it holds its flavor and texture over time.

chopped tomato salad

2 large ripe tomatoes, cut into ⅓-inch dice, or 2 cups cherry or grape tomatoes, quartered

1 red bell pepper, cut into ⅓-inch dice

1 medium cucumber, peeled and cut in ⅓-inch dice

½ cup finely chopped fresh parsley leaves

2 or 3 fresh mint leaves, finely chopped

¼ teaspoon sea salt

⅛ teaspoon Aleppo-style pepper or red pepper flakes

Grated zest and juice of 1½ lemons (about ¼ cup juice)

3 to 4 tablespoons extra virgin olive oil

¼ to ⅓ cup Toasted Sunflower Seeds (page 260)

At home, we refer to this salad as "Israeli Salad," because it's the salad served across Israel, for breakfast, lunch and dinner. This is the salad to make at the peak of summer, especially with produce gathered from your garden or local farmers' market. The secret to this salad is to cut everything into small dice, so the tomato, cucumber and peppers are all the same size. This turns the salad into a relish of sorts, delicious as a breakfast salad with fried eggs, tucked into a pita with falafel balls, or served with hummus and scooped up with flatbread. Don't refrigerate this salad, or the tomatoes will get mealy.
SERVES 4

Stir together the tomatoes, bell pepper, cucumber, parsley, and mint in a large bowl. Stir in the salt, Aleppo-style pepper, lemon zest and juice, and oil. Taste and adjust the seasonings to your taste. Top with sunflower seeds. This salad is best served fresh, at room temperature.

SUBSTITUTIONS

I give the option of using large tomatoes or cherry or grape tomatoes, because tomatoes are not all the same. In the Pacific Northwest where I live, the weather is not hot enough for delicious tomatoes, so I always make this salad with grape tomatoes.

MAKE IT YOUR OWN

Add different herbs to the salad, like basil, dill, or chervil, depending on what you have on hand.

If you like raw onion, add 1 small red onion, very finely chopped.

Other ideas for additions to this salad: chopped radishes, celery hearts, or carrots; halved pitted kalamata olives; crumbled feta or queso fresco; pickled onions or other pickled vegetables.

To make a tahini dressing for the salad, whisk together the lemon juice, olive oil, salt and Aleppo-style pepper with a couple of tablespoons of tahini. Adjust the seasonings, if needed.

cabbage and fennel salad

WITH NIGELLA AND PUMPKIN SEEDS

1 small head green or
red cabbage

Sea salt

Grated zest of 2 lemons

Juice of 1½ to 2 lemons
(about ⅓ cup juice)

1 head fennel, trimmed,
quartered, and cored,
fronds reserved

1 large unpeeled carrot

¼ cup fresh parsley leaves

¼ cup fresh cilantro leaves

⅛ to ¼ teaspoon
Aleppo-style pepper

⅛ teaspoon freshly ground
black pepper

¼ to ⅓ cup extra virgin
olive oil

⅓ cup Toasted Pumpkin
Seeds (page 260)

1 tablespoon nigella seeds

Flaky salt, for serving

MAKE AHEAD

This is a great make-ahead
salad that will keep in the
refrigerator for up to 4 days. If
you use red cabbage, the colors
will start to fade and bleed after
about a day, but it still tastes
good.

This cabbage salad is a fresh alternative to coleslaw, piquant with lemon and fresh herbs. It also features nigella seeds, which have a cumin-like flavor. You can use either red or green cabbage in this slaw, or a combination of both. The red cabbage is a beautiful color, and the green cabbage is a little more tender. This is one of those big, versatile salads that can be made on a Sunday and enjoyed for the next three or four days. I've eaten it for lunch, paired with soft-boiled eggs, some avocado and feta cheese. Or atop a burger. It's especially good on tacos. Go ahead and make the whole recipe and reap the rewards of leftovers. · MAKES ABOUT 6 CUPS

1 Core, quarter, and thinly slice the cabbage. Place the cabbage in a large bowl. Sprinkle ½ teaspoon sea salt over the cabbage, then add the lemon zest and juice. Using your (clean) hands, massage the salt and lemon into the cabbage, until the strands of cabbage begin to soften.

2 Thinly slice the fennel bulb, using either a knife or a mandoline. Chop enough of the fennel fronds to make about ¼ cup. Grate the carrot on the largest holes of a box grater. Finely chop the parsley and cilantro.

3 Add the sliced fennel, carrot, fennel fronds, parsley, and cilantro to the cabbage and toss together to combine. Add the Aleppo-style pepper, black pepper, and oil and toss again until well mixed and coated. Taste and adjust the salt, lemon, or peppers, if needed. (You might need another ½ teaspoon or more of sea salt, but adjust to your own taste.)

4 Add the pumpkin seeds and nigella seeds and toss again to combine. Transfer to a serving bowl and top with just a little flaky salt.

MAKE IT YOUR OWN

If you're out of lemon, apple cider vinegar is a great substitute.

If you'd like a more neutral-flavored oil, avocado oil works great.

Experiment with adding different herbs to the salad—mint, basil, and chervil all work well.

Don't have pumpkin seeds on hand? Use sunflower seeds, or add toasted sesame seeds and a little sesame oil. Maybe even a little tahini. You'll have a completely different salad!

OF NOTE FOR SPECIAL DIETS

Massaging the cabbage with salt and lemon juice not only makes it more delicious, but also more gentle for the stomach. Raw foods can be hard for some people to digest, and breaking down those fibers with salt makes the cabbage easier to digest.

roasted beet and citrus salad

WITH GOAT CHEESE AND DUKKAH

2 large red beets, trimmed

2 blood or Navel oranges

1 tablespoon fresh lemon juice

Flaky salt (preferably Maldon)

Freshly ground black pepper

Extra virgin olive oil

½ cup pitted Castelvetrano olives

1 tablespoon Spicy Dukkah (page 264), plus more to taste

4 ounces Humboldt Fog or similar semi-soft goat cheese

MAKE AHEAD

The beets can be roasted up to 4 days ahead of time. Store them, peeled but uncut, in an airtight container in the refrigerator. Cut them right before making the salad so the juices don't run. Once assembled, the salad is best eaten the same day. The beets will dye and strongly flavor the rest of the ingredients as the salad sits.

When fall arrives, I enjoy the transition from crisp greens and juicy tomatoes to earthy root vegetables and tart citrus. I love the color and flavor of blood oranges, but I can't always find them. Navel oranges will also work well. This salad manages to celebrate the change in seasons while still being bright and refreshing. It easily functions as a light lunch, a starter before dinner, or a side dish. · SERVES 2 TO 4

1 Preheat the oven to 400 degrees F.

2 Wrap the beets in aluminum foil and place them on a baking sheet. Roast the beets for about an hour, until very tender. (A fork should be able to easily pierce to the center.)

3 Let the beets cool completely, then peel them and cut them into wedges. Place the beets in a large bowl.

4 Using a Microplane, grate the zest of both the oranges into a small bowl. Cut the remaining peel and the pith off oranges with a sharp knife. Holding an orange over the bowl with the beets, use a small paring knife to cut between the membranes, cutting out the orange segments. Let the segments drop into the bowl with the beets. Repeat with the other orange.

5 Hold the orange membranes over the bowl that contains the zest and squeeze out any remaining juice. You should have about 2 tablespoons orange juice in the bowl. Add the lemon juice, a generous pinch of salt, and a few grinds of black pepper. Whisk in 2 to 3 tablespoons oil, depending on how tart you like your salad dressing.

6 Add the olives and dukkah. Add the dressing and very gently toss everything together.

7 Divide the salad between serving bowls. Top with the cheese, either sliced or crumbled (your choice). Garnish with additional salt and more dukkah, if you like.

shaved brussels sprouts salad

WITH GRAPEFRUIT, POMEGRANATE SEEDS, AND DUKKAH

1 to 1½ pounds Brussels sprouts

2 large pink grapefruits

2 tablespoon pomegranate molasses

¼ to ½ teaspoon sea salt

Freshly ground black pepper

¼ to ⅓ cup extra virgin olive oil

½ cup pomegranate seeds

¼ to ½ cup Spicy Dukkah (page 264)

MAKE AHEAD

You can make this salad a day ahead. In fact, it might be even better on day two, when all of the flavors have had a chance to mingle together.

MAKE IT YOUR OWN

If grapefruits are expensive (as they sometimes are), substitute 3 navel oranges. You might then want to add a little lemon juice or sherry vinegar to the dressing to add a little tartness.

If you can't find pomegranates, substitute dried tart cherries or dried cranberries. They won't have the same crunch, but they'll give that sweet-tart flavor.

Winter salads can be less than inspiring, but not this one. The bitterness of the Brussels sprouts and grapefruit is balanced by the sweetness of pomegranate molasses and pomegranate seeds. It's a welcome bright and crunchy respite from a season laden with rich dishes. The dukkah is an essential ingredient to the flavor of this salad. If using a purchased dukkah, make sure it is flavorful and a little spicy. · SERVES 6

1   Wash and dry the Brussels sprouts. Trim them, cutting off the bottom stem and peeling off any dry, discolored, or wilted outer leaves. Cut the sprouts in half through the stem, lay them down flat, and slice them very thin. Alternatively, if you have a mandoline, leave them whole and use it to slice them. You can also run them through the shredder plate of a food processor.

2   Place the shredded sprouts in a large bowl. Using a Microplane, grate the zest of one grapefruit onto the sprouts.

3   Cut the top and bottom off each grapefruit with a sharp knife, then cut off all the peel and pith. One grapefruit at a time, holding it over a small bowl to catch any juice, cut between the membranes and the flesh of the fruit. Add the grapefruit segments to the bowl with the sprouts. Repeat with the other grapefruit.

4   Squeeze the grapefruit membranes over the small bowl, extracting all the juice. You should have ¼ to ⅓ cup grapefruit juice. Discard the membranes. Add the pomegranate molasses to the grapefruit juice, along with ¼ teaspoon salt and pepper to taste. Whisk in ¼ cup oil. Taste and add more olive oil and salt, if needed. (I like the dressing on the brighter side, but adjust to your taste.)

5   Pour the dressing over the sprouts and grapefruit segments. Add the pomegranate seeds and ¼ cup of the dukkah and toss everything together. Transfer the salad to a serving bowl and top with the remaining dukkah.

CHAPTER FIVE

SOUPS

braised beef chili

2 pounds beef chuck roast, cut into 2-inch cubes

2 teaspoons sea salt, divided

2 tablespoons ghee or avocado oil, plus more if needed

1 large onion, sliced

2 cloves garlic, sliced

1 tablespoon My Spice Blend (page 262)

1 tablespoon sweet paprika

1 tablespoon dried oregano

½ teaspoon freshly ground black pepper

¼ teaspoon Aleppo-style pepper or red pepper flakes, or more if you like spice

2 tablespoons tomato paste

One 12-ounce bottle gluten-free beer or dry cider

Two 28-ounce cans whole tomatoes

1 Charred Red Bell Pepper (page 265), sliced

3 Charred Poblano Peppers (page 265), sliced

¼ cup chopped fresh cilantro

When I was growing up in Kentucky, when the late afternoon sun faded to an evening just chilly enough to need a sweater and the leaves became ombré, transitioning from green to yellow-orange or crimson red, it became chili season. Made from ground beef and kidney beans, my Mom's chili—spiced with a commercial chili powder blend—was thick enough to eat with a fork, and always served with cornbread. My Granny's version was brothy and contained spaghetti, Cincinnati-style. I loved them both, but created my own. If you are used to traditional bean-and-ground-beef chili, this version is a delightful departure: a beanless chili made from slowly braised beef chuck. It has enough meat to make it hearty but not heavy, and is redolent with spices. Let the chili simmer until the tomatoes have reduced down almost to a sauce-like consistency. Leave the pot on the stove, put out bowls with all of the toppings, and let your family and friends help themselves. PHOTOGRAPH ON PAGE 118 · SERVES 6 TO 8

1 Season the beef all over with 1 teaspoon of the salt. Heat a large heavy-bottomed pot or Dutch oven over medium-high heat. Add the ghee and let it melt. Add half of the beef, or as much as will fit without crowding. (If there's too much in the pot, it will steam, not brown.) Let it sear undisturbed for several minutes, until it develops a deep caramelized crust on the bottom. Using tongs, turn the beef and let it brown on the other sides. Remove the beef to a bowl. Repeat with the rest of the beef, adding more ghee, if necessary.

2 Reduce the heat to medium-low. If the pot seems dry, add a little more ghee. Add the onion and garlic and the other teaspoon of salt. Cook, stirring often, until the onions have started to brown, 8 to 10 minutes. Add the spice mix, paprika, oregano, black pepper, and Aleppo-style pepper. Stir, letting the spices toast for a minute or two with the onions. Add the tomato paste and cook it with the onion mixture until it starts to brown.

3 Increase the heat to medium. Add the beer and scrape up any caramelized bits off the bottom of the pot with a wooden spoon. Using your hands, crush the tomatoes, tearing them into rough pieces and adding them to the pot. Add any tomato juice left in the cans. Add back the beef plus any juices in the bowl. Stir in the charred red and poblano peppers. Bring the chili to a low simmer and cover the pot. Let cook slowly for at least 2 hours, stirring occasionally, until the beef is very tender.

4 Remove the lid and let the chili simmer for another hour, stirring occasionally, allowing it to reduce and thicken.

5 Stir in the chopped cilantro. Serve in warmed bowls, to top with shredded cheese, avocado, cilantro, yogurt, and pumpkin seeds. Offer homemade corn or cassava tortillas or cornbread on the side.

6 Store in an airtight container (without the toppings) in the refrigerator for up to five days or in the freezer for up to 3 months.

for serving

Shredded sharp cheddar cheese

Sliced avocado

Fresh cilantro, chopped or sprigs

Whole milk Greek yogurt, sour cream or crème fraîche

Toasted Pumpkin Seeds (page 260)

Corn Tortillas (page 42), Cassava Tortillas (page 43) or Cornbread (page 37)

TIME SAVER

If you don't want to take the time to char the peppers, you can just slice them and add them after you brown the onions. The skins will separate from the peppers and you won't have that subtle, smoky flavor. But the chili will still be delicious.

MAKE AHEAD

The soup can be made up to 4 days in advance. Don't add the matzo balls or fresh herbs until you are ready to serve. The matzo balls can also be made a day in advance.

OF NOTE FOR SPECIAL DIETS

This recipe is not kosher, because I use butter to make the matzo balls. You can substitute schmaltz or extra virgin olive oil to make them dairy-free.

Matzo ball soup will forever make me think of my father-in-law, Moe. Despite the great success he achieved in life, he didn't like fancy things or fussy food. No matter how many times I made him dinner, he always gave me detailed instructions on how to make his favorite foods. For matzo ball soup, he would ask, "Did you put lots of dill in it?" Yes Moe, I will always put dill in it, just for you.

matzo ball soup WITH LOTS OF DILL (FOR MOE)

2 large eggs

2½ tablespoons unsalted butter, melted

½ teaspoon salt, plus more for the soup

⅛ teaspoon freshly ground black pepper, plus more for the soup

¼ cup plus 2 tablespoons finely chopped fresh parsley

About 2½ gluten-free matzo squares, finely ground in the food processor to yield about ⅔ cup matzo meal, or ⅔ cup purchased gluten-free matzo meal

¼ cup sparkling water or club soda

2 quarts Chicken Stock (page 277) or good purchased bone broth

4 small carrots, very thinly sliced on the diagonal

2 small parsnips, very thinly sliced on the diagonal

2 tablespoons finely chopped fresh dill sprigs

This is the perfect soup to make with the leftovers from the Slow-Roasted Chicken on page 195. Use the bones to make a homemade stock and then make this soup. Matzo ball soup is really all about the broth, which should be clear and very flavorful. Adding sparkling water to the matzo mixtures keeps the matzo balls light and fluffy, which is my preference. For Passover, we serve the matzo ball soup without chicken, just with a few thin slices of carrots and parsnips and lots of herbs. To make it more substantial, add some shredded chicken. Just don't forget the dill. • SERVES 6

1 To make the matzo balls, whisk the eggs in a medium bowl to blend them. Whisk in the butter, salt, pepper, and 2 table-spoons of the parsley. Add the matzo meal and sparkling water, and stir to combine everything thoroughly. Cover the bowl and chill for at least 1 hour or up to 1 day.

2 Line a baking sheet with parchment paper. Using a teaspoon or a small cookie scoop, shape the batter into balls about 1½ inches in diameter. Place them on the baking sheet. You should have about 12 to 14 matzo balls.

3 Bring a large pot of lightly salted water to a gentle boil. Carefully drop in the matzo balls, cover partially with a lid, and reduce the heat to low. Simmer until the matzo balls are tender and cooked through, about 30 minutes. If you cut a matzo ball in half, it should be the same color all the way through.

4 Using a slotted spoon, transfer the matzo balls to a clean baking sheet. If you're making them ahead, let them cool, then cover the baking sheet tightly and put them in the refrigerator, where they will keep for up to a day. If you'll be adding them directly to the soup, just set them aside.

5 To make the soup, pour the chicken stock into a large pot and bring to a boil. Reduce to a simmer and add the carrots and parsnips. Cook for 10 to 15 minutes, until the vegetables are just tender. Taste and add salt and/or pepper, if necessary. Add the matzo balls and allow them to warm through, about 10 minutes. Add the remaining ¼ cup parsley and the dill. Serve warm.

the soup version of a green smoothie

4 to 6 cups purchased bone broth or Chicken Stock (page 277)

Sea salt

1 small head cauliflower, trimmed, cut into florets

1 small carrot, unpeeled, coarsely chopped

2 stalks celery, coarsely chopped

5 ounces tender greens (such as spinach, baby kale, Swiss chard, baby collards, mizuna, dandelion; about 4 cups)

1 cup fresh parsley sprigs

Grated zest of 1 lemon

¼ cup hemp hearts

⅛ to ¼ teaspoon Aleppo-style pepper

Freshly ground black pepper

In general, I am a savory over sweet person, so I rarely make smoothies. Instead, this is my version of a green smoothie. The cauliflower makes the soup thick and creamy without any dairy. The carrot adds just a hint of sweetness. For the greens, I generally just toss in one 5-ounce clamshell of "supergreens" so I don't have to buy and wash a variety of greens. This is the soup I'm always happy to have in the refrigerator when I don't have time for lunch. I can heat it up, pour it into a thermos, and drink it on the go. If I'm home, I might dress it up a bit with a drizzle of extra virgin olive oil or chili oil (page 267) and maybe some pumpkin seeds. It's nutritious and filling.
MAKES 8 TO 10 CUPS

1 Pour 4 cups of the bone broth to a large pot set over medium heat. If the broth is low-sodium, add salt, starting with ¼ teaspoon and increasing from there, to taste. Add the cauliflower, carrot, and celery. Bring to a boil, then reduce to a simmer. Cook for 10 to 15 minutes, until the vegetables are very tender.

2 Add the greens, parsley, lemon zest, hemp seeds, Aleppo-style pepper, and black pepper. Using an immersion blender, blend the soup in the pot until smooth. If you don't have an immersion blender, puree the soup in batches in a high-speed blender. (When pureeing hot liquids, only fill the container halfway, as hot liquids will expand.) If the soup seems too thick, add another cup or two of bone broth. Taste and add salt, if needed. Store the soup in an airtight container in the refrigerator for up to 5 days or in the freezer for up to 3 months.

PLANT-BASED GREEN SMOOTHIE SOUP · Substitute vegetable stock for the bone broth and add another ¼ cup hemp seeds for additional protein.

turmeric, chicken, and rice

2 tablespoons extra virgin olive oil or avocado oil

1 small onion, thinly sliced

1 clove garlic, thinly sliced

Sea salt

1 tablespoon turmeric, or more to taste

2 teaspoons My Spice Blend (page 262)

¼ teaspoon freshly ground black pepper

⅛ to ¼ teaspoon Aleppo-style pepper or red pepper flakes

1¼ cups Arborio or Bomba rice

2 quarts Chicken Stock (page 277) or purchased bone broth

1 bunch kale or Swiss chard, stemmed and chopped (about 2 cups)

4 boneless, skinless chicken thighs (about 1½ pounds)

½ cup finely chopped fresh parsley leaves

for serving (optional)

Sliced avocado

Toasted Pumpkin Seeds (page 260)

Finely chopped fresh parsley

Chili Oil (page 267)

Chicken broth—especially homemade—is rich with vitamins and minerals, and science shows it does indeed help with curing colds. Turmeric is an anti-inflammatory spice, and it works especially well when paired with black pepper, which enhances its healing properties. I love to use short-grain rice, like Arborio or Bomba, in this soup, because as it cooks it becomes thick and creamy without dairy. It turns the soup into a kind of brothy risotto, which feels so nourishing and warms the belly. When I'm sick, I limit the vegetables to greens, but add any other vegetables that sound good to you. · SERVES 4

1 Pour the oil into a medium-sized pot set over medium-low heat. Add the onion and garlic and ¼ teaspoon salt. Cook over medium-low heat, stirring occasionally, until the onion is almost caramelized, about 25 minutes.

2 Stir in the turmeric, spice blend, black pepper, and Aleppo-style pepper. If the pot is dry, add a little more oil so you can coat the spices in the oil. Let them toast for a minute or two. Add the rice and stir to coat the rice in the oil, onions, and spices.

3 Add the chicken stock, greens, and chicken thighs and stir. Add ½ teaspoon more salt if the stock is low-sodium. Raise the heat and bring the soup to a boil, then immediately reduce the heat to low, cover the pot, and cook for 25 minutes, until the rice is done and the chicken is very tender.

4 Using a slotted spoon or tongs, transfer the chicken to a cutting board or plate. Shred the chicken with two forks and add it back to the soup. Stir in the parsley. Serve warm, with toppings for diners to add at the table.

MAKE AHEAD

The soup will keep in an airtight container in the refrigerator for 3 or 4 days. If you are storing and reheating the soup, know that the rice will absorb a lot of the stock overnight. I actually love this soup reheated—it becomes even more risotto-like. But you can always add more stock when reheating the soup, if you want to thin it out again.

chicken poblano soup

6 boneless, skinless chicken thighs (about 2 ¼ pounds)

Sea salt

2 tablespoons avocado oil, plus more if needed

1 medium onion (about 6 ounces), thinly sliced

2 cloves garlic, sliced

⅛ to ¼ teaspoon Aleppo-style pepper or red pepper flakes

1 tablespoon My Spice Blend (page 262)

2 tablespoons tomato paste

2 quarts Chicken Stock (page 277) or purchased bone broth

1 Charred Red Bell Pepper (page 265), diced

2 Charred Poblano Peppers (page 265), diced

One 14-ounce can whole tomatoes, pureed with their juices

1 bay leaf

¼ cup masa harina

1 cup loosely packed fresh cilantro, chopped

for serving

Cubed avocado

Shredded sharp cheddar cheese

Greek yogurt

Thinly sliced scallions or chives

Fresh cilantro leaves

Corn Tortillas (page 42) or Cornbread (page 37)

This is the soup I take to potlucks. It's my standard for a warm, comforting meal before a sugar-filled night of trick-or-treating. If we were a football-watching family, I would serve this soup for the Super Bowl. Charring both red bell and poblano peppers lends a subtle smoky flavor and heat. Whisking in masa harina gives the soup body and a subtle corn flavor. What makes the soup extra special is a buffet of toppings—chopped avocado, shredded sharp cheddar cheese, Greek yogurt, thinly sliced chives and cilantro leaves. Let everyone serve themselves. · SERVES 6 TO 8

1 Remove the chicken from the refrigerator about 30 minutes before you're going to cook. Season it with ¼ teaspoon salt.

2 Place a Dutch oven or similar heavy pot over medium heat. Add the oil. When the oil is hot, add the chicken thighs in a single layer. Let the thighs brown well and develop a crust before you try to turn them, 6 to 8 minutes. They should lift easily with tongs. Turn and brown on the other side, another 4 to 6 minutes. When the chicken is browned, remove it from the pot to a bowl and set aside.

3 Reduce the heat to medium-low. Add the onion and garlic to the pot along with ¼ teaspoon salt and stir. Cook the onions and garlic slowly, stirring often, until the onions are completely wilted and starting to caramelize, about 25 minutes. If the pot gets too dry, add another tablespoon of oil.

4 Add the pepper and spice blend and stir to coat the spices in oil and onions. Increase the heat to medium. Push the onions to the edges and put the tomato paste in the middle of the pot. Let the tomato paste fry in the oil for 2 minutes, or until it starts to brown. Add the chicken stock and stir with a wooden spoon to scrape up any browned bits off the bottom of the pot. Add the charred peppers, tomatoes, and bay leaf. Return the chicken and any juices back to the pot. Whisk in the masa harina. Cover the pot and reduce the heat to low. Cook for 40 minutes, until the chicken is very tender and easy to shred

5 Using a slotted spoon or tongs, transfer the chicken to a cutting board or plate. Fish out and discard the bay leaf. Shred

the chicken with two forks, and add it back to the soup. Stir in the cilantro.

6 To serve, put out bowls of avocado, cheese, yogurt, scallions, and extra cilantro. Let everyone top their soup as desired. Serve with tortillas or cornbread.

PLANT-BASED POBLANO SOUP • Substitute Vegetable Stock (page 276) for the chicken stock. Omit the chicken thighs. Add 2 to 3 cups drained cooked black beans, hominy, or a mixture of both, when you add the charred peppers and tomatoes. After you add the masa harina, cook the soup, uncovered, for 20 to 25 minutes.

TIME SAVER

To make this soup come together a little faster, you can skip the step of charring the peppers and just add sliced raw peppers after the onions caramelize. The skins will separate while the peppers cook and it will lose the smoky flavor. But I have made it that way many times. You can also substitute already cooked shredded chicken for the chicken thighs. Add the shredded chicken at the same time you add the masa harina and cook the soup for 20 to 25 minutes.

PLANT-BASED MISO-TAHINI RAMEN • I often make this ramen using vegetable stock instead of bone broth and tofu instead of chicken. For the tofu, toss 15 ounces cubed extra-firm tofu (I like the Wildwood brand) in tapioca starch to coat. Pour about ¼ inch of avocado oil into a cast-iron skillet and heat it to 350 degrees F. Fry the tofu in batches, turning until lightly golden brown on all sides. Remove the tofu to a plate lined with a paper towel to drain. Season lightly with sea salt. Top the ramen soup with the tofu.

spicy miso-tahini ramen

2 quarts purchased chicken bone broth or Chicken Stock (page 277)

2 tablespoons white miso

2 tablespoons coconut aminos

¼ cup raw tahini

2 teaspoons Chili Oil (page 267), plus more for serving

Sea salt (optional)

4 boneless, skinless chicken thighs (about 1½ pounds)

1 large bunch Swiss chard, stemmed and coarsely chopped

4 rice ramen noodle cakes (I like Lotus Foods brand)

2 small zucchini, trimmed and spiralized

Fresh cilantro sprigs

Crispy Shiitake Chips (page 273)

Nigella seeds and/or Toasted Sesame Seeds

When I was in Tokyo, I took a ramen cooking class, where we learned about the history and different styles of ramen. After making and eating many bowls of ramen, I discovered that miso ramen was my favorite. This is a much simplified version of the traditional ramen made with dashi (an umami-rich both, often made with kombu), but it still hits all those flavor and texture notes—the deep umami from the miso, creamy rich-ness from tahini and bone broth (instead of traditional pork stock), and spice from chili oil. I love to add spiralized zucchini along with the rice ramen noodles, but it's optional. This dish easily comes together in about 30 minutes, so it's perfect for weeknight meals. It's also deeply satisfying. · SERVES 4

1 Pour the bone broth into a large pot and place over high heat. Once the broth is at a simmer, whisk in the miso, coconut aminos, tahini, and chili oil until the miso is dissolved. Taste and add salt, if needed. The amount you need will depend on the saltiness of the broth. Add the chicken thighs.

2 Once the broth is at a boil, reduce the heat to low. Cover the pot and cook for 20 to 25 minutes, until the chicken is tender and easy to shred.

3 Using a slotted spoon or tongs, transfer the chicken to a cutting board or plate. Shred the chicken, using two forks. Return it to the pot and add the Swiss chard.

4 Bring the broth back to a boil. Add the noodles and cook for 4 minutes. As the noodles soften, separate the strands using two forks or tongs. After 4 minutes, add the zucchini. Cook for another 2 minutes, until the zucchini has wilted.

5 Divide the soup between four bowls. Garnish with cilantro, shiitake chips, sesame or nigella seeds and additional chili oil.

USING YOUR FREEZER

My first foray into a career in food was as a personal chef. I cooked in my clients' homes, preparing a week's worth of meals at one time and storing them in the refrigerator and freezer with reheating instructions. During that time, I learned some creative ways to use the freezer. Here are those tips.

Vegetable Scraps I save scraps of onion skins, ends of carrots and celery, fennel stalks, cores, and fronds, and herbs beginning to wilt. I toss them all into a reusable food storage bag and store them in the freezer. When I'm ready to make stock, I just pour the contents of the bag into the water—on their own or with chicken bones. Nothing goes to waste.

Leftover Wine If I can't get through a bottle of wine before it starts to turn, I pour the contents into a glass jar and store it in the freezer. I keep one jar for white and one jar for red, and keep adding to it. When a recipe calls for wine, I use the frozen wine. I can't taste the difference in recipes.

Plant-Based Milks Almond milk and coconut milk both freeze well, sealed tightly in glass jars. Thaw overnight in the refrigerator to use.

Saucy Leftovers Saucy foods freeze well—roasted tomatoes, bolognese sauce, lasagna, braised meats. Store them tightly sealed in a glass container and let them thaw in the refrigerator overnight before using.

Condiments I make double batches of condiments like harissa and zhug and store the extra in the freezer. Thaw in the refrigerator overnight.

Pancakes and Waffles Let leftover pancakes and waffles cool completely, then layer them between pieces of parchment paper. Store in a reusable gallon-sized food storage bag. For an easy breakfast, pop them in the toaster and heat until warmed through. Theo eats this for breakfast almost every weekday morning.

Cookie Dough and Pie Dough Scoop raw cookie dough onto a baking sheet, then place the sheet in the freezer. When the cookie dough balls are frozen solid, remove them from the sheet and place in a reusable food storage bag. Whenever you want cookies, just bake them from frozen (they might take a few minutes longer). Wrap pie dough disks in plastic wrap and store in a food storage bag. Thaw in the refrigerator overnight when you want to make a pie.

Pasta Dough I store pasta dough in the freezer three different ways. First, I freeze unrolled dough. I portion unrolled dough into single-serving 3-ounce portions, wrap each one tightly in plastic wrap, and place it in a reusable food storage bag. That way I can pull out as many portions as I need. Second, I freeze rolled-out sheets of pasta dough to use for lasagna. Third, I divide cut pasta into 3-ounce portions and coil each into a nest. I place the nests on a baking sheet, cover them, and freeze. Once they're frozen, I drop the nests into a reusable food storage bag. Boil sheets and cut pasta from frozen.

CHAPTER SIX

VEGETABLES, GRAINS, & MORE

seared asparagus mimosa

WITH PROSCIUTTO

Ice water

1 bunch asparagus, bottoms trimmed

Extra virgin olive oil

1 lemon

3 ounces sliced prosciutto

3 large eggs, hard-boiled and cut in ¾-inch cubes

2 teaspoons finely chopped fresh tarragon

Flaky salt

Freshly ground black pepper

In France, a mimosa salad or vinaigrette includes hard-boiled eggs. When the first tender asparagus appears at the farmers' market, this is the dish I want to eat. Instead of folding the diced eggs into a vinaigrette, I like layering everything separately. It prevents the eggs from getting smooshed and makes the dish more beautiful. This asparagus dish is so versatile—it can be served for breakfast, lunch or dinner. If friends are stopping by on a spring afternoon, I'll often make this and a charcuterie board as a light snack, served with champagne.

SERVES 4 TO 6

1 Fill a large bowl with ice water. Fill a large pot with 2 inches of water. Bring it to a boil, then reduce to a steady simmer. Drop in the asparagus and blanch for 1 minute, until bright green but still crisp. Remove the asparagus with tongs and immediately plunge the stalks into the ice water. Once the asparagus have chilled, remove from the water and dry on a clean kitchen towel.

2 Heat a large skillet over medium heat. Add the prosciutto in a single layer, cooking 1 to 2 minutes on each side, until it has crisped. Remove the prosciutto to a plate. Wipe out the skillet.

3 Return the pan to medium-high heat. Pour in 2 tablespoons oil, then add a single layer of asparagus spears. (You may need to cook the asparagus in batches.) Cook for 1 minute, just until slightly charred. Remove the asparagus to a serving platter. Repeat with any remaining asparagus. Use a Microplane to zest the lemon over the spears. Cut the lemon in half and squeeze the juice from one half over the asparagus. (Store the remaining half in the refrigerator for another use.)

4 Arrange the eggs on top of the asparagus spears. Crumble on the prosciutto, then sprinkle the tarragon over the top. Add just a little flaky sea salt and a few grinds of pepper. Serve warm or at room temperature.

honey-roasted carrots and parsnips
WITH RICOTTA

5 or 6 thin carrots (about 1 pound), tops trimmed to ½ inch

5 or 6 thin parsnips (about 1 pound)

¼ teaspoon sea salt

2 tablespoons honey, plus more for drizzling

2 tablespoons unsalted butter, melted

Grated zest of 1 lemon

½ teaspoon fresh thyme leaves

¼ teaspoon red pepper flakes

¾ cup whole milk ricotta

¼ cup roasted pistachios, chopped

Flaky salt

Freshly ground black pepper

I love to make this dish in the spring when the first finger-thin carrots appear at the farmers' market and the wintered-over parsnips are tender and sweet. Roasting the carrots and parsnips together with butter and honey gives them a deep, rich caramelization that's balanced by the fresh, creamy ricotta. If the parsnips are large, cut them lengthwise in half or quarters, to be the same size as the carrots. This is a beautiful dish to serve for a weekend brunch. · SERVES 4 TO 6

1 Preheat the oven to 425 degrees F. Line a rimmed baking sheet with parchment paper.

2 Peel the carrots and parsnips. Place them in a large bowl and toss with the sea salt.

3 In a small bowl, whisk together the honey, butter, lemon zest, thyme, and pepper flakes. Drizzle the honey mixture over the carrots and parsnips and toss to coat.

4 Place the carrots and parsnips on the baking sheet in a single layer. Roast for 25 to 30 minutes, until the carrots are beginning to brown and caramelize. Don't be tempted to remove them earlier. The carrots and parsnips should be very soft and slightly charred. Transfer the carrots and parsnips to a serving dish.

5 Top with the ricotta and pistachios. Drizzle with additional honey and garnish with flaky salt and black pepper. Serve warm or at room temperature.

DAIRY-FREE ROASTED CARROTS AND PARSNIPS ·
Substitute extra virgin olive oil or coconut oil for the butter. Instead of ricotta, top with cashew cream. To make the cashew cream, combine 1 cup raw cashews, ½ cup water, 1 tablespoon fresh lemon juice, and ½ teaspoon sea salt in a high-speed blender and blend until very smooth.

crispy beets

WITH LABNEH

6 medium-sized beets

Sea salt

2 bay leaves

½ teaspoon black peppercorns

Extra virgin olive oil

1 to 1½ cups Labneh (page 274)

Gremolata (page 271), for serving

2 to 3 tablespoons Toasted Pumpkin Seeds (page 260)

2 tablespoons pomegranate seeds

1 tablespoon pomegranate molasses

MAKE AHEAD

The beets can be simmered a few hours before searing. Leave them at room temperature until you're ready to assemble the dish. Because beets leak their juices as they rest, it doesn't really work to cook them days in advance and refrigerate them—they won't get crispy.

MAKE IT YOUR OWN

The beets and labneh are a blank canvas for a variety of flavors and textures. Drizzle it with Zhug (page 271) or Chili Oil (page 267). Instead of pumpkin seeds, use chopped toasted hazelnuts or walnuts.

It had never occurred to me to eat beet skins until I saw a recipe in Francis Mallmann's *Seven Fires* cookbook. The method for this recipe is similar to the Smashed Roasted Potatoes on page 162 and the sweet potatoes on page 166, in that the beets are simmered in water until tender and then smashed and seared in a hot skillet. The extra surface area from smashing the beets ensures a larger, crispy crust. The earthy beets pair beautifully with creamy labneh, topped with a bright gremolata. · SERVES 6

1 Put the beets in a medium pot. Cover with water by at least 1 inch. Add 1 tablespoon salt, the bay leaves, and peppercorns. Place the pot over high heat and bring to a boil. Reduce the heat to medium-low and simmer for 30 to 40 minutes, until the beets are very tender. (You should be able to easily pierce the beets with a fork.)

2 Drain the beets, discarding the cooking water and spices. Let the beets sit until they are cool enough to handle. Line a baking sheet with parchment paper. Place the beets on the parchment paper. Using the bottom of a glass or a large measuring cup, gently flatten the beets. It's okay if some of the pieces break.

3 Heat a large cast-iron skillet over medium-high heat. Pour in enough oil to just cover the bottom. Add one layer of beets, being careful not to crowd the pan. (You may need to cook the beets in two or more batches.) Season the beets with salt. Let the beets fry in the oil for about 2 minutes, until the bottoms are crispy and browned. Turn them and season the cooked side with salt. Once the beets are browned on both sides, remove them from the pan to a plate. Repeat with remaining beets.

4 Spoon the labneh onto a large plate or into a large, shallow bowl. Use the back of a spoon to swirl the labneh over the plate to make a bed for the beets. Arrange the beets on top of the labneh. Garnish with the gremolata, pumpkin seeds, pomegranate seeds and pomegranate molasses.

roasted radicchio

WITH GOAT CHEESE, CRUSHED PISTACHIOS, AND POMEGRANATE

3 heads Treviso radicchio

3 tablespoons extra virgin olive oil

¼ teaspoon sea salt

Freshly ground black pepper

3 to 5 ounces Humboldt Fog or other soft ripened goat cheese, crumbled

2 to 3 tablespoons pomegranate seeds

2 to 3 tablespoon crushed unsalted roasted pistachios

Grated zest from ½ a lemon

Pomegranate molasses

MAKE AHEAD

You can roast the radicchio a few hours before dinner and leave it at room temperature. Add the garnishes right before serving.

MAKE IT YOUR OWN

Play with the combination of toppings for this dish. Just think about having something creamy, something crunchy, and something a little sweet to balance the bitterness.

I love bitter greens, but they can be polarizing. If you generally find radicchio too assertive, try this recipe. Roasting the radicchio mellows the bitterness, caramelizing the sugars to a toasty sweetness. I used the long Treviso radicchio here, but you can also use Chioggia, the round radicchio more commonly found. I love it paired with something creamy and something crunchy, for texture. Here, I chose Humboldt Fog, but a mild blue cheese like Maytag Blue would also be delicious. Since radicchio is a cold-weather vegetable, in-season pomegranate pairs well. And the pistachios add a nice sweetness and crunch. Serve this as a side or an alternative to a salad. Leftovers make a great lunch. · SERVES 6

1 Preheat the oven to 425 degrees F. Line a baking sheet with parchment paper.

2 Remove the wilted outer leaves of the radicchio, then cut it in half lengthwise. Lay the radicchio, cut side up, on the baking sheet. Drizzle with half of the olive oil and sprinkle evenly with half of the salt. Turn the radicchio cut side down and drizzle with the remaining oil and salt. Bake for 10 to 15 minutes, until the radicchio has wilted and the edges are charred. Remove from the oven.

3 Place the radicchio on a serving platter, cut side up. Add a few grinds of pepper. Top with the cheese, pomegranate seeds, and pistachios. Grate a little lemon zest over the top, then drizzle with just a bit of pomegranate molasses. Serve warm or at room temperature.

charred kale

3 tablespoons extra virgin olive oil, plus more for serving

2 bunches lacinato (Tuscan) kale, stemmed, leaves torn into 2- or 3-inch pieces

⅛ teaspoon sea salt

⅛ teaspoon Aleppo-style pepper or red pepper flakes

Grated zest of 1 lemon

Flaky salt, for serving

MAKE AHEAD

Sautéed greens will stay warm on the stove, held over low heat, for at least an hour. Alternatively, you can make these greens up to a day ahead and just reheat them gently on the stovetop, adding a little water if needed.

MAKE IT YOUR OWN

I love a basic bowl of kale, but feel free to create your own mix of greens. Swiss chard, collards, and mustard greens are all fair game. Just stay away from spinach and arugula, as they will turn to mush in the longer cooking time.

I am a perfect candidate for one of those tees promoting kale: Kale Yeah! or Kale 'Em With Kindness. I'm here for it. I love kale. But even if you're not a kale lover, this recipe might change your mind. By starting at relatively high heat, some of the kale leaves char in the olive oil, adding some crispy edges and a little smoky flavor. The end result is a combination of silky and crispy kale, rich with olive oil. A little lemon zest and flaky salt are all it needs. · SERVES 4

1 Heat a large skillet over medium-high heat. Add the olive oil and as much kale as will fit in it without overflowing. Add the sea salt, pepper, and lemon zest and stir.

2 Cook the kale until some of the bottom leaves begin to char. Stir and add more kale, if you have any not already in the pan. Add more olive oil if the skillet looks dry. Let the kale cook allowing some of the leaves to char in the pan. Use tongs to turn the kale in the pan occasionally. Cook for 8 to 10 minutes, until the kale is wilted and tender with some charred leaves. Transfer the kale to a serving bowl and drizzle with additional olive oil and a good sprinkling of flaky salt.

braised collard greens

2 to 3 tablespoons extra virgin olive oil

1 large onion (about 8 ounces), sliced

¼ teaspoon sea salt

2 bunches collard greens, stemmed, leaves chopped

1 tablespoon apple cider vinegar

Freshly ground black pepper

I feel like collard greens are an underappreciated green. The leaves are large and tough, so it takes a while to coax them to their silky potential. While collard greens are often flavored with ham hock, I like the naked flavor of just the greens, without the smoky, salty pork. The almost-caramelized onion provides depth of flavor, brightened by a splash of apple cider vinegar at the end. These greens are a great accompaniment to the shrimp and grits (page 229). · SERVES 4

1 Heat a large, deep skillet or Dutch oven over medium-high heat. Add the olive oil, onion, and salt. Cook until the onion is just starting to caramelize, about 25 minutes.

2 Stir in a little water. Add the collards. You may have to let them wilt a little bit before you add more, so they all fit in the pot. Partially cover the pot and let the collards cook, stirring occasionally, for at least an hour, until they are very soft and tender. Add more water during cooking as needed to keep the pot from getting dry.

3 Stir in the vinegar. Taste and adjust for salt as needed. Add several good grinds of pepper and serve.

simply seared broccolini

Ice water

½ teaspoon sea salt

2 large bunches broccolini, ends trimmed

2 to 3 tablespoons extra virgin olive oil, plus more for drizzling (optional)

Grated zest of 1 lemon

Aleppo-style pepper

Flaky salt

MAKE IT YOUR OWN

While I love this simple preparation, you can certainly dress up the broccolini in a variety of ways. Top with Toasted Sunflower Seeds (page 260), crumbled feta, and Chili Oil (page 267). Or toasted hazelnuts, blue cheese, and a drizzle of honey. It's also delicious as a light lunch, topped with a fried egg.

Sometimes, I just want a simple green side dish to accompany a rich ribeye or salmon. This broccolini is what I make. Instead of roasting, I love to blanch broccolini, preserving its bright green color and verdant flavor, and then quickly char it in a hot skillet. I find that kids really love this dish, too. Theo calls them "trees," holding the broccolini by the stalk and nibbling the tender, sweet florets. · SERVES 4 TO 6

1 Fill a large bowl with ice water. Fill a large pot with 2 inches of water and add the sea salt. Bring it to a boil, then reduce to a steady simmer. Drop in the broccolini and blanch for 4 minutes. Remove the broccolini with tongs and immediately plunge it into the ice water.

2 Once the broccolini has chilled, remove it from the water and lay it out to dry on a clean kitchen towel.

3 Place a large skillet over medium-high heat. Pour in the oil, then add a single layer of broccolini. (You may need to cook it in batches.) Cook the broccolini for 1 to 2 minutes, just until slightly charred. Place the broccolini on a serving platter. Repeat charring any remaining broccolini.

4 Sprinkle the lemon zest over the broccolini, followed by a little pepper and flaky salt. Drizzle with more olive oil, if desired.

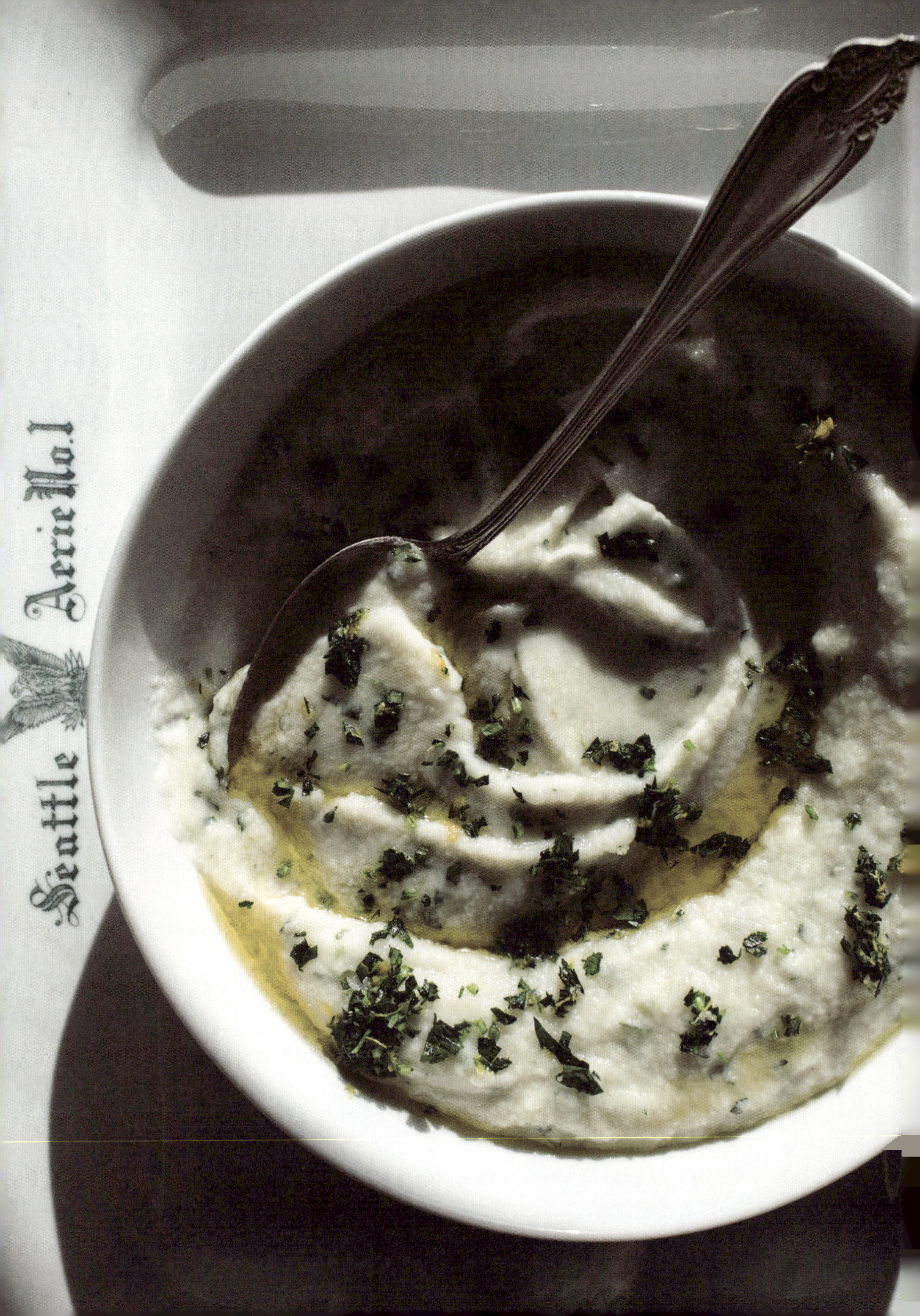
Seattle Aerie No.1

whipped cauliflower

Sea salt

1 large head cauliflower, trimmed, cut into florets

2 to 3 tablespoons extra virgin olive oil

⅛ teaspoon Aleppo-style pepper

¼ cup freshly grated Parmigiano-Reggiano cheese

2 tablespoons fresh parsley leaves

Gremolata (page 271), optional

MAKE AHEAD

You can keep this warm on the stove over very low heat for up to an hour. Alternatively, cook and puree the cauliflower a couple of days ahead and store it in an airtight container in the refrigerator. Reheat gently over low heat before serving.

MAKE IT YOUR OWN

Vary the flavor with different herb and cheese combinations. Try fresh thyme and goat cheese, dill and cream cheese, or parsley and pecorino Romano.

I love the simplicity of the olive oil, but I have made this with browned butter, and it is rich and nutty.

In general, I don't like foods masquerading as other foods. Like cauliflower rice, which is decidedly not rice. However, this is not one of those recipes. While it's tempting to compare this dish to mashed potatoes, it's a delicious side that stands on its own. The cruciferous head of cauliflower is turned into something creamy and smooth. I love using this as a bed for Crispy Cast-Iron Salmon (page 222) or fried chicken (page 56). And it's especially delicious topped with a lemony gremolata, but that's optional. · SERVES 4 TO 6

1 Fill a large pot with 2 inches of water. Bring to a boil over high heat, then reduce the heat to medium-low. Add ¼ teaspoon salt and the cauliflower. Cook the cauliflower until very tender but not mushy, about 15 minutes.

2 Using a slotted spoon, transfer the cauliflower to a food processor. Add the oil and pepper, and puree until very smooth. Add the parmesan and parsley and blend again until the cheese is melted. Taste and adjust for salt, if needed.

3 Pour the water out of the pot. Transfer the pureed cauliflower back to the pot. Cover and keep warm on very low heat until you're ready to serve. Serve topped with the gremolata, if desired.

whole roasted cauliflower

WITH GREEN TAHINI, SUNFLOWER SEEDS, AND ZHUG

1 large head cauliflower

1 tablespoon sea salt

¼ cup extra virgin olive oil

1 to 1½ cups Herby Green Tahini Sauce (page 85)

Flaky salt

3 to 4 tablespoons Toasted Sunflower Seeds (page 260)

¼ cup chopped parsley and/or cilantro, for serving

Zhug (page 271), for serving

MAKE AHEAD

The cauliflower can be simmered in the water up to a day ahead. Drain the cauliflower and let cool completely. Cover and keep in the refrigerator until you're ready to roast it.

MAKE IT YOUR OWN

This cauliflower lends itself to creativity. Substitute plain Tahini Sauce (page 85) for the green tahini, or use Fresh Chile Harissa (page 273), Gremolata (page 271), or Olive Oil–Roasted Tomatoes (page 268) instead of zhug. Or use any combination of those.

Miznon, a casual restaurant in Tel Aviv, made the whole roasted cauliflower iconic. I remember the first time I ate it, sitting outside under the night sky, the street lights illuminating the brightly-colored plastic tables and music blaring from the kitchen. The blackened cauliflower arrived at the table wrapped in parchment paper. We tore the tender florets apart with our hands, scooping them through small bowls of tahini, chopped fresh tomato, and zhug. In this version, I serve the cauliflower over green tahini sauce, showered with sunflower seeds and accompanied by zhug. It can serve as a plant-based main dish or side dish. · SERVES 2 TO 4

1 Trim the green leaves from the cauliflower. Trim the stem so the cauliflower can stand upright. Place the cauliflower in a large pot and add enough water to cover it. Add the sea salt. Bring to a boil, then reduce to a simmer. Cook the cauliflower for 10 to 15 minutes, turning it a few times, until you can insert a skewer or a fork very easily through the center. (If the cauliflower is not fully submerged, put the lid on the pot to partially cover and keep the cauliflower in the water.

2 Using a slotted spoon or tongs, transfer the cauliflower to a colander set over a bowl or in the sink. Let the cauliflower drain for 10 or 15 minutes.

3 While the cauliflower is draining, preheat the oven to 500 degrees F.

4 Place the cauliflower in a cast-iron skillet. Pour the oil over the cauliflower. Place the skillet in the oven on the center rack. Roast for about 30 minutes, until the outside is caramelized and beginning to blacken in spots.

5 Spread the tahini sauce on a serving platter. Carefully remove the cauliflower from the skillet and place it on top of the sauce. Sprinkle with flaky salt and garnish with the sunflower seeds and fresh herbs. Serve zhug on the side.

roasted cauliflower

WITH TOASTED SUNFLOWER SEEDS, PARSLEY, AND CHILI OIL

1 large head cauliflower, trimmed, cut into florets

3 to 4 tablespoons extra virgin olive oil

¼ teaspoon sea salt

⅛ teaspoon Aleppo-style pepper or pinch of red pepper flakes

¼ cup Toasted Sunflower Seeds (page 260)

1 tablespoon finely chopped fresh parsley

Chili Oil (page 267; optional)

MAKE AHEAD

If I'm making this for a dinner party, I prep the oil-coated cauliflower early in the day and let it hang out on the baking sheet on the counter. Then I can just put it in the oven about 40 minutes before I'm ready to serve.

MAKE IT YOUR OWN

Roasted cauliflower is a blank canvas. Use your imagination to create a dish that reflects the flavors in your meal. I love to serve this over a bed of tahini, combined with the Smashed Roasted Potatoes (page 162). If you like sweet and savory combinations, think about adding crunchy nuts or seeds and dried fruit, like currants, sliced dried figs or chopped dates.

Deeply roasted cauliflower is my go-to vegetable for almost every type of meal. Almost everyone loves it, and it can be used in a variety of ways, on its own, as a side dish, or tucked into a taco. It can be mixed with roasted potatoes for a breakfast hash. Its versatility is as appealing as its flavor. This version, with sunflower seeds and chili oil, is the one I make most often. There are only two tricks to perfecting cauliflower: enough oil and enough time. Make sure the cauliflower is thoroughly coated with oil. Don't be shy. The amount you need depends on the size of the cauliflower. And leave the cauliflower in the oven long enough for it to develop a deep golden crust. Leaving it in the oven for an additional 10 minutes as the oven cools is the secret to the perfect texture. SERVES 4 TO 6

1 Preheat the oven to 425 degrees F. Line a rimmed baking sheet with parchment paper.

2 Place the cauliflower florets on the baking sheet and drizzle with oil. Sprinkle with the salt and pepper. Using your hands, rub the oil, salt, and pepper into the cauliflower until well coated.

3 Roast for 25 to 30 minutes, until the cauliflower is deeply browned.

4 Once the cauliflower is lightly charred and fork-tender, turn off the oven. Let the cauliflower sit in the oven for another 10 minutes as the oven cools. It will continue to caramelize and soften perfectly.

5 Transfer the cauliflower to a serving platter. Garnish with the sunflower seeds and parsley, and drizzle with chili oil, if desired.

charred eggplant

WITH OLIVE OIL AND ZA'ATAR

2 large eggplants

2 to 3 tablespoons extra virgin olive oil

1 tablespoon za'atar

Flaky salt

This charred eggplant is often traditionally made by placing it over hot coals, turning it occasionally until the skin is completely blackened and the inside collapses, making the flesh creamy and slightly smoky. Roasting it in a very hot oven is a hands-off method to achieve a similar result. Serve this eggplant with Sourdough Flatbread (page 34) as an appetizer. Or serve it as part of a mezze-style meal. It pairs beautifully with Hummus (page 89) or Cauliflower Hummus (page 90), Tahini Sauce (page 85), and Chopped Tomato Salad (page 111). SERVES 4 TO 6

1 Preheat the oven to 500 degrees F.

2 Place the eggplants on a baking sheet and pierce them a few times with the tip of a knife or a fork. Roast the eggplants, turning them occasionally with tongs, until they are charred and completely collapsed, 30 to 40 minutes.

3 Let the eggplants cool on the baking sheet. When cool, transfer the eggplant to a shallow serving bowl. Slice down the top of each eggplant, from the stem to the bottom. Open up the eggplants like you're opening a baked potato. Drizzle the olive oil over the flesh of both eggplants. Sprinkle with the za'atar and flaky salt, and serve.

roasted cabbage

WITH CARAWAY SEEDS, TOMATOES, AND CRÈME FRAÎCHE

1 medium head cabbage, cut into 8 wedges

¼ teaspoon sea salt

⅛ teaspoon Aleppo-style pepper

1 tablespoon caraway seeds

3 tablespoons extra virgin olive oil

1 cup Olive Oil–Roasted Tomatoes, lemon removed (page 268; see Cooking Tip)

Crème fraîche, for serving (optional)

COOKING TIP

If you don't already have the roasted tomatoes on hand in the refrigerator, you can make them while the cabbage is roasting. Then add them to the cabbage for its last few minutes of cooking time.

Cooked cabbage doesn't have a great reputation for being delicious, but this recipe will negate that rumor. Roasting wedges of cabbage in a hot oven turns them sweet, with crispy caramelized edges. The caraway seeds lend a slight anise note, and the deeply roasted tomatoes add a bright acidity. While the creamy, tart crème fraîche is optional, it's a lovely accompaniment. • SERVES 4 TO 6

1 Preheat the oven to 425 degrees F.

2 Place the wedges of cabbage in a cast-iron skillet or baking dish. Season with the salt and pepper. Scatter the caraway seeds over the cabbage and drizzle with the olive oil. Roast for 25 to 30 minutes, until the cabbage is charred and very tender.

3 Remove the skillet from the oven and arrange the tomatoes on and around the cabbage. Place the skillet back in the oven for 6 to 8 minutes, until the tomatoes are warmed and bubbling. Serve hot, garnished with crème fraîche if you like.

potato latkes

2 large russet potatoes
(about 1 pound)

1 small onion, peeled

2 tablespoons superfine
brown rice flour

¼ cup tapioca starch

1 teaspoon sea salt

1 teaspoon baking powder

¼ teaspoon freshly ground
black pepper

Extra virgin olive oil or
avocado oil, for frying

Flaky salt

MAKE AHEAD

You can make these a few hours ahead of time. Transfer the latkes to a wire rack set over a rimmed baking sheet, placing them in a single layer. Keep them warm in a 175 degree F oven until you're ready to serve.

SERVING TIPS

While latkes can be served as part of a main meal, they lend themselves to before-dinner snacking. I love creating a latke toppings bar with both sweet and savory options. Here are a few ideas: applesauce or sliced apples, pomegranate seeds, crème fraîche or sour cream, labneh, smashed avocado, smoked salmon, caviar, chopped dill, chopped parsley, grated lemon zest.

People who make potato latkes are very opinionated about what makes the best recipe: What type of potato to use. Onion or no onion. The type of fat used for frying. It's a heated debate, but I think this method makes the crispiest, most perfect latkes. First, use russet potatoes, which have a high starch content. Add just a little bit of finely grated onion, to flavor the latkes but not overpower them. Squeeze as much moisture out of the potatoes and onion as you can, so the potato mixture is quite dry. Lastly, add just a little tapioca starch with the brown rice flour, which gives the latkes an extra crispy crust that stays crisp longer. When I'm making these, I usually have people hovering about the stove, reaching for the crispy latkes as soon as they hit the plate. • MAKES ABOUT 2 DOZEN LATKES

1 Peel the potatoes. Using the grater blade of a food processor, grate the potatoes and onion. Alternatively, grate the potatoes and onion on the largest holes of a box grater. Pour the mixture into the center of a clean kitchen towel. Squeeze out and discard as much liquid from the mixture as possible.

2 Scrape the potato-onion mixture into a large bowl. Add the flour, tapioca starch, salt, baking powder, and pepper and toss together until well combined.

3 Line a large plate with paper towels. Heat a cast-iron or carbon steel skillet over medium heat. Pour in a thin layer of oil, about ¼ inch deep. Once the oil is hot, drop a large tablespoon of the latke batter into the oil, flattening it a little with the back of the spoon. Repeat with additional batter, leaving an inch or two between the latkes. Cook the latkes on one side until browned and crispy, 4 to 5 minutes. Turn with a thin, flexible spatula. Cook on the other side until browned, 2 to 3 minutes. As each latke is browned and crispy on both sides, remove it to the plate to drain briefly. Sprinkle with flaky salt while still warm. Repeat with remaining latke batter, adding more oil as needed. To keep them warm until serving, see the tip to the left.

fresh corn polenta

6 ears corn, shucked

2 tablespoons unsalted butter

2 cloves garlic, thinly sliced

½ cup finely grated Parmigiano-Reggiano cheese

2 tablespoons chopped fresh parsley

Aleppo-style pepper

Sea salt

WHAT CAN YOU DO WITH CORN STOCK?

Use the leftover corn stock in soups or stews, just like vegetable stock. It is delicious added to the Chicken Poblano Soup on page 128. The stock will keep in the refrigerator for up to 4 days, or in the freezer for up to 3 months.

Elie and I had one of our favorite meals in a rather unexpected location: a nondescript restaurant next to a gas station in the northeastern corner of Israel, almost within sight of the Syrian and Lebanese borders. We enjoyed a memorable dinner including a crock of fresh corn polenta, sweet and creamy with the perfume of parmesan. Because this dish is simple and relies on only a few good ingredients, it is best made in the late summer, when corn is at its peak. If your corn is on the starchy side, add the tiniest bit of sugar to sweeten it up. **SERVES 4 TO 6**

1 Set a small bowl upside down in the middle of a very large mixing bowl. Set the wide end of 1 ear of corn on the small bowl. Use a sharp knife to cut off all the kernels from the corn. Repeat with a second ear of corn. Remove the small bowl. Using a box grater, grate the kernels from the remaining 4 ears, letting all the grated kernels and corn "milk" collect in the bottom of the bowl. Use the edge of a spoon or the back of a knife to scrape out any additional milk.

2 Place the corn cobs in a pot big enough to hold them all. Add enough water to cover. Bring to a boil, then reduce to a simmer. Simmer the corn cobs for about an hour to create a flavorful corn stock.

3 After the stock has been simmering for about 40 minutes, start cooking the corn. Place a large skillet over medium heat. Add the butter. When the butter has melted and is starting to foam, add the garlic and sauté for 30 seconds to a minute, until fragrant, being sure not to let the garlic or butter brown.

4 Add the corn kernels and corn milk to the skillet, stirring to combine everything. Add a good pinch of salt , about ⅛ teaspoon, and let the corn simmer for about 20 minutes, stirring occasionally.

5 Stir in a ladleful of the corn stock. The corn should be saucy, but not soupy. Simmer the polenta for another 10 minutes or until the corn is at the desired tenderness.

6 Add the parmesan, and taste for seasoning, adding more salt if necessary. Stir in the parsley and a good pinch of pepper and serve warm.

smashed roasted potatoes

WITH CRISPY SHALLOTS

1½ to 2 pounds baby red, white, and purple potatoes

Sea salt

4 to 5 tablespoons extra virgin olive oil

1 cup avocado oil

4 small shallots, thinly sliced

1 tablespoon chopped fresh parsley, for serving

MAKE AHEAD

You can boil, smash, and season the potatoes several hours in advance. Let the potatoes hang out on the baking sheet until you're ready to put them in the oven.

SERVING TIPS

I love to pair this dish with Roasted Cauliflower (page 153), over a bed of Tahini Sauce (page 85). That can make a plant-based main course or a beautiful dish for a picnic. You can also serve these potatoes as a snack before dinner, with aioli or Fresh Chile Harissa (page 273).

These potatoes are one of my favorite recipes to serve at brunch or dinner, especially if kids are present. First, they are incredibly easy, and much of the work can be done ahead of time. Second, everyone loves them. The inside of the potatoes are fluffy and tender, and the ragged edges from gently smashing the potatoes gives extra surface area for crispy browned potato skins. A shower of crunchy fried shallots makes the dish feel special. · SERVES 4 TO 6

1 Preheat the oven to 450 degrees F. Line a rimmed baking sheet with parchment paper.

2 Place the potatoes in a large pot and cover with cold water. Bring to a boil, then reduce to a simmer. Cook the potatoes until they are very tender but not cracking and falling apart, 25 to 30 minutes. They are done when you can easily pierce them with a fork.

3 Drain the potatoes, then dry them on a clean kitchen towel. Place the potatoes on the baking sheet. Using the palm of your hand or the flat bottom of a measuring cup or glass, gently smash each potato slightly, until it's flattened but not falling apart. Season with about ¼ teaspoon salt, then generously drizzle with olive oil. Roast the potatoes for about 30 minutes, until they are golden and have very crispy edges.

4 While the potatoes are roasting, make the fried shallots. Place a fine-mesh sieve over a medium bowl and line a plate with paper towels. Place the shallots and avocado oil in a small saucepan. Cook the shallots over medium-high heat for 10 to 15 minutes, until they are nicely browned. Be careful—the transition from brown to burnt can happen quickly. Pour the shallots and oil into the sieve to drain thoroughly. Transfer the shallots to the plate to cool. Season the shallots with salt.

5 To serve, place the potatoes on a serving platter, top with the fried shallots, and garnish with fresh parsley.

olive oil–fried brussels sprouts

1½ pounds Brussels sprouts

Extra virgin olive oil

¼ teaspoon sea salt

⅛ teaspoon Aleppo-style pepper or red pepper flakes

Grated zest of 1 lemon

Freshly ground black pepper

Flaky salt

I love Brussels sprouts with bacon as much as the next person. Or Brussels sprouts cooked in butter. But there is something about the simple preparation of these Brussels sprouts that I find addictive. Every time I make them, I find myself snacking on them right out of the pan. I think making Brussels sprouts on the stovetop is superior to roasting. It allows you to take each Brussels sprout out when it's just done, so you don't end up with any mushy pieces. I like my Brussels sprouts browned and just barely cooked through, tender but still with a little crunch. If you like yours a little more done, just leave them in the pan longer. Lastly, to get a good caramelization on the Brussels sprouts, you'll need to use a cast-iron or carbon steel skillet. A nonstick skillet won't brown and crisp them the same way. · SERVES 4

1 Prepare the Brussels sprouts by cutting off the bottom stem and removing any dry, discolored, or wilted outer leaves. Cut the sprouts in half lengthwise.

2 Heat a large cast-iron or carbon steel skillet over medium-high heat. Add enough oil to cover the entire bottom of the pan with a thin layer. When the oil is shimmering, add enough of the sprouts, cut side down, to just cover the skillet in a single layer. You don't want to crowd the pan, or the sprouts will steam and not brown. Don't be tempted to add them all at once.

3 Sprinkle with half of the sea salt. Let the sprouts cook for 2 to 3 minutes undisturbed until the bottom is caramelized. Use tongs to flip the sprouts to the other side. Let them cook for 2 to 3 minutes, until the other side is browned. If the pan gets dry, add a little more oil. Use the tongs to stir the sprouts, making sure each of them is browned all over. Taste one; if it seems almost done, but still has just a little bite, remove all the sprouts to a bowl. Repeat with the remaining sprouts.

4 Pour all the sprouts onto a serving platter. Sprinkle with the lemon zest. Add a little pepper and a sprinkling of flaky salt. Serve warm.

crispy smashed parmesan sweet potatoes

2 or 3 medium-sized Jewel or Garnet sweet potatoes, unpeeled

1 tablespoon sea salt

3 to 4 tablespoons extra virgin olive oil

¾ to 1 cup freshly grated Parmigiano-Reggiano cheese

⅛ teaspoon Aleppo-style pepper

Chili Oil (page 267; optional)

These sweet potatoes may use the same method as the Smashed Roasted Potatoes on page 162, but the result is an entirely different dish. Showering the cooked sweet potato slices with a mountain of grated parmesan cheese and then roasting them in a hot oven results in browned sweet potatoes with a rich, cheesy crust. They are delicious served as is, or drizzled with chili oil for heat. · SERVES 6

1 Preheat the oven to 425 degrees F. Line a rimmed baking sheet with parchment paper.

2 Slice the potatoes crosswise into rounds about 2 inches thick. Place them in a large pot and cover with cold water. Add 1 tablespoon salt. Bring to a boil, then reduce to a simmer. Simmer the potatoes until they are tender all the way through but not falling apart, 10 to 15 minutes.

3 Drain the sweet potatoes in a colander set in the sink for 10 to 15 minutes, until quite dry.

4 Place the sweet potato rounds on the baking sheet. Drizzle the sweet potatoes with half of the olive oil. Turn them and drizzle the other half of the olive oil on the other side. Use the flat bottom of a measuring cup or glass to gently smash each sweet potato slightly. It's okay if some of the sweet potatoes break apart. You just want more surface area for the potatoes to crisp.

5 Sprinkle the parmesan evenly over the tops of the sweet potatoes. Bake for 20 to 25 minutes, until the sweet potatoes are browned, the skins are crisp, and the parmesan is melted and browned. Drizzle with chili oil, if you like, and serve warm.

roasted vegetable panzanella

½ loaf gluten-free bread (about 8 ounces), cut into ½-inch cubes (I like the Happy Campers brand)

4 tablespoons (½ stick) unsalted butter, melted

Pinch of red pepper flakes

2 teaspoons fresh thyme leaves

4 tablespoons chopped fresh sage leaves

Sea salt

Freshly cracked black pepper

¼ to ½ cup finely grated Parmigiano-Reggiano cheese

2 large carrots

1 large or 2 small parsnips

1 medium butternut squash

1 large head fennel

1 large red onion

1 pound shiitake mushrooms

¼ cup extra virgin olive oil

1 pound Brussels sprouts

1 pound bacon, cut crosswise into strips

4 or 5 dates, pitted and sliced

1 cup pecans halves, toasted and chopped

Leaves from ½ bunch fresh flat-leaf parsley

¼ cup chopped fennel fronds

This recipe is inspired by my friend Mataio, an incredible chef and mentor who invented an irresistible version of Thanksgiving stuffing (or dressing). In this dish, deeply roasted fall vegetables come together with crispy, buttery croutons, smoky bacon, nuts and dried fruit, and the traditional herbs of sage and thyme. It's a colorful, beautiful addition to the table. And while it does make an impressive side dish for Thanksgiving, I often make it for dinner throughout the fall and winter. It's a satisfying meal in and of itself. This recipe is a bit of time commitment, but well worth the effort. · SERVES 8 TO 10

1 Preheat the oven to 425 degrees F. Line two or three rimmed baking sheets with parchment paper.

2 In a large bowl, combine the bread, butter, pepper flakes, parmesan, 1 teaspoon of the thyme, and 2 tablespoons of the sage. Season with ½ to 1 teaspoon salt and ⅛ teaspoon black pepper, and toss everything together. Spread the croutons in a single layer on a baking sheet. Bake for 10 to 15 minutes, until the cheese has melted and the croutons are nicely browned and crispy. Let cool completely. (If you only have two baking sheets, remove the croutons, still on the parchment paper, from the baking sheet and reline the sheet with clean parchment.)

3 While the croutons are baking and cooling, prepare the vegetables, cutting the vegetables to approximately the same size and adding them to the same large bowl as they are ready. Peel and dice the carrots, parsnips, and butternut squash. Trim the fennel, reserving the fronds, and reserving the stalks for another use (like freezing for stock). Dice the fennel bulb. Peel the onion and cut into thin wedges. Remove the stems from the mushrooms. (Save the stems for vegetable stock.) Tear mushroom caps into halves or quarters.

4 Season the vegetables with 1 teaspoon salt and ¼ teaspoon black pepper. Add the remaining thyme and sage and the oil and toss everything together. Divide the vegetables between

RECIPE CONTINUES

You can make the croutons several days in advance. Store them in an airtight container at room temperature. The roasted vegetables can be made 1 day in advance. Reheat them in a 350 degree F oven until just warm. The bacon can also be cooked 1 day in advance and stored in the refrigerator. Rewarm it in the microwave or in a skillet before adding it to the dish.

COOKING TIP

I don't season the Brussels sprouts at first, because they are cooked in bacon fat and everything else is highly seasoned. If you want to add a little sea salt, by all means do.

SERVING TIP

I love this panzanella left over—most often, I just eat it cold. But you can also warm it in a skillet and top it with a fried egg for lunch.

two baking sheets, spreading them in a single layer. Roast for 30 to 35 minutes, until the vegetables are soft and have begun to caramelize, with crispy edges. Depending on your oven, you may want to rotate the baking sheets halfway through for even roasting. Remove the vegetables from the oven and set aside.

5 While the vegetables are roasting, line a plate with paper towels. Put the bacon in a large cast-iron or other heavy skillet and place over medium-low heat. Slowly render out all fat, then continue cooking, stirring occasionally, until the bacon is crispy, about 10 to 12 minutes. Using a slotted spoon, remove the bacon to the plate. Carefully pour all but 2 tablespoons of the bacon fat into a glass jar and reserve for another use.

6 Trim the Brussels sprouts, cutting off the bottom stem and peeling off any dry, discolored, or wilted outer leaves. Cut each in half through the stem end. Return the skillet with the bacon fat to medium heat. Lay the sprouts in the skillet a single layer, cut side down, and cook until well browned, about 5 to 6 minutes. Turn them with tongs and cook briefly on the other side. Depending on the size of your skillet, you may need to do this in several batches, adding more bacon fat. (Be careful not to overcook. Brussels sprouts are better slightly underdone than overdone.) Add the sprouts to the roasted vegetables.

7 When you are ready to serve, combine all vegetables in a very large bowl along with the bacon. Add the dates, pecans, parsley, fennel fronds, and reserved croutons. Toss everything together and transfer to a serving dish. Store any leftovers in an airtight container in the refrigerator for up to 5 days.

PLANT-BASED ROASTED VEGETABLE PANZANELLA · Use a vegan gluten-free bread, omit the cheese and bacon, and cook the Brussels sprouts in olive oil. I've made it this way many times, and it's delicious.

roasted kabocha squash
WITH PECANS AND POMEGRANATES

1 kabocha squash

¼ cup extra virgin olive oil

¼ to ½ teaspoon sea salt

¼ cup chopped toasted pecans

¼ cup pomegranate seeds

Chili Oil (page 267)

Pomegranate molasses, for drizzling

WHAT CAN YOU DO WITH LEFTOVER SQUASH?

Depending on the size of the squash, you might have more wedges than you need. Scoop out the roasted flesh to use in place of the canned pumpkin in the Maple-Pumpkin Bread (page 250) or any other recipe that calls for pumpkin. If you're not using the squash right away, store it in the refrigerator in an airtight container for up to 5 days.

When squashes and pumpkins first start appearing at the market, I'm usually still resistant to the change in season. But the beauty of the Kabocha squash always gets me. I pick one up at the farmer's market, and I'm coaxed into fall with this dish. It's simple enough for a weeknight meal, but elegant enough to grace a holiday table. Roasted wedges of deep orange kabocha squash are topped with a shower of pomegranate seeds, toasted pecans, and chili oil, making it savory, tart, and spicy. If you can't find kabocha squash at your grocery store or farmers' market, substitute a sweet pumpkin. PHOTOGRAPH ON PAGES 134 AND 135 · SERVES 6

1 Preheat the oven to 375 degrees F.

2 Place the squash in the oven for about 15 minutes, to make it soft enough to cut. Remove from the oven and let cool until you can handle it.

3 Increase the oven temperature to 425 degrees F. Line a baking sheet with parchment paper.

4 Use a sharp knife to cut out the stem of the squash. Cut the squash in half, through the hole where the stem was. Scoop out all of the seeds and discard. Cut the squash into wedges 2 to 3 inches across.

5 Place the squash wedges on one cut side on the baking sheet. Drizzle with half of the oil and half of the salt. Turn the squash wedges over and drizzle with the remaining oil and salt. Use your hands to rub the oil and salt into each piece.

6 Roast for 20 to 25 minutes, turning the wedges halfway through the cooking time, until the squash is deeply golden brown and caramelized. Don't be tempted to take the squash out before it's browned. If your oven needs more time, keep it in longer.

7 Place the wedges on a serving platter and garnish with the pecans and pomegranate seeds. Drizzle a little chili oil and pomegranate molasses over the top.

slow-roasted delicata squash

WITH FRIED SAGE

2 large delicata squash

⅛ to ¼ teaspoon sea salt

2 tablespoons extra virgin olive oil

2 tablespoons unsalted butter

2 cloves garlic, peeled

3 or 4 sprigs fresh thyme

3 or 4 sprigs fresh sage

MAKE AHEAD

Since the squash cooks slowly in the oven, it's a hands-off dish to make when you are having people over. If you want to make it a couple of hours ahead, just keep it warm, covered with foil, in a very low oven.

Almost every recipe for delicata squash calls for halving the squash and slicing it into thin half-moons. Instead, I love to roast the halves whole, slowly letting them caramelize with butter, garlic, and herbs. As the squash roasts in the oven, the butter browns, becoming fragrant and nutty. The garlic, sage, and thyme slowly fry in the browned butter, perfuming the dish. As the skin of the squash crisps, the inside becomes creamy and scoopably soft. I usually serve this squash in its roasting dish. • SERVES 4

1 Preheat the oven to 350 degrees F.

2 Cut the delicata squash in half lengthwise. Scoop out the seeds and discard. Season with salt.

3 Put the oil and butter in an oven-safe skillet. Heat in the oven for a few minutes, until the butter melts. Place the squash, cut side down, in the skillet. Nestle the garlic, thyme, and sage around the squash.

4 Roast for 30 to 45 minutes, until the squash is deeply cara-melized on the bottom, the flesh is very soft, and the skin has crisped. Remove the skillet from the oven. I love to serve this in the skillet it was cooked in. The garlic cloves will be very soft and browned. The sage leaves should have crisped and fried in the oil, and are delicious. This dish is best served warm.

roasted sweet potatoes

WITH FIGS AND POMEGRANATES

2 or 3 large Jewel or Garnet sweet potatoes, unpeeled and cut into 2- to 3-inch chunks

¼ teaspoon sea salt

⅛ teaspoon Aleppo-style pepper

1 tablespoon pomegranate molasses

2 tablespoons extra virgin olive oil

1 pint fresh figs, stemmed and halved

¼ cup toasted pecans, chopped

¼ cup pomegranate seeds

3 ounces Humboldt Fog cheese (optional)

SUBSTITUTIONS

Tossing the sweet potatoes in a little pomegranate molasses gives them a tart sweetness and ensures a deep caramelization. If you can't find pomegranate molasses, use honey.

If figs are not in season, you can substitute dried figs. Don't cook them; just slice them and add them with the nuts before serving.

If you can't find pomegranates, you can leave off the pomegranate seeds or substitute dried tart cherries.

Elie and I attended a dinner at Wood Stone, a local manufacturer of pizza ovens, where the chef made the entire dinner in the wood-burning oven, from the bread to the apple pie. My favorite dish was one of sweet potatoes tossed with pomegranate molasses and topped with figs. This is my interpretation of that dish. I added chopped pecans, pomegranate seeds, and crumbled Humboldt Fog cheese, which easily turns this into a satisfying main dish for a light lunch or dinner. If you're serving this as a side dish at dinner, you could certainly leave off the cheese. · SERVES 6

1 Preheat the oven to 425 degrees F. Line a rimmed baking sheet with parchment paper.

2 Place the sweet potatoes on the baking sheet and season with salt and pepper. Drizzle the pomegranate molasses and oil over the sweet potatoes. Using your hands or a spoon, toss the sweet potatoes to evenly coat them. Make sure the sweet potatoes are all in a single layer and not touching each other. Roast for 15 minutes.

3 Remove the baking sheet from the oven. Stir the sweet potatoes, then add the figs. Try to find room to place the figs cut side down on the baking sheet. Make sure everything is still in a single layer. Place the baking sheet back in the oven for another 10 to 15 minutes, until the sweet potatoes are tender and caramelized and the figs have softened and started to brown. Depending on your oven, you may want to rotate the pan or stir the sweet potatoes a few times during cooking to prevent them from burning.

4 Transfer the sweet potatoes and figs to a serving platter. Garnish with the pecans, pomegranate seeds, and the Humboldt Fog, if using.

creamy polenta or grits

2 tablespoons unsalted butter

1 clove garlic, sliced

8 cups water

2 teaspoons sea salt

1 bay leaf

1¼ cups uncooked polenta or grits (not instant or quick-cooking)

Freshly ground black pepper

MAKE IT YOUR OWN

For extra creamy polenta (grits), replace 4 cups of the water with whole milk and stir in 2 to 3 tablespoons butter at the end.

For parmesan polenta (grits), stir in 1 cup freshly grated Parmigiano-Reggiano cheese at the end.

For cheesy polenta (grits), stir in 1 to 2 cups grated sharp cheddar cheese at the end.

SERVING TIPS

Polenta (grits) is delicious topped with anything braised and with runny eggs. Here are a few ideas.

Top with Back-Pocket Braised Chicken (Pictured opposite).

Top with Charred Kale (page 144) and a fried or poached egg. A little crumbled bacon would be delicious.

Top with Sort-of-Barbacoa beef (page 215), Toasted Pumpkin Seeds (page 260), and Chili Oil (page 267).

Polenta and grits are similar—their main difference comes down to the type of corn. Grits are generally made from dent corn, while polenta comes from flint corn. Flint corn holds its texture more than dent corn, but they can be cooked and eaten the same way. So warm and satisfying, soft and creamy polenta—or grits—is one of my ultimate comfort foods. You can use it as a base for shrimp and grits (page 229), drown it with a succulent braised chicken (page 200), or top it with sautéed greens and a fried egg for a belly-warming breakfast. For perfectly spoonable polenta, don't follow the package instructions, which will usually give you a 2:1 ratio of water to polenta. For soft polenta, you need a ratio of at least a 6:1 ratio of liquid to polenta. It also needs to cook for at least an hour, to allow the polenta to hydrate and become soft and creamy. Anson Mills Coarse White Grits are my favorite, but Bob's Red Mill Corn Grits are good, too. Just be sure to look for one made from non-GMO corn. · MAKES ABOUT 8 CUPS

1 Heat a Dutch oven or similar large heavy-bottomed pot over medium heat. Add the butter. When it has melted, add the garlic and cook for a few seconds. Before the garlic has a chance to brown, pour in the water and salt and stir. Add the bay leaf.

2 Bring to a boil, then reduce to a bare simmer. Slowly pour in the polenta or grits and whisk well. Partially cover the pot. (Covering the pot prevents the polenta from spitting at you, but still allows the steam to escape.) Cook for at least an hour, keeping the heat very low, and whisking often to prevent clumping and stop from the polenta (grits) from sticking to the bottom of the pot.

3 When done, the polenta (grits) should be spoonably soft, with no gritty bite. It should taste well-seasoned and delicious. Fish out and discard the bay leaf. Add pepper to taste, and adjust the salt, if necessary.

4 The polenta (grits) can be stored in an airtight container in the refrigerator for up to 5 days. The polenta will firm up as it sets. Warm in a pot set over low heat, adding a little water or milk to loosen the polenta (grits), if necessary.

ON GATHERING

Inviting people over to sit around the table is ultimately about meaningful connection with other human beings. In *The Art of Gathering,* Priya Parker writes, "Gatherings crackle and flourish when real thought goes into them, when (often invisible) structure is baked into them, and when a host has the curiosity, willingness, and generosity of spirit to try."

As hosts, we spend so much time thinking about the aesthetic and sensory details of the table setting, menu, lighting and music, and we often leave the chemistry of the gathering to chance. I know I'm guilty. We have all been to dinners where we walk away feeling a missed opportunity to have connected in a more meaningful way. And we have all been to gatherings where we walk away feeling elated, connected, inspired. Those evenings are magical. What if we put as much effort into the structure of the evening as we did to the other details?

Even a simple dinner party with friends can only benefit from thought and planning. Setting an intention for a gathering gives me a chance to reflect on how I want people to feel as they leave our house to travel back home. Perhaps it is to feel celebrated, or to feel deeply loved. Perhaps it is to feel inspired, that they learned something new or learned more about themselves. Sometimes the intention is to introduce people to each other, to create new connections. Or perhaps, I want my guests to know they matter, that the gathering would not be the same without their presence.

The structure of a gathering depends on the setting, number of guests and the intention. But it's always a good idea to start with introductions (if guests don't know each other). I can't tell you how many dinners I've attended where I didn't get to know the names of the other people seated around the table. As an introvert, I'm often shy to introduce myself to people I don't know. I doubt I'm alone in this.

When the meal begins, we say a prayer or blessing, even if the guests are not religious. Often, if kids are present, I ask them to sing a blessing song. It creates a moment of pause, of communal gratitude.

Not always, but often, I will pose a question to my guests as they are gathered at the table. It can set the tone for digging deeper than current events or other superficial topics of conversation. Questions of intentions, memories, meaningful experiences, spirituality. The questions can be fun, such as "If you could only eat five foods for the rest of your life, what would they be?" Or the questions can be more probing, like "Who are the three people in your life who have influenced you the most, and why?" Offering questions to our guests creates a safe environment for sharing. Paying attention to these small details creates that invisible structure that creates a gathering that sparkles. One guests will remember.

CHAPTER SEVEN

LARGER DISHES

pasta bolognese

A.K.A. CHRISTMAS BOLOGNESE

Extra virgin olive oil

4 ounces pancetta, diced

1 pound shiitake mushrooms, stemmed, caps sliced

1 large onion, coarsely chopped

2 stalks celery, coarsely chopped

2 large carrots, coarsely chopped (no need to peel)

2 cloves garlic, peeled

Sea salt

1 pound 80/20 ground beef

Freshly ground black pepper

¼ to ½ teaspoon Aleppo-style pepper

4 sprigs fresh thyme

2 bay leaves

1 cup whole milk

¼ to ½ teaspoon freshly grated nutmeg, to taste

1 cup dry white wine

One 28-ounce can whole San Marzano tomatoes

¼ cup finely chopped fresh parsley leaves

18 ounces Homemade Gluten-Free Tagliatelle (page 45)

Freshly grated Parmigiano-Reggiano cheese, for serving

I call this recipe "Christmas Bolognese" because it has become the dish we serve every year for Christmas Day dinner. It is a lush, celebratory pasta, one that also feels appropriate for a date night at home, or to mark a special occasion. The barely pink sauce is rich and luscious with an earthy undertone from the addition of browned shiitake mushrooms and brightened by sweet, aromatic nutmeg. Although the sauce takes a long time from start to finish, the hands-on time is minimal. As ingredients are cooking or reducing or simmering, there's space for other kitchen tasks, or simply breathing in the joy of the day. PHOTOGRAPH ON PAGES 180-181 · SERVES 6

1 Pour 2 tablespoons oil into a large heavy-bottomed pot or Dutch oven set over medium heat. Add the pancetta and cook until the pancetta is beginning to brown, about 3 or 4 minutes.

2 Add the shiitake mushrooms and cook, stirring occasionally, until the mushrooms have completely wilted, released all their moisture, and started to brown, 10 to 15 minutes. Add a bit more oil if the pan gets too dry. Using a slotted spoon, transfer the mushrooms and pancetta to a bowl; set aside.

3 While the mushrooms are cooking, pulse the onion, celery, carrot, and garlic in a food processor until the very finely chopped.

4 Reduce the heat to medium-low. Pour another 2 tablespoons oil into the pot. Add the vegetable mixture and ½ teaspoon salt. Slowly cook the vegetables, stirring occasionally, until completely soft and just starting to brown, 10 to 15 minutes.

5 Add the beef, another ½ teaspoon salt, the black and Aleppo-style peppers, thyme, and bay leaves. Raise the heat to medium and cook for about 10 minutes, stirring often, until the beef is cooked through.

6 Stir in the reserved pancetta and shiitake mushrooms and any juices in the bowl. Stir in the milk. Let the sauce simmer, stirring frequently, until the liquid has completely evaporated, about 10 minutes.

7 Stir in ¼ teaspoon of the nutmeg and the wine. Simmer until the wine has almost completely evaporated, about 10 minutes.

8 While the wine is reducing, place the tomatoes in a food processor or blender and blend until almost smooth. Add the tomatoes to the sauce and stir. Taste and add more salt, pepper, and/or nutmeg, as desired. Don't add too much salt, as you will add some of the salted pasta cooking water at the end.

9 Let the sauce simmer, uncovered, for at least 1 hour or preferably 2 to 3 hours, until it is thick and luscious. Stir the sauce occasionally as it simmers and add a little bit of water if it starts to look too thick or too dry.

10 Fish out and discard the bay leaf and thyme stems. Stir in the parsley.

11 Bring a large pot of water to a boil. Add a three-finger pinch of salt to the water. Add the tagliatelle and stir. Cook for 3 to 4 minutes, until just shy of done. Using a slotted spoon or sieve, transfer the tagliatelle to the pot of sauce. Add a ladleful of the pasta cooking water and stir again. Let the pasta finish cooking in the sauce, absorbing all the flavors. Serve with grated parmesan.

MAKE AHEAD

The bolognese sauce can be made a few days ahead of time and stored, covered, in the refrigerator. Reheat it gently on the stovetop before adding the pasta. You can also freeze the sauce, without the pasta, for up to 3 months.

SUBSTITUTIONS

If you can't find pancetta, substitute bacon. It will give the sauce a little bit of a smoky flavor, but I've made it that way many times. It's not overpowering. Alternatively, substitute chopped prosciutto, also easy to find. If you don't eat pork, just leave it out.

COOKING TIPS

Finely chopping the vegetables in the food processor ensures they will melt into the sauce as it simmers. They should basically disappear.

Don't rush the process of reducing the milk. If you add the wine too soon, the sauce might curdle. (I've done it.) It will still taste okay, but it won't look very pretty.

a pasta for crab season

Sea salt

3 tablespoons extra virgin olive oil, plus more for serving

2 cloves garlic, sliced

3 cups cherry or grape tomatoes, halved

⅛ teaspoon Aleppo-style pepper or red pepper flakes

1 pound jumbo lump crab meat

¼ cup finely chopped fresh parsley leaves

4 or 5 basil leaves, finely chopped

Grated zest of 1 lemon

12 ounces Homemade Gluten-Free Linguine or Tagliatelle (page 45) or purchased dried

Freshly ground black pepper

Flaky salt

During the pandemic, we became boaters, which, in the Pacific Northwest, means we also became crabbers. It is such a fun activity to do with kids—the thrill of dropping the crab pot and the anticipation of how many will be in it as it's pulled up. One Dungeness crab yields enough meat to feed all three of us, and this pasta is my favorite way to eat it. Crab season coincides with tomato season, so a simple sauté of fresh, ripe tomatoes, garlic, and vibrant herbs is the perfect accompaniment to the briny, sweet crab. If you have Sun Gold tomatoes in your garden, those are perfect in this dish. · SERVES 4

1 Bring a large pot of salted water to a boil.

2 Heat a medium-sized skillet over medium heat. Add the oil and garlic. Sauté the garlic for 30 seconds to 1 minute before stirring in the tomatoes, ¼ teaspoon sea salt, and the Aleppo-style pepper. Increase the heat to medium-high and cook for about 5 minutes, stirring occasionally, until the tomatoes just start to wilt but are still holding their shape. They should release their juices to make a little pan sauce. Add the crab, parsley, basil, and lemon zest. Stir gently to combine, being careful not to break up the crab meat. Keep warm over low heat until the pasta is ready.

3 When the water is boiling, add the pasta. If you are using fresh pasta, cook it for 3 to 4 minutes, until the pasta is just al dente. If you're using dried pasta, cook according to the package directions. To test if the pasta is done, remove one piece from the water and bite into it. It should be the same color throughout, without any chalky white line in the center.

4 When the pasta is done, use a slotted spoon or tongs to remove it from the water and drop it straight into the pan with the crab. Add about ¼ cup of the pasta cooking water. Stir gently to combine the pasta with the crab and tomatoes.

5 Divide the pasta between four warm shallow bowls. Top with freshly ground black pepper, a drizzle of olive oil, and a sprinkling of flaky salt.

baked cheesy radicchio pasta
WITH TOASTED BUCKWHEAT

Extra virgin olive oil

2 ounces thinly sliced prosciutto

1 small onion, thinly sliced

1 small head fennel, trimmed, cored, and thinly sliced

1 clove garlic, thinly sliced

1 large head radicchio, cored and sliced

Aleppo-style pepper or red pepper flakes

2 teaspoons caraway seeds, toasted

1 cup Chicken Stock (page 277) or purchased bone broth

8 ounces Taleggio cheese, sliced

Sea salt

1 pound Homemade Gluten-Free Strozzapreti (page 45), or purchased gluten-free pasta

Freshly ground black pepper

Grated zest of one lemon

½ cup freshly grated Parmigiano-Reggiano cheese

¼ cup Toasted Buckwheat (page 261)

MAKE AHEAD

You can assemble the pasta an hour or two ahead of time and leave it at room temperature until ready to bake.

This baked pasta was inspired by Susan Spungen's Pink Pasta in her cookbook *Open Kitchen*. In this dish, beautiful bitter radicchio is mellowed by cheesy pasta. While the sharp, peppery caraway seeds may seem unusual, I was inspired by the creamy cabbage pastas of Eastern Europe. I think it pairs beautifully with the radicchio and cheese. Please don't leave off the buckwheat—it provides an interesting, earthy crunch. If you don't want to make the fresh Strozzapreti, substitute with a dried gluten-free pasta of similar shape. · SERVES 6

1 Preheat the oven to 375 degrees F.

2 Heat 2 tablespoons oil in a very large oven-safe skillet (like a 12-inch carbon steel or cast iron) over medium heat. Add prosciutto and cook until browned. Add the onions and cook, stirring often, until the onions begin to caramelize, about 20 to 25 minutes. Add another tablespoon of olive oil and the fennel and garlic. Cook for another 3 to 4 minutes, until the fennel and garlic have softened.

3 Add the radicchio and cook until the radicchio has started to wilt. Stir in the Aleppo-style pepper and caraway seeds, stirring to let the caraway seeds become fragrant. Stir in the stock and bring to a low simmer. Stir in the Taleggio until the cheese has melted. Turn off the heat.

4 Bring a large pot of water to a boil and add a three-finger pinch of salt. Add the pasta and cook for 1 to 2 minutes, until barely al dente. Using a sieve, scoop the pasta out of the water and add it to the radicchio mixture. If the pasta seems dry, add a little bit of the pasta water, ¼ to ⅓ cup. Season with a good amount of black pepper, add the lemon zest and stir well.

5 In a small bowl, stir together the parmesan and buckwheat. Sprinkle this mixture over the top of the pasta. Transfer the skillet to the oven and bake for 25 to 30 minutes, until the pasta is golden brown on top and bubbling. Store any leftovers in an airtight container in the refrigerator for up to 5 days. This pasta does not freeze particularly well.

butternut squash–chicken bolognese

WITH TAGLIATELLE

2 pounds butternut squash, peeled, seeded, and cubed

Extra virgin olive oil

Sea salt

1 medium onion (about 6 ounces), coarsely chopped

2 stalks celery, coarsely chopped

2 small carrots, coarsely chopped

1½ pounds ground chicken thighs (see Tip)

Freshly ground black pepper

¼ teaspoon Aleppo-style pepper or red pepper flakes

1 bay leaf

1 tablespoon chopped fresh sage leaves

¼ teaspoon freshly grated nutmeg

1 cup unoaked dry white wine or rosé

1 quart Chicken Stock (page 277) or purchased bone broth, plus more if needed

1½ pounds Homemade Gluten-Free Tagliatelle (page 45)

Finely chopped fresh parsley, for serving

Freshly grated Parmigiano-Reggiano cheese, for serving

I get so much inspiration from reading cookbooks, and then I take an idea and play with it to make it my own. (I hope this book encourages you to do the same.) This recipe was inspired by the Pumpkin Bolognese in Joshua McFadden's book *Six Seasons*. Although it takes a bit of time, you'll be rewarded with a warming dish that almost tastes like Thanksgiving in pasta form. The butternut squash cooks down into a luxurious sauce that perfectly coats the fresh pasta. In some ways, this recipe is easier than a traditional bolognese, because without milk, you don't have to worry about the sauce curdling. This recipe is dairy-free if you leave off the Parmigiano-Reggiano. · SERVES 6 TO 8

1 Preheat the oven to 425 degrees F. Line two rimmed baking sheets with parchment paper.

2 Divide the squash between the two baking sheets. Drizzle the squash on each baking sheet with about 2 tablespoons oil and sprinkle with ¼ teaspoon salt. Rub the oil and salt into the squash, using your hands. Make sure the cubes are in a single layer and not overlapping. Roast for 20 to 25 minutes, until the squash is soft and caramelized. Let cool.

3 Place the onion, celery, and carrot in a food processor. Pulse until the vegetables are finely chopped.

4 Heat 2 tablespoons oil in a heavy-bottomed pot or Dutch oven and add the onion mixture and about ¼ teaspoon salt. Keeping the heat at medium-low, slowly cook the onion mixture until the mixture is completely soft and just starting to brown, 10 to 15 minutes.

5 Stir in the chicken. Raise the heat to medium and cook for about 5 minutes, stirring often, until the chicken is cooked through. If the pan becomes dry, add a little more oil.

6 Stir in the black pepper, Aleppo-style pepper, bay leaf, sage, and nutmeg. Add the wine and simmer until the wine has almost completely evaporated, about 5 minutes.

RECIPE CONTINUES

MAKE AHEAD

The sauce can be made up to 3 days in advance and stored in the refrigerator in a covered container. Warm gently on the stove before serving. The sauce can be frozen in airtight containers for up to 3 months. Thaw overnight in the refrigerator before warming.

A TIP ON GROUND CHICKEN

It's often hard to find good-quality ground chicken thighs, so I grind my own, using the meat grinder attachment to my KitchenAid mixer. I buy boneless, skinless chicken thighs from pasture-raised chickens and use the plate for a coarse grind. If you can't find ground chicken thighs or grind them yourself, substitute ground chicken breast or ground turkey.

7 While the wine is reducing, puree the squash in the food processor. Add the squash puree and the stock to the sauce and stir. Check the sauce for seasoning, adding a little more salt or pepper if needed. Note that you will be adding some of the salted pasta water to the sauce, so err on the side of less salt. Keeping the heat low, let the sauce simmer gently for about an hour, stirring occasionally. If it starts to thicken too much, add a little water or more stock.

8 When you're ready to serve, fish out and discard the bay leaf from the sauce. Bring a large pot of water to a boil. Add a three-finger pinch of salt to the water. Add the tagliatelle and stir. Cook for 3 to 4 minutes, until just shy of done. Using a slotted spoon or sieve, transfer the tagliatelle to the pot of sauce. Stir in a ladleful of the pasta cooking water and let the pasta finish cooking in the sauce, absorbing all the flavors.

9 Divide between warm bowls and serve, topped with fresh parsley and a shower of parmesan.

margherita pizza WITH PROSCIUTTO

pizza dough

1¼ cups (270 grams) room-temperature filtered water

1 tablespoon (12 grams) psyllium husk powder

2 tablespoons (20 grams) ground flaxseed

1 teaspoon (6 grams) sea salt

½ cup (125 grams) Gluten-Free Brown Rice Sourdough Starter (page 278)

1 cup plus 2 tablespoons (157 grams) superfine brown rice flour

⅓ cup (56 grams) potato starch

2 tablespoons (17 grams) tapioca starch

1 tablespoon extra virgin olive oil, plus more for the pan

Cornmeal, for the pan

sauce and toppings

2 cups cherry or grape tomatoes

Fresh basil leaves

⅛ to ¼ teaspoon red pepper flakes, plus more for sprinkling

7 or 8 ounces buffalo mozzarella (mozzarella di bufala), torn or sliced

4 ounces thinly sliced prosciutto

Elie and I have made a sport of finding the best pizza in any city we visit. We have been known to travel far and wait in long lines for the perfect wood-fired, naturally leavened slice. When I went gluten free, I obsessed over developing a naturally leavened pizza crust and on relying as little as possible on starches. This recipe is the result of that labor of love. This pizza gives a satisfying crunch as you cut the first slice, with a flavorful, slightly tangy, and chewy crust. I love the simplicity of a fresh tomato sauce, but you could blend the Olive-Oil Roasted Tomatoes, lemon removed (page 268) or Oven-Dried Tomatoes (page 268) into a thick, rich sauce.
MAKES TWO 12-INCH PIZZAS

1 To make the pizza dough: Pour the water into a large bowl. Add the psyllium husk powder, ground flaxseed, and salt and whisk well, making sure there are no lumps. The mixture will quickly start to gel.

2 Add the starter, flour, potato starch, tapioca starch, and oil and mix until the ingredients come together into a shaggy dough. A dough whisk works well for this.

3 Turn out the dough onto a clean surface and knead it a few times, just until it comes together into a ball. Place the dough back in the bowl and cover it with a clean towel. Let the dough rise at room temperature for about 4 hours, or in the refrigerator for up to 24 hours. (A longer, slower ferment in the refrigerator will result in a tangier dough.) When it is ready, the dough will have puffed up, but not doubled in size.

4 Preheat the oven to 500 degrees F.

5 Make the sauce: Put the tomatoes, 4 or 5 basil leaves, and pepper flakes to taste in a high-speed blender or food processor. Blend until smooth.

6 Make the pizzas: Divide the dough into two even halves. Dust the counter with a little brown rice flour. Working with one half at a time, use a rolling pin to roll the dough very thin, about ¼ inch thick. The dough should be about 14 or 15 inches in diameter, larger than your skillet.

RECIPE CONTINUES

TIPS FOR PERFECT PIZZA

I find that using all superfine brown rice flour is best for creating a dough that most resembles a Neapolitan-style pizza crust.

Be judicious with the sauce and toppings—keeping a light hand will ensure a crisp bottom.

Because gluten-free doughs are more delicate, it's not easy to use a pizza peel to transfer the pizza to a hot stone without tearing the dough. That's why I place the rolled-out dough in a carbon steel or cast-iron skillet, then roll in the edges of the dough to create a crust.

Gluten-free doughs require a longer baking time, so par-baking the dough before the toppings are added gives it a longer time to develop a blistered crust without overcooking the toppings.

7 Sprinkle a little cornmeal in the bottom of a 12-inch cast-iron or carbon steel skillet. Use your rolling pin to help you lift the dough into the skillet. Take the dough that hangs over the skillet and roll it into the pan, creating a raised edge. (Think about this as if you were making a pie crust.) Place the skillet in the oven for 15 to 20 minutes to par-bake the crust. The bottom of the crust should be starting to brown.

8 Remove the skillet from the oven and drop a few spoonfuls of the sauce onto the crust, using the back of a spoon to spread it evenly. Top with half of the mozzarella, then half of the prosciutto.

9 Bake the pizza for another 10 minutes, until the crust has browned and the cheese is melted and bubbly. If desired, finish the pizza under the broiler for just a minute or two, until the crust has slightly charred. Remove the pizza to a cutting board and top with additional torn basil leaves. Repeat with the remaining dough, sauce, cheese, and prosciutto, either using a second skillet or cooling down the skillet before making the second pizza in it. Slice and serve, offering the extra tomato sauce and more red pepper flakes on the side.

Three Different Pizzas

A simple margherita pizza is the one we make most often, so that's the recipe I included here. But here are a few other ideas for toppings to use on the par-baked crust. The quantities listed are for two pizzas.

LAMB, MUSHROOM, AND GOAT CHEESE · Sauté 4 ounces ground lamb with red pepper flakes, dried oregano, and 1 cup sliced shiitake mushrooms. Spoon over the tomato sauce. After baking, top with creamy goat cheese.

KALE AND SOPRESSATA · Sauté the chopped leaves from 1 small bunch kale in a little olive oil with red pepper flakes and sliced garlic. Spoon the sautéed kale over the tomato sauce. Top with thin slices of sopressata and fresh mozzarella and bake.

WILD MUSHROOM, PROSCIUTTO, AND FONTINA · Sauté a blend of wild mushrooms (about 8 ounces) in a little olive oil with garlic, fresh thyme, and red pepper flakes. Omit the tomato sauce. Spoon the mushrooms over the pizza dough, top with prosciutto and Fontina cheese and bake.

CLASSIC CHICKEN SOUP • Heat about 2 quarts chicken stock in a large pot. Add chopped carrots, celery, and shredded or chopped leftover chicken meat. Add a cup of uncooked gluten-free pasta (your choice of shape). Cook until the vegetables are soft and the pasta is done. Stir in a couple of big handfuls of baby spinach, some chopped fresh parsley, and several grinds of black pepper.

slow-roasted chicken

One 5-pound chicken

5 or 6 sprigs fresh thyme

3 or 4 sprigs fresh sage

Sea salt

1 sprig fresh rosemary

1 lemon, halved

Extra virgin olive oil

Freshly ground black pepper

A FEW TIPS

There are two tricks to a delicious roast chicken. One, generously salt the chicken, inside and out. And two, baste it a few times while it's cooking. It will help keep the breast moist and help the skin get crispy.

MAKE IT YOUR OWN

I like to keep the seasonings simple, with just salt and pepper. But you can experiment with adding sumac, Baharat (page 264), or other spices. You can also sprinkle the skin with raw sesame seeds, which adds a delicious nuttiness.

WHAT TO DO WITH LEFTOVER CHICKEN

Use the bones and scraps to make the chicken stock on page 277.

This is my favorite way to roast a chicken. If you love rotisserie chicken, you'll love this recipe. Roasted slowly in a low oven, it develops crispy skin and meat that is fall-off-the-bone tender. It's one of those no-fail recipes that works every time, so it's great for when you have friends over. SERVES 6

1 Preheat the oven to 300 degrees F.

2 Unwrap the chicken and remove the packet of giblets from the cavity, if there is one. Do not wash the chicken, as that can spread bacteria easily to the kitchen counter and sink. Just place the chicken in a roasting pan—one with sides at least a few inches high—and pat it well with paper towels until it's dry. This will help the skin crisp. If there were giblets, place them in the bottom of the pan.

3 Loosen the skin over the breast, gently running your fingers between the skin and the meat. Place a few of the thyme and sage sprigs under the skin on each side of the breast.

4 Pour about 1 tablespoon salt into the cavity of the chicken and rub it all around. Sprinkle salt all over the skin. Place the remaining thyme and sage and the rosemary in the cavity of the chicken along with the 2 lemon halves. Coat the outside of the chicken with 3 to 4 tablespoons oil, using your hands to rub it in. Grind pepper over the skin. Tie the legs together with kitchen twine. Position the chicken on its back in the roasting pan.

5 Roast the chicken for about 3 hours, basting it occasionally with the pan juices. The chicken is done when the skin is deeply browned. If you hold the end of the chicken leg and gently twist, it should feel like it would be easy to pull off.

6 Transfer the chicken to a cutting board and let it rest for 10 minutes before carving and serving. Pull the lemons out of the cavity and place on the serving platter with the chicken. I love to squeeze the roasted lemon over the chicken pieces.

chicken-zucchini meatballs

WITH ROASTED TOMATOES

1 large zucchini

2 pounds ground chicken thighs (see A Tip on Ground Chicken, page 190)

2 to 3 tablespoons chopped fresh parsley, plus more for garnish

2 to 3 tablespoons chopped fresh cilantro

2 teaspoons sea salt

1 tablespoon My Spice Blend (page 262)

¼ teaspoon red pepper flakes

Extra virgin olive oil

1 cup Chicken Stock (page 277) or purchased bone broth

1 cup cherry or grape tomatoes, halved

Aleppo-style pepper

SUBSTITUTIONS

If you can't find ground chicken thighs, or can't grind your own, you can substitute ground chicken breast with good results. I have made these with ground turkey, but I don't think the flavor is quite as good.

MAKE AHEAD

You can make the meatball mixture up to 24 hours in advance. Store it, tightly covered, in the refrigerator until you're ready to cook.

Flavorful ground chicken thighs combine with shredded zucchini, fresh herbs, and aromatic spices to make a moist and tender meatball. You will be surprised at how well they hold together without egg or breadcrumbs—neither is needed. These meatballs have become one of my signature dishes, and I often make them for large dinners. · MAKES 16 TO 20 MEATBALLS

1 Preheat the oven to 425 degrees F.

2 Grate the zucchini on the largest holes of a box grater into a large bowl. Add the chicken, parsley, cilantro, salt, spice blend, and pepper flakes. Use your hands to evenly combine. The mixture will be a little wet, but don't worry—it will hold together. Shape the meatball mixture into 16 to 20 golf ball-sized meatballs.

3 Heat a large oven-proof skillet over medium heat. Pour in about 2 tablespoons oil. Place the meatballs in a single layer in the skillet, being sure not to crowd them too much. If they won't all fit in the pan, cook them in batches.

4 Cook the meatballs until browned on the bottom, 3 or 4 minutes. This will sear the meatballs, so they'll be easy to turn. Turn and cook on the other side, another 3 to 4 minutes. If you need to cook the meatballs in batches, remove all the meatballs from the pan and place them in a bowl. Repeat with remaining meatball mixture. Add all of the meatballs back to the pan with any accumulated juices. (At this point, it's okay if they are crowded.)

5 Pour the stock over the meatballs and scrape up any caramelized bits that have stuck to the pan, being careful not to break the meatballs apart. Scatter the tomatoes over the top. Place the skillet in the oven and bake for 25 to 30 minutes, until the meatballs are cooked through, the sauce has reduced a little bit, and the tomatoes have started to collapse. Garnish with more parsley and a little Aleppo-style pepper.

SERVING TIPS

Most of the time, I serve these meatballs on their own with Tahini Sauce (page 85) and Zhug (page 271).

The meatballs pair well with the Roasted Cauliflower (page 153) and Fresh Corn Polenta (page 161).

For a comfort food dish, serve them over Creamy Polenta (page 176)

Turn them into meatballs for pasta by omitting the spice blend, substituting basil for the cilantro, and adding a little sliced garlic with the tomatoes.

Use leftovers for a delicious meatball sandwich: Top a soft gluten-free bun with a couple of meatballs and a little sliced or shredded Drunken Goat cheese. Broil until the cheese is melted. Dollop with zhug and place the toasted bun top. Serve warm.

MAKE IT YOUR OWN

Think of this roasted chicken thigh recipe as more of a method. Once you have the technique of searing and roasting the chicken thighs, you can substitute different aromatics and vegetables according to the season and your preferences. Here are a few ideas. Instead of mushrooms, sauté shaved fennel with the shallots and garlic and garnish with fresh tarragon after roasting. Instead of shallots and garlic, sauté several sliced leeks, adding fresh tarragon after roasting. Substitute a sliced red onion for the shallots and garlic, adding a pint of cherry or grape tomatoes after the wine. Garnish with fresh basil or oregano.

pan-roasted chicken thighs

WITH MUSHROOMS AND THYME

6 skin-on, bone-in chicken thighs (about 2 pounds total)

Sea salt

2 tablespoons unsalted butter

2 tablespoons extra virgin olive oil

1 clove garlic, sliced

1 large shallot, sliced

8 ounces wild mushrooms, stemmed if tough, caps sliced

½ cup dry white wine

½ to 1 cup Chicken Stock (page 277) or purchased bone broth

⅛ teaspoon Aleppo-style pepper

Freshly ground black pepper

4 or 5 sprigs fresh thyme

When I'm creating menus for having people over, I always think about creating an array of dishes that can be made ahead or don't take a lot of fussing. This is one of those dishes. You do a little prep up front before your friends arrive, and then pop the skillet in the oven before dinner. Chicken thighs are extremely forgiving, so they won't be ruined if they stay in the oven a bit too long. The recipe calls for skin-on, bone-in thighs, but I often make this with boneless, skinless thighs instead, especially if I'm going to serve this dish over polenta. · SERVES 6

1 Remove the chicken from the refrigerator at least 30 minutes before you're going to cook them. Preheat the oven to 425 degrees F.

2 Season the chicken with ½ teaspoon salt. Heat a large cast-iron or carbon steel skillet over medium heat. Add the butter and oil. Place the chicken, skin side down, in the skillet. Let them cook undisturbed for 6 to 8 minutes. Using tongs, try to lift 1 chicken thigh. If it releases easily and is golden brown on the bottom, turn it to the other side. If not, leave it alone for another minute or two before turning. Repeat with all the chicken thighs. Once all the chicken thighs have browned on both sides, transfer them from the pan to a bowl.

3 Pour off all but 2 tablespoons fat from the pan. Add the garlic, shallots, mushrooms, and about ⅛ teaspoon salt. Cook, stirring occasionally, until the mushrooms are wilted and starting to brown, 6 to 8 minutes.

4 Add the wine. Using a wooden spoon, scrape up any caramelized bits from the bottom of the pan. Let the wine reduce to just a tablespoon or two, then stir in the stock, Aleppo-style pepper, and a few grinds of black pepper. Nestle in the chicken thighs and the thyme. Pour over any accumulated juices from the bowl.

5 Roast for 35 to 40 minutes, until the chicken is very tender and the sauce has reduced. Serve warm.

back-pocket braised chicken

6 boneless, skinless chicken thighs (about 2¼ pounds)

Sea salt

2 tablespoons unsalted butter

2 tablespoons extra virgin olive oil

1 onion, thinly sliced

2 cloves garlic, sliced

⅛ to ¼ teaspoon Aleppo-style pepper or red pepper flakes

¼ cup white wine

1 cup Chicken Stock (page 277) or purchased bone broth

1 red bell pepper, sliced

2 cups cherry or grape tomatoes

4 sprigs fresh thyme

1 bay leaf

1 handful fresh parsley sprigs, chopped (about 1 cup)

I call this a "back-pocket" recipe, because it's really more of a method. Once you learn how to sear and braise chicken thighs in a flavorful, aromatic broth, you can spin the method using whatever you have on hand. If the thighs are resistant to shredding after braising, put the lid back on and continue to cook. They should be fall-apart tender. I love to serve the braised chicken over Creamy Polenta (page 176), but see the suggestions on the next page for other ideas. PHOTOGRAPH ON PAGE 177 · SERVES 4 TO 6

1 Remove the chicken from the refrigerator at least 30 minutes before you're going to cook, to allow it to come to room temperature. Season the chicken with ½ teaspoon salt.

2 Place a Dutch oven or similar large, heavy pot over medium heat. Add the butter and oil. When the butter has melted and started to foam, add the chicken. Let the thighs brown well and develop a crust, 6 to 8 minutes, before you try to turn them. They should lift easily with tongs. Turn and brown on the other side, another 4 to 6 minutes. When the chicken is browned, remove it to a bowl.

3 Reduce the heat to medium-low. Add the onion and garlic to the pot with ¼ teaspoon salt and stir. Cook, stirring often, until the onions are completely wilted and starting to caramelize, about 20 to 25 minutes. If the pot gets too dry and the onions start to stick, add another tablespoon of oil.

4 Add the Aleppo-style pepper. Increase the heat to medium. Add the wine and stir, scraping up any caramelized bits from the bottom of the pot. Let the wine simmer for a few minutes, until almost all of the liquid has reduced.

5 Stir in the chicken stock, bell pepper, tomatoes, thyme, and bay leaf. Return the chicken to the pot with any accumulated juices. Cover the pot and reduce the heat to low. Let the chicken cook for at least 30 minutes or up to an hour, until it is very tender.

6 Using a slotted spoon or tongs, transfer the chicken to a cutting board or plate. Fish out and discard the bay leaf and thyme stems. Shred the chicken with two forks, then stir it back into the sauce. Add the parsley and stir everything together to combine. Serve hot.

WHAT CAN YOU DO WITH BRAISED CHICKEN?

This braised chicken is so versatile. Here are a few ideas.

Spoon the chicken over Creamy Polenta (page 176) and serve with Charred Kale (page 144).

Turn leftovers into Chicken Melts: Spoon the braised chicken mixture onto the bottom of a soft gluten-free bun. Cover with shredded sharp cheddar cheese and place under the broiler until the cheese is melted. Cover with the bun top and serve warm.

Make Chicken Tacos: Omit the wine. Stir in about ¼ cup chopped cilantro at the end. Serve with Corn Tortillas (page 42) and other desired toppings.

Make Arroz con Pollo: Omit the wine and increase the chicken stock to 1 quart. Add 1 cup Arborio or Bomba rice. Cover the pot and cook on low for 25 minutes, or until the rice is cooked through. Stir in fresh cilantro and serve with sliced avocado and fresh corn tortillas.

Make Braised Chicken with Coconut Milk: When you add the onion and garlic, add 1 tablespoon My Spice Blend (page 262) and 1 tablespoon chopped fresh ginger. Omit the wine, increase the chicken stock to 1 quart, and add a 13-ounce can full-fat coconut milk. When you return the seared chicken back to the pot, add 1 cup Arborio or Bomba rice, cover, and cook for 25 minutes, until the rice is cooked through. Shred the chicken. Stir in about ¼ cup chopped cilantro just before serving.

whole stuffed cabbage

2 cups grape or cherry tomatoes

Extra virgin olive oil

Sea salt

1 large head savoy cabbage or green cabbage

1 large onion (about 7 or 8 ounces), thinly sliced

2 cloves garlic, thinly sliced

2 cups shiitake or cremini mushrooms, stemmed and sliced

1 pound ground chicken thighs (See A Tip on Ground Chicken, page 190)

1 teaspoon ground turmeric

1½ teaspoons Baharat Spice Mix (page 264)

1¼ cups short-grain rice (such as Arborio or Bomba)

1 quart Chicken Stock (page 277) or purchased bone broth

Gremolata (page 271), for serving

Crème fraîche, for serving

When I travel to other countries, I almost always book a cooking class at my destination. Learning how to cook the traditional foods of a place provides a way to learn more deeply about the values and traditions—the story of ingredients, spices, and cooking methods are all shaped by the culture. I have taken multiple classes from one host, Pnina, a woman of the Druze faith, who lives near the Sea of Galilee. She is not only a wonderful cook, but is also a gracious and open-hearted human being and a great ambassador for the idea that we are all more alike than we are different. One of my favorite dishes I've cooked with Pnina is maqluba, a traditional dish of meat, vegetables and spices cooked with rice and then flipped upside down out of the pot for serving. In this version, the savory blend of ground chicken and shiitake mushrooms are perfumed with baharat, flavoring the rice. Lining the pan with cabbage leaves to create a blanket for the filling makes for a beautiful presentation, an idea inspired by the maqluba recipe in *Tel Aviv: Food. People. Stories.* by Haya Molcho. · SERVES 6 TO 8

1 Preheat the oven to 425 degrees F.

2 Place the tomatoes in a baking dish. Add 2 tablespoons oil and ¼ teaspoon salt. Stir the tomatoes to coat them in the oil. Roast for 20 to 25 minutes, until the tomatoes are soft and beginning to darken. Remove from the oven and set aside.

3 Fill a large pot with water and add a tablespoon of salt. Remove any tough or wilted leaves from the outside of the cabbage and discard. Trim the stalk so the cabbage sits flat on it. Place the cabbage in the water. Bring to a boil, then reduce the heat and simmer the cabbage for 20 minutes, turning it occasionally, until a skewer can be easily inserted to the core. Carefully remove the cabbage from the water and place it in a colander in the sink to drain and cool.

4 Heat a large Dutch oven over medium-low heat. Add 2 tablespoons oil, the onion, garlic, and ¼ teaspoon salt. Cook, stirring often, until the onions are completely wilted and soft, about 10 minutes. Add the shiitake mushrooms and cook until they have softened and started to brown, about 15 minutes.

RECIPE CONTINUES

This recipe does have quite a few steps. If you would like to cut down on some of the time in the kitchen, here are a few suggestions.

Instead of making the baharat, purchase a pre-made baharat blend.

If you don't want to take the time to roast the tomatoes, just add halved cherry or grape tomatoes when you add the chicken stock and cook with the rice.

Instead of making gremolata, serve the cabbage with lemon wedges and a sprinkling of chopped fresh parsley.

MAKE AHEAD

This dish can be made a day before serving. Store the assembled dish, tightly covered, in the refrigerator. Reheat, uncovered, in a 350 degree oven until bubbling and hot, about 30 minutes.

5 Increase the heat to medium. Add the chicken and cook for about 5 minutes, stirring and breaking up any lumps of ground meat with a wooden spoon. Stir in the turmeric and baharat, coating the meat and vegetables in the spices and letting them become fragrant, about 1 minute. Add the rice and stir to coat. Add the chicken stock and reserved tomatoes and stir well. Bring the filling to a boil, then immediately reduce to a simmer. Cover and cook for about 20 minutes, until the rice is just done. Turn off the heat and remove the lid, letting the rice sit until the cabbage is ready to stuff.

6 While the filling is cooking, finish preparing the cabbage. Place the cabbage on its stalk end on a cutting board. Quarter it without cutting all the way through, so it holds together at its stalk and opens out like a flower. Remove the small inner leaves and reserve.

7 Drizzle a tablespoon of oil into a 12- or 14-inch skillet or oven-safe dish. Place the cabbage in the skillet, stalk end down. Drizzle another tablespoon of oil over the leaves. Roast the cabbage for 20 to 25 minutes, until the cabbage is starting to brown. Remove the skillet from the oven.

8 To assemble the stuffed cabbage, pour the rice filling into the middle of the cabbage, spreading it out to cover the cabbage. Layer the reserved cabbage leaves over the filling, turning in the overhanging cabbage leaves to cover the edges. (Think about it as a pie, with the cabbage being the top crust. You don't have to be too fussy about it.)

9 Preheat the broiler to high.

10 Place the skillet under the broiler until the top of the cabbage is deeply brown. Keep a close eye on it so it doesn't burn. Remove the skillet from the broiler and let rest for about 10 minutes to cool slightly.

11 You can serve the cabbage one of two ways: Cut the cabbage into wedges and serve on individual plates, topping each serving with a little gremolata and crème fraîche. Alternatively, turn the whole cabbage out onto a serving platter, spoon gremolata on top, and carve the cabbage at the table. Serve with extra gremolata and crème fraîche on the side.

stacked chicken enchiladas

WITH TURMERIC TORTILLAS

4 boneless, skinless chicken thighs (about 1½ pounds)

½ teaspoon sea salt

2 tablespoons extra virgin olive oil or avocado oil, plus more if needed

1 large onion, thinly sliced

2 cloves garlic, thinly sliced

1 small jalapeño chile, seeded and thinly sliced, or 1 pinch of red pepper flakes

1 tablespoon My Spice Blend (page 262)

1 cup Chicken Stock (page 277) or purchased bone broth, plus more if needed

2 cups cherry or grape tomatoes

2 Charred Poblano Peppers (page 265), sliced

1 large or 2 small Charred Red Bell Peppers (page 265), sliced

1 cup loosely packed fresh cilantro sprigs

2 firmly packed cups baby spinach

12 Turmeric Tortillas (page 42)

8 ounces sharp cheddar cheese, shredded (about 2 cups)

for serving

Sliced avocado

Toasted Pumpkin Seeds (page 260)

Fresh cilantro leaves

Chili Oil (page 267; optional)

While these enchiladas are not traditional, they are inspired by the stacked enchiladas of northern Mexico. Layering the enchiladas keeps the tortillas crispy on the edges yet soft and saucy in the middle. Instead of a dried chile–based enchilada sauce, this one relies on sautéed onions, peppers, tomatoes, and spices, blended into a light, flavorful sauce. Covered with cheese and baked until bubbling and just starting to brown, these enchiladas are a much-requested recipe in our home.
SERVES 4

1 Remove the chicken thighs from the refrigerator and season with ¼ teaspoon salt. Let them come to room temperature.

2 Heat a large pot over medium heat and pour in the oil. Add the chicken in a single layer and sear undisturbed for 6 to 8 minutes, until the bottoms of the thighs are deeply golden brown. Use tongs to turn them, then brown the other side, 3 or 4 minutes. Transfer the chicken to a bowl.

3 Reduce the heat to medium-low. If the bottom of the pot is dry, add another tablespoon or two of oil. Add the onion, garlic, jalapeño, and the remaining ¼ teaspoon salt and cook slowly until almost caramelized, 10 to 15 minutes.

4 Add the spice blend and stir to coat the vegetables with the spices. Add the chicken stock and using a wooden spoon, scrape up any browned bits on the bottom of the pot.

5 Stir in the tomatoes and charred peppers. Nestle the chicken thighs into the sauce and pour over any accumulated juices from the bowl. Turn the heat to low, cover the pot, and simmer for at least 30 minutes or up to an hour, until the tomatoes have collapsed and the chicken is very tender and can be easily shredded with a fork. Reduce the heat under the pot to very low.

6 Remove the chicken thighs to a clean bowl. Transfer half of the vegetables and most of the liquid from the pot to a blender. It's okay—actually preferable—to leave a little liquid in the pot, to keep everything saucy. Add the cilantro to the mixture in the blender. Blend until smooth. Taste and adjust for salt

RECIPE CONTINUES

TIME SAVERS

If you don't want to take the time to char the peppers, just slice and sauté them with the onions. The skins will separate and you won't have the additional smoky flavor, but it's still good.

Use 1½ to 2 cups shredded leftover chicken in place of the chicken thighs. Cook the vegetables without the chicken, puree the sauce, then stir the chicken into the vegetables just before adding the spinach.

and spice level. If the sauce seems too thick, add a little extra stock. If it seems thin, it's okay. It will reduce in the oven.

7 Shred the chicken and add it back to the pot. Add the spinach, stirring until it wilts. Turn off the heat.

8 Preheat the oven to 350 degrees F.

9 Pour a little bit of the enchilada sauce each of into four individual skillets or one large baking dish, enough to coat the bottom. Place a tortilla in each skillet, or lay out 4 tortillas in the baking dish. Top the tortillas with about half of the chicken and vegetable mixture and one-third of the cheese. Repeat layering each stack with another tortilla, the remaining chicken mixture, and another third of the cheese. Place the final tortilla on top of each stack. Pour the remaining sauce over the top of the stacks, letting some run down the sides. Top with the remaining cheese.

10 Bake for 30 to 35 minutes, until the cheese has melted and started to brown, but the sauce has not evaporated. Garnish as desired with avocado, pumpkin seeds, cilantro, and chili oil, if using.

VEGETARIAN OR PLANT-BASED ENCHILADAS · Make these enchiladas vegetarian by using vegetable stock and replacing the chicken with about 2 cups of any cooked vegetables you have on hand, chopped. I've made them with roasted sweet potatoes and with roasted eggplant. If you eat beans, braised black beans would be delicious. Top with a cashew cream (recipe on page 139).

pulled pork barbecue sandwiches

1 teaspoon cumin seeds, toasted and ground

1 teaspoon dry mustard powder

1 teaspoon Aleppo-style pepper

1 tablespoon smoked paprika

1 teaspoon freshly ground black pepper

2 tablespoons kosher salt

5 pounds boneless pork shoulder (a.k.a. pork butt), tied

2 to 3 tablespoons ghee

for serving

about 2 cups Bourbon Barbecue Sauce (recipe follows)

Cabbage and Fennel Salad with Nigella and Pumpkin Seeds (page 112)

12 gluten-free hamburger buns

MAKE AHEAD

This just gets better as it sits. Make it up to 3 days in advance. Store the barbecue, in the sauce, in an airtight container in the refrigerator. Reheat on the stovetop on low heat before serving. It also freezes well. Add extra sauce to the pork and freeze for up to 3 months.

Many years ago, we visited Austin with friends over the New Year holiday, with a plan to eat our way through the city. Franklin Barbecue was high on the agenda—a restaurant famous for selling out early, its long line of devoted customers often camping out overnight to ensure a taste of the celebrated barbecue. On a cold Texas night, our friend Mataio was first in line. When we arrived in the morning, a jovial tailgating party of Franklin followers greeted us. When the doors opened, we were the first ones through, rewarded with a little taste of burnt ends while we ordered one of everything—brisket, beef ribs, pork ribs, pulled pork, sausages and smoked turkey, served with sides of coleslaw and potato salad and a local IPA.

It's impossible to recreate a Franklin Barbecue brisket without a smoker. But here is a recipe in homage to their incredible craft. The meat is tender and succulent, and the barbecue sauce is just shy of sweet. Serve with a dry cider or gluten-free beer. MAKES 12 SANDWICHES, PLUS LEFTOVERS

1 Mix together the cumin, mustard powder, Aleppo-style pepper, paprika, black pepper, salt, and sugar. Rub all over the pork shoulder. Cover and refrigerate overnight.

2 Preheat the oven to 275 degrees F.

3 Heat a large Dutch oven over medium-high heat. When the pot is very hot, add the ghee. Let it melt, then add the pork shoulder. Sear the pork undisturbed for a few minutes. You will know it is ready to turn when it lifts easily from the pot and is deeply caramelized on the bottom. Turn and repeat the searing on all sides.

4 Cover the pot with a lid and place in the oven. Roast the pork for 6 hours or until it is very tender and falling apart.

5 Remove the pork to a cutting board and let it sit until cool enough to handle. Shred the pork, removing any large pieces of fat. Discard the juices and fat left in the pot. Transfer the pork to a large serving platter. Coat it lightly with barbeque sauce. To serve, create a buffet with the pulled pork, extra barbecue sauce, cabbage salad, and buns. Let everyone make their own sandwich.

RECIPE CONTINUES

bourbon barbeque sauce

2 tablespoons extra virgin olive oil

1 medium onion, finely chopped

3 cloves garlic, minced

¼ teaspoon red pepper flakes

1 teaspoon sea salt

2 teaspoons cumin seeds, toasted and ground

1 teaspoon ground allspice

½ teaspoon ground ginger

One 28-ounce can crushed tomatoes

½ cup Kentucky bourbon (such as Maker's Mark), or apple cider if you don't drink alcohol

2 tablespoons Dijon mustard

½ cup blackstrap molasses

⅓ cup dark brown sugar

⅓ cup apple cider vinegar

Freshly ground black pepper

This recipe makes enough barbecue sauce for the pork, plus leftovers. I freeze the extra sauce in 8 ounce containers.
MAKES ABOUT 4 CUPS

1 Heat a large pot over medium-low heat. Add the oil, onions, garlic, pepper flakes, and salt. Cook for 15 to 20 minutes, stirring occasionally, until the onions are just starting to caramelize.

2 Stir in the cumin, allspice, ginger, tomatoes, bourbon, mustard, molasses, sugar, and vinegar. Simmer for about an hour, stirring occasionally to prevent burning, until the sauce has thickened. Taste and adjust the seasonings, if necessary. If you like, you can blend the sauce in batches in a high-speed blender until smooth, or use an immersion blender.

slow-roasted leg of lamb

One 5-pound boneless leg of lamb, tied

1 tablespoon sea salt

2 to 3 tablespoons ghee or avocado oil

1 cup dry white wine

1 cup Chicken Stock (page 277) or Vegetable Stock (page 276), plus more if needed

4 cloves garlic, peeled

1 medium onion (about 6 or 7 ounces), quartered

5 sprigs fresh thyme

2 bay leaves

½ teaspoon freshly ground black pepper

¼ teaspoon Aleppo-style pepper or red pepper flakes

MAKE AHEAD

You can make the lamb a day or two ahead of time. Store it in the refrigerator in its cooking liquid. When you're ready to serve, remove the fat that has solidified and then gently reheat the lamb in the liquid.

When I was growing up, we raised sheep on our small farm. Farming gave me a deep appreciation for where our food comes from and for the sacred cycle of life. At home, lamb was usually reserved for special dinners like Christmas or Easter, when my Dad would slowly roast a leg of lamb to a perfect medium-rare, the centerpiece of the holiday table. While I appreciate the beauty of a roast that can be carved into perfect thin slices, I prefer lamb slowly roasted until the succulent meat almost falls apart. · SERVES 8, WITH LEFTOVERS

1 About an hour before you're going to put the lamb in the oven, take it out of the refrigerator to come to room temperature. Generously season on all sides with salt.

2 Preheat the oven to 300 degrees F.

3 Heat a large Dutch oven over medium-high heat. Melt the ghee in the pot. When it's hot, add the lamb and cook on the first side until deeply brown and seared, about 5 minutes. Using tongs to turn the lamb, sear it on all of the sides. Remove the lamb to a large bowl.

4 Pour in the wine and stock. Scrape up any browned bits from the bottom of the pan with a wooden spoon. Return the lamb to the Dutch oven. Add the garlic, onion, thyme, and bay leaves. Sprinkle the black pepper and Aleppo-style pepper over the lamb. Make sure there is enough liquid to come halfway up the side of the lamb. If you need more liquid, add a little water or more stock. Cover the pot with a lid and place it in the oven. Let the lamb cook slowly for 4 ½ hours.

5 Check on the lamb. It should easily pull apart with a fork. If it is not yet very tender, return it to the oven for another 30 minutes and check again.

6 Remove from the oven and let rest for 30 minutes, to allow all of the juices to reabsorb. Using tongs, carefully lift the lamb out of the pot and place on a cutting board. Slice the meat across the grain. It's okay if the slices aren't perfect. The meat will be so tender that it might fall off in pieces, rather than slices. Transfer to a serving platter. If you like, strain the juices through a fine mesh strainer and skim off the fat. Serve the juice on the side.

WHAT CAN YOU DO WITH SLOW-ROASTED LAMB?

Here are a few of my favorite ways to serve this lamb.

Drain the meat from the juices, shred, and stir in 1½ cups of Olive Oil-Roasted Tomatoes (page 268) and ¼ cup finely chopped parsley. Spoon over Creamy Polenta (page 176).

Make Lamb Tacos (pictured): Drain the meat from the juices, shred, and mix with 2 cups of Olive Oil Roasted Tomatoes (page 268). Serve with Roasted Cauliflower (page 153 and Toasted Pumpkin Seeds (page 260), Fresh Chile Harissa (page 273) and Homemade Corn Tortillas (page 42).

Create a Middle Eastern feast by serving the sliced lamb with Zhug (page 271), Tahini Sauce, (page 85) Lemony Eggplant (page 93), and Sourdough Flatbread (page 34).

Serve sliced lamb with Deviled Eggs (page 82), Smashed Roasted Potatoes (page 162), and Frisée, Radicchio, and Fennel Salad (page 104) for Easter brunch.

sort-of-barbacoa tacos

WITH ALL THE FIXINGS

barbacoa beef

6 dried guajillo chiles, stemmed and seeded

2 cups beef stock or Chicken Stock (page 277), plus more if needed

4 large oranges, halved

One 5-pound grass-fed boneless chuck roast, tied

1 tablespoon sea salt

2 to 3 tablespoons ghee or avocado oil

1 large onion, sliced

4 cloves garlic, sliced

1 tablespoon My Spice Blend (page 262)

½ teaspoon Aleppo-style pepper

½ teaspoon freshly ground black pepper

3 Charred Poblano Peppers (page 265), sliced

all the fixings

Corn Tortillas (page 42)

Olive-Oil Avocado Dip (page 86)

Fresh Tomato Salsa (page 270) or Roasted Tomato Salsa (page 270)

Chili Oil (page 267)

Fresh Chili Harissa (page 273)

Toasted Pumpkin Seeds (page 260)

Cabbage and Fennel Salad (page 112)

True barbacoa is beef or lamb that has been cooked slowly over an open fire until the meat is faintly smoky and very succulent. If you're like me and don't have a fire pit at your house, this recipe is a great close second. The juice of roasted oranges adds a little smoky sweetness to the meat, and the flavor of the orange peel perfumes the dish and adds a pleasant bitterness. For a more complex flavor, I like the mix of both dried and charred fresh chiles. This is one of my favorite meals to make for friends, a casual, unfussy dinner with lots of flavor. · SERVES 8, WITH LEFTOVERS

1 Remove the chuck roast from the refrigerator about an hour before you're going to roast it. Season the beef on all sides with salt.

2 Heat a dry cast-iron skillet over medium-high heat. Add the guajillo chiles, pressing down on them with the back of a wooden spoon so they char and toast. Once they are blackened in spots, transfer the chiles to a high-speed blender. Add the beef stock and blend until smooth. Set aside.

3 Preheat the broiler to high.

4 Place the oranges, cut side up, on a rimmed baking sheet. Place under the broiler and broil until charred, 3 to 4 minutes. Let cool enough to handle, then juice the oranges. (You should have 1 to 1½ cups orange juice.) Reserve the juice and 2 of the orange shells.

5 If the broiler is at the top of the oven, reduce the oven temperature to 300 degrees F. If it's separate, heat the oven to 300 degrees F.

6 Heat a large Dutch oven over medium-high heat. Make sure the pot is very hot, then add the ghee. Let it melt, then add the beef. Sear the beef undisturbed for a few minutes. You will know it is ready to turn when it lifts easily from the pot and is deeply caramelized on the bottom. Turn and repeat searing on all sides.

RECIPE CONTINUES

The beef can be made up to 3 days in advance. Store it, tightly covered, in the refrigerator and reheat before serving. You can freeze any leftovers for up to 3 months. Thaw in the refrigerator and reheat in a covered pot set over low heat before serving.

SERVING TIP

If your friends like to help in the kitchen, this is a great meal for that. While the beef is cooking, let everyone help make the tortillas, smashed avocado, tomato salsa, toasted pumpkin seeds and the cabbage and fennel salad. You'll probably already have chili oil and harissa in the refrigerator. When you're ready for dinner, let everyone mix and match to make their own tacos at the table.

7 Reduce the heat to low. Using tongs, remove the beef to a large bowl. Add the onion, garlic, spice mix, and Aleppo-style and black peppers to the fat in the pot. Stir to coat the vegetables and spices in the fat. Stir in the reserved orange juice and the chile–beef broth puree. Add the poblanos. Nestle the beef into the liquid. It should come halfway up the sides. If it doesn't, add more beef broth or a little water. Pour in any accumulated juices from the bowl. Add the reserved orange shells.

8 Cover the Dutch oven with a lid and place it in the oven. Let the beef cook undisturbed for 4 hours.

9 After 4 hours, check the beef. It should be very tender and shred easily with a fork. If it's not tender enough, cover again and let it cook for another 30 minutes. When the beef is done, remove the pot from the oven and let it sit, covered, for 30 minutes to allow all the juices to reabsorb. Remove the orange halves and discard.

10 Remove the beef from the pot to a cutting board, cut away the strings, and shred the meat with two forks. Strain the fat and juices from the pot into a container with straight sides (like a 4-cup liquid measuring cup). Skim the fat from the top. Return the meat and juice back to the pot, stirring together. Taste the beef. Depending on the saltiness of your beef broth, you may need to stir in more salt. It should taste well-seasoned but not salty. Scoop the shredded beef into a large serving bowl. Put out plates and bowls with the tortillas, avocado, salsa, chili oil, harissa, pumpkin seeds, and salad for everyone to make their own perfect tacos.

slow-roasted brisket

FOR PASSOVER OR ANY FAMILY DINNER

One 5-pound flat-cut brisket

1 tablespoon sea salt

2 to 3 tablespoons avocado oil

2 bay leaves

4 or 5 sprigs fresh thyme

2 tablespoon My Spice Blend (page 262)

2 tablespoons Fresh Chile Harissa (page 273)

1 cup dry white wine

4 cups beef stock or Chicken Stock (page 277)

½ teaspoon freshly ground black pepper

2 large red onions, cut into wedges through the root

20 small carrots (not "baby carrots"), peeled and trimmed

Gremolata (page 271), for serving

MAKE AHEAD

If you want to make the brisket ahead of time, make it without the carrots (you can just add a few, to flavor the sauce). The carrots aren't as delicious left over. Refrigerate the unsliced brisket in the cooking juices. Reheat in a covered pot over low heat until warmed all the way though. Roast carrots separately for serving.

When Elie and I married, we became a dual-faith family. Although Elie doesn't actively practice Judaism, we honor its cultural and family traditions. I have come to cherish the twin celebrations of Passover and Easter, Hanukkah and Christmas. As we began to host celebrations in our home, I created this dish to be our family brisket. Slow-roasting the brisket ensures the beef will be tender and succulent. Waiting to add the carrots and onion in the last hour of cooking prevents the vegetables from overcooking, while still letting them absorb all the flavor of the broth. I hope Theo will remember this brisket like I remember the Easter lamb of my childhood—a sensory memory of love and laughter and the warm strength of clasped hands as we prayed together. · SERVES 8 TO 10

1 Take the brisket out of the refrigerator about an hour before you start cooking, to come to room temperature. Season the brisket all over with the salt.

2 Preheat the oven to 300 degrees F.

3 Heat a large Dutch oven over medium heat. Pour in the oil, then add the brisket. Sear the brisket undisturbed for 3 to 4 minutes. To check if the brisket is ready to turn, lift one edge with tongs. If it releases easily, turn the brisket to the other side. If not, leave it for a few more minutes. When it's ready, turn and brown the other side.

4 Remove the brisket from the pot to a large platter. Add the bay leaves, thyme, and spice mix to oil in the pot. Stir, letting the spices toast in the oil for a minute or two. Add the wine and harissa and use a wooden spoon to scrape up any caramelized bits from the bottom of the pan. Stir in the beef stock. Return the brisket to the pot. Sprinkle the pepper on top.

5 Cover the pot and place it in the oven. Let it cook slowly for 2 hours.

6 After 2 hours, add the onions and carrots. Cover again and cook for another hour, until the brisket is very tender and the vegetables can be easily pierced with a fork.

RECIPE CONTINUES

7 Remove from the oven. Using tongs, carefully lift the brisket out of the pot and place it on a cutting board. Strain the cooking juices through a fine mesh strainer into a container with straight sides (like a 4-cup liquid measuring cup). Skim off the fat. Return the juice back to the pot and bring to a simmer, reducing until the sauce thickens slightly.

8 Slice the brisket across the grain and place the slices on a serving platter, along with the onions and carrots. Spoon the gremolata on top. Serve the sauce on the side.

WHAT CAN YOU DO WITH LEFTOVER BRISKET?

Make brisket sandwiches. I love layering slices of cold brisket on a soft gluten-free bun spread with Dijon mustard and topping them with tangy sauerkraut.

Shred the brisket and use it for tacos, tucked into Corn Tortillas (page 42) and topped with Fresh Chile Harissa (page 273).

Make Brisket Sort-of-Pho: Heat vegetable stock in a pot, adding thin slices of brisket to heat in the stock. Add sliced baby bok choy or a big handful of chopped greens. Cook until vegetables are tender. Add cooked rice noodles. Top each serving with thin slices of jalapeño, a big handful of fresh cilantro or basil sprigs, bean sprouts, and a squeeze of lime.

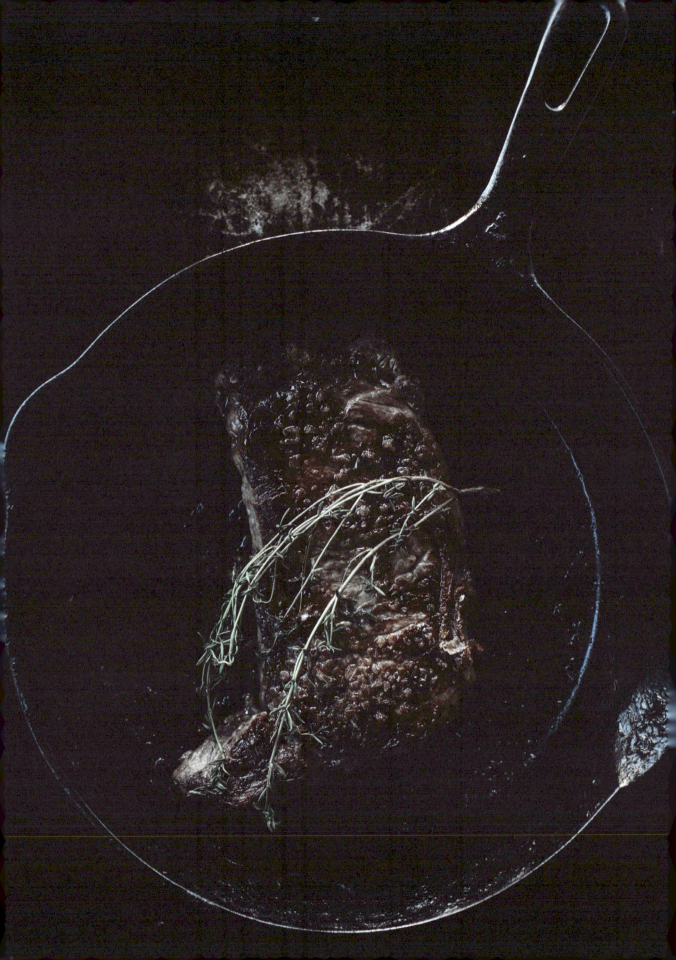

cast-iron ribeye

One 1-pound boneless grass-fed ribeye steak

2 teaspoons flaky or coarse sea salt

1 tablespoon ghee

Freshly ground black pepper

A FEW TIPS

I like a boneless ribeye, as opposed to bone-in, because it cooks evenly and there's almost no waste.

Searing the steak in a cast-iron skillet gives it a delicious, salty crust that you can't get from grilling. I use ghee for this, because ghee is the best fat for high-heat cooking. Plus, it gives the steak even more flavor, without burning like butter would.

Add the pepper after the steak is cooked so it doesn't burn.

A good grass-fed ribeye is so flavorful, it doesn't really need much else. Perhaps a little gremolata spooned on top.

To turn this ribeye into steak tacos, thinly slice the beef and serve with homemade tortillas (page 42), Fresh Chile Harissa (page 273) and fresh cilantro.

If you have leftovers, thinly slice the beef and turn it into a steak sandwich, with caramelized onions and lots of homemade mayonnaise (page 274).

This ribeye is my idea of fast food. A beautiful ribeye, seasoned simply with coarse salt and seared in a very hot cast-iron skillet until it develops a deep crust, is incredibly simple but full of flavor. Ready in only 10 minutes, it's the perfect big-impact weeknight meal. I always choose grass-fed beef, which is better for the animals, better for the environment, and better for us. It is more expensive, though, so we just eat less. The three of us share a one-pound steak, with the rest of the meal focused on vegetables. Often, we'll turn the ribeye into steak tacos, which is Theo's favorite meal.
SERVES 2 OR 3

1 Remove the steak from the refrigerator at least 30 minutes before you're ready to cook.

2 Heat a cast-iron skillet over medium-high heat until very hot. Sprinkle the salt on both sides of the steak. Add the ghee to the pan and let it melt. (It might give off a whiff of smoke. That's okay.) Lay the steak in the pan. Take a lid that is wider than the skillet and partially cover the steak, letting the steam escape. (This prevents the steak from splattering fat all over the stovetop, and also helps keep the heat in.) Let the steak cook undisturbed for 4 minutes.

3 Remove the lid. Using tongs, turn the steak. Partially cover the steak again. Let the steak cook for another 3 minutes for medium-rare or 4 minutes for medium. Remove the steak to a cutting board and let it rest for 10 minutes before slicing against the grain. This steak is best eaten right after it's cooked, while still hot.

crispy cast-iron salmon

WITH GREMOLATA

Six 4- to 6-ounce center-cut skin-on wild salmon fillets (preferably king salmon)

½ teaspoon sea salt

Grated zest of 2 lemons

2 to 3 tablespoons extra virgin olive oil or avocado oil, plus more if needed

Gremolata (page 271), for serving

COOKING TIP

Perfectly cooked salmon is delicious; overcooked salmon is dry and fishy. It might take you a little bit of practice to find the perfect amount of time for the salmon, the stove, the heat, the pan. If you've never cooked salmon before, you might want to practice with just one piece first, to see how you like it. In general, I find a 1-inch-thick center-cut fillet of salmon cooks perfectly with 7 to 8 minutes of total cooking time. You can gently flake the center of the fish with a fork to check for doneness, or use an instant-read thermometer. The salmon should be about 125 to 130 degrees F.

After living in the Pacific Northwest for the past ten years, I have learned a lot about the different varieties of salmon. King salmon is my favorite—fatty, succulent, and delicious. If you can't find king salmon, sockeye is a close second. (Avoid farmed salmon if you can, as many studies show salmon farming harms the marine environment and those salmon contain higher levels of pollutants and lower levels of omega-3 fats.) In my opinion, the most delicious method for cooking salmon is to sear center-cut fillets in a cast-iron skillet until they are crispy on the outside and just barely done on the inside. Serve them plain, or topped simply with fresh gremolata. PICTURED WITH WHIPPED CAULIFLOWER (PAGE 149). · SERVES 6

1 Remove the salmon from the refrigerator at least 30 minutes before cooking, to come to room temperature. Check for pin bones by running your fingers down the length of each fillet. If you find any bones sticking out, remove them with fish tweezers or needle-nose pliers. (You can ask your fishmonger to remove pin bones for you.)

2 Season the salmon with the salt and lemon zest. Heat a large cast-iron or carbon steel skillet over medium-high heat. Pour in the oil. Once the oil is very hot, add the salmon, skin side down. (If all of the salmon won't fit in the skillet at one time, cook it in batches.) Let the salmon cook undisturbed for 4 minutes. Using a spatula, carefully turn the salmon. Let it cook for another 3 to 4 minutes, until seared on the outside but still translucent on the inside. (It will continue to cook after you remove it from the heat.) Transfer to serving plates and top with gremolata. If you need to cook the salmon in batches, wipe out the skillet to remove the old oil and repeat with fresh oil and the remaining salmon. Serve warm.

olive oil–poached halibut

WITH LEMONY EGGPLANT AND OLIVE GREMOLATA

Four 6-ounce wild-caught halibut fillets, skin removed

½ teaspoon sea salt

Extra virgin olive oil

Freshly ground black pepper

Gremolata (page 271)

1 cup pitted Castelvetrano olives, chopped

Lemony Eggplant, warmed (page 93)

SERVING TIPS

Here are a few alternate ways to serve the halibut.

Top with the Fresh Chile Harissa (page 273) and serve with Smashed Roasted Potatoes (page 162).

Add pitted kalamata olives to Roasted Tomato Salsa (page 270) and spoon on top of the halibut. Serve with Fresh Corn Polenta (page 161).

Serve the halibut over Whipped Cauliflower (page 149), spooning the gremolata on top.

I love halibut seared in a hot skillet until it develops a deep brown crust. But I don't always want my kitchen to smell of fish cooking. I tried all different ways of cooking halibut—baking, broiling, poaching in water—to come up with another method that gave me a deliciously rich and moist halibut. This is it! When cooking halibut, testing the internal temperature with an instant-read thermometer is the best way to be sure it's done (and not overdone). For halibut, 125 to 130 degrees F is just right. You'll also need a deep-fry thermometer to check the oil temperature. · SERVES 4

1 Season the halibut with the salt. Place the halibut in a single layer in a medium pot or Dutch oven. Pour in enough oil to cover the halibut by a couple of inches. Attach a deep-fry thermometer to the side of the pot. Turn on the heat to medium and heat until the oil reaches 150 degrees F. Cook the halibut, maintaining that oil temperature, for 8 to 10 minutes, until the halibut reaches an internal temperature of 130 degrees F.

2 Line a plate with paper towels. Using a slotted spoon, remove the halibut from the oil and place it on the plate to drain. Season the halibut with pepper to taste. Discard the oil.

3 Stir the olives into the gremolata. Spoon the eggplant onto a serving platter. Place the halibut pieces on top, then spoon the olive gremolata over the fish. Serve warm.

halibut tacos WITH ALL THE FIXINGS

halibut

1½ pounds skin-on wild-caught halibut fillets

4 tablespoons avocado oil, plus more if needed

¼ to ½ teaspoon sea salt

⅛ to ¼ teaspoon Aleppo-style pepper

Grated zest of 1 lemon

all the fixings

12 to 18 Corn Tortillas (page 42)

Cabbage and Fennel Salad (page 112)

Olive Oil–Avocado Dip (page 86)

Fresh Tomato Salsa (page 270)

Toasted Pumpkin Seeds (page 260)

Chili Oil (page 267)

MAKE AHEAD

While it might seem overwhelming to make all of the salads and toppings, everything except the halibut and tortillas can be made in advance. The pumpkin seeds and chili oil can be made weeks ahead. The day before, make the cabbage and fennel salad and the avocado dip. Several hours before, make the tomato salsa. Make the corn tortillas and cook the halibut right before serving.

The firm, meaty texture of halibut lends itself to tacos. By cubing and seasoning the fish, and searing it in a cast-iron pan, the halibut will have a crispy, flavorful crust. When halibut is not in season, or you don't want to pay a hefty price for it, rock cod or ling cod are great substitutes. This is not a taco recipe authentic to one region or place. Instead, it's a combination of all the flavors and textures I want in a taco—bright, crispy, crunchy, creamy, salty, and spicy, all in one bite. Serve these tacos family style, letting everyone help themselves. SERVES 6

1 Remove the halibut from the refrigerator 30 minutes before you plan to start cooking. (Letting the halibut come to room temperature will help prevent it from sticking to the pan.)

2 Using a sharp knife, remove the skin from the halibut and discard. (Some grocery stores will do this for you.) Cut the halibut into 1½-inch cubes and place them in a bowl. Pour 2 tablespoons of the oil over the halibut. Use your hands to rub the oil on every piece. Add the salt, pepper, and paprika and rub the spices into the halibut.

3 Heat a large cast-iron or carbon steel pan over medium heat until very hot. (Starting with a hot skillet will also prevent the halibut from sticking and allow the halibut to develop a good sear.) Pour the remaining 2 tablespoons oil into the pan, enough to coat the bottom. Add the halibut in a single layer with none of the pieces touching. If all of the halibut won't fit in the pan, cook it in two batches. Let the halibut cook undisturbed for 2 minutes.

4 Using tongs, try to lift a piece. If it lifts easily, turn it to brown the other side. If it doesn't, leave it alone to continue browning. Repeat this with all of the pieces. It will take only 4 to 5 minutes for the halibut to just cook through. Cut one piece in half to check for doneness. Remove the pieces from the skillet when the center is still slightly translucent. (The fish will continue to cook off the heat.) Place the cooked halibut in a shallow bowl. If you're cooking in batches, repeat with rest of the halibut. If the pan is dry, add more avocado oil.

5 Serve the fixings in individual bowls and let everyone mix-and-match to make their own tacos.

COOKING TIP

I tend not to salt this halibut heavily, because there is also salt in all the fixings. Once you've made this recipe a time or two, you'll know how much salt you like.

a fresh take on shrimp and grits

8 Roma (plum) tomatoes, halved lengthwise

1 head fennel, trimmed, cored, and cut into wedges

Sea salt

3 tablespoons extra virgin olive oil

2 tablespoons unsalted butter

2 cloves garlic, sliced

¼ teaspoon red pepper flakes

4 cups Vegetable Stock (page 276)

¼ teaspoon freshly ground black pepper

2 to 3 tablespoons ghee

1½ pounds extra large wild shrimp, peeled and deveined, tails left on

Creamy Polenta or Grits, warmed (page 176)

1 lemon

¼ cup finely chopped fresh parsley

MAKE AHEAD

Both the polenta and sauce can be made up to a day in advance, leaving only the shrimp to cook just before serving. Store them in separate containers in the refrigerator. Reheat before serving.

COOKING TIP

Shrimp come in different sizes, based on the number of shrimp in one pound. This might be obvious, but if you buy a smaller shrimp, just reduce the cooking time.

In this fresh version of the iconic dish, roasted tomatoes and fennel are blended into a light sauce, and quickly seared shrimp finish poaching in that sauce. It's a lighter, brighter version of traditional shrimp and grits. While the instructions may seem long, the whole dish actually comes together quite quickly once the vegetables are roasted. • SERVES 6

1 Preheat the oven to 425 degrees F. Line a rimmed baking sheet with parchment paper.

2 Place the tomatoes and fennel on the baking sheet. Season with ¼ teaspoon salt and drizzle with the oil. Roast for 15 to 20 minutes, until the tomatoes are wilted and starting to caramelize and the fennel is browning. Remove the baking sheet from the oven and set aside.

3 Heat a medium-sized pot over medium heat. Add the butter. Once it has melted and started to foam, add the garlic and pepper flakes. Cook for about 1 minute, until the garlic is fragrant but not browned. Add the vegetable stock and the reserved tomatoes and fennel. Bring to a boil, then reduce to a simmer. Cook for about 10 minutes, just to allow all of the flavors to come together. Add the black pepper.

4 Using an immersion blender, blend the sauce into a smooth puree. Alternatively, blend it in batches in a high-speed blender. (Don't fill the blender container more than halfway, as hot liquids expand when they are blended.) Pour the pureed sauce back in the pot and keep warm.

5 Heat a large skillet over medium-high heat. Season the shrimp with another ¼ teaspoon salt. Melt the ghee in the skillet. Add a single layer of shrimp and cook for 2 minutes. Turn and cook for another 2 minutes on the other side. Remove the shrimp to a bowl. (The shrimp will not quite be done, but they will finish cooking in the sauce.) Repeat with remaining shrimp.

6 Add the shrimp and any accumulated juices to the sauce and simmer for a few minutes, until the shrimp are cooked through.

7 Divide the polenta between warmed bowls. Top with the shrimp and a ladleful of the sauce. Use a Microplane to grate a little bit of lemon zest over each bowl. Top with the parsley and serve warm.

WHAT THE PANDEMIC TAUGHT ME ABOUT HAVING PEOPLE OVER

In some ways, I owe this book to the global pandemic. In early 2020, cocooned in my home with my husband and son, cooking every meal and snack while devising ways to use each broccoli stalk and overripe banana, this book was born. Writing a cookbook had always been a dream, one I kept tabling for "when I have more time." On an uncharacteristically warm spring day, sitting on the sidewalk in front of our home and chatting six feet away from neighbors about silver linings, I decided there may never be a better time.

As I cooked through the pandemic, I also started to think differently about hosting. Before this, I would have said I was a fan of the big party. For years, we hosted a Christmas Eve open house, inviting friends from all corners of our lives. The evening always felt celebratory, but at the end of the night, I felt like I'd had 99 fragmented conversations between refilling the shrimp and making introductions. On Christmas Eve of 2020, Elie, Theo, my mom, and I put on our pajamas and rolled tamales. It felt freeing.

As restrictions dictated the size of gatherings, I realized that small can be better. I don't need to invite everyone I know, just so no one feels left out. Instead, I've come to prefer intimate meals with people I really care about, or those I want to get to know better. When people come to our home, they simply want connection, conversation, meaning. That's why we gather.

Obviously, food and cooking are important parts of my life. But I also learned, it doesn't have to be dinner. In 2020, we hosted dozens of coffee dates in the garden. Elie made lattes and I offered slices of Lemon Olive Oil Cake (page 253). We sat and talked and got to know neighbors and friends in a new way.

Brunch became my favorite way to gather. Especially with a young child, stretching a brunch from late morning to afternoon feels luxurious and unhurried. I would make a platter of sourdough pancakes and soft scrambled eggs, or skillets of shakshuka. The adults sat at the table for hours as the kids played around us. Afterward, everyone helped clean up. At this stage of life, it felt both manageable and joyous.

Despite these revelations, I know I will always love a dinner party. The magic that comes as the sun sets and the room glows from the warmth of candles. But I will do it differently in the future. Fewer people. Deeper conversations. More connection.

CHAPTER EIGHT

SWEETS

everyday cookie

½ cup raw unblanched almonds

¼ cup ground flaxseed

¼ cup water

½ cup coconut oil, melted

½ cup almond butter

½ cup coconut sugar

¼ cup dark brown sugar

2 teaspoons pure vanilla extract

1 cup almond flour

1½ cups gluten-free old-fashioned rolled oats

½ teaspoon baking soda

½ teaspoon sea salt

3 ounces 80% bittersweet chocolate, chopped (about ½ cup)

MAKE IT YOUR OWN

I am the only person in my house who likes raisins and coconut in cookies. If you do, too, you can make a granola cookie by switching out the chocolate for raisins and replacing up to ½ cup of the oats with coconut flakes.

Every time we drive to Vancouver to visit family, our first stop is always TurF, a whole foods café and fitness studio. I love their vegan, gluten-free Everyday Cookie, a perfect crispy on the outside, chewy on the inside, "just sweet enough but not too sweet" almond and oats–packed cookie studded with dark chocolate. It's so good. Theo helped me develop our version. It took us well over a dozen tries to create a cookie that comes close to the original. This is it. · MAKES 18 COOKIES

1 Preheat the oven to 350 degrees F. Line two baking sheets with parchment paper.

2 Place the almonds on one of the baking sheets. Bake for 10 to 12 minutes, until you can smell the almonds toasting. Remove from the oven but leave the oven on. Let the almonds cool, then pulse them in a food processor until finely chopped. Set aside.

3 Whisk together the ground flaxseed and water in a large bowl. Add the coconut oil, almond butter, coconut sugar, brown sugar, and vanilla and whisk until smooth. Combine the reserved chopped almonds, almond flour, oats, baking soda, and salt in another large bowl. Stir the wet ingredients into the dry ingredients until combined. Stir in the chocolate. The dough will be just wet enough to hold together.

4 Scoop out about ¼ cup of the dough and form it into a ball. Place the ball on one of the prepared baking sheets and press to flatten it to between ½ and ¾ inch thick. Repeat with the remaining dough, leaving space between the cookies. (You should have 9 cookies per sheet.) Bake for 15 to 17 minutes, until the edges are starting to crisp and turn golden.

5 Remove from the oven and let the cookies cool on the baking sheets for about 5 minutes before transferring them to a wire rack to cool completely. Once cooled, store in an airtight container for up to a week.

tahini cookies

8 tablespoons (1 stick) unsalted butter, at room temperature

½ cup coconut sugar

½ cup raw tahini

1 teaspoon pure vanilla extract

1¼ cups sorghum flour

1¼ teaspoons baking powder

¼ teaspoon sea salt

Black or white sesame seeds, for decorating

A TIP

If you don't have time to soften the butter, you can just whip the butter and sugar together until soft. The cookies will be a little taller with a softer center.

We once stayed at Shulamit Yard, located in Rosh Pina near the Sea of Galilee. The proprietor, Shuli, had an unassuming and gracious sense of hospitality, inviting us into her home and community. Shuli made us beautiful breakfasts each morning in her open-air kitchen, slowly turning eggplant over an open flame or toasting granola in butter on the stovetop. She also kept a jar of tahini cookies in the front living room of the inn, a not-too-sweet snack for any time of the day. I adapted the cookie recipe she shared with me to make it gluten-free. I found out from Shuli's daughter that she is no longer with us on earth, but these shortbread-like cookies will always remind me of her generous, kind spirit. · MAKES ABOUT 18 COOKIES

1 Preheat the oven to 350 degrees F. Line two baking sheets with parchment paper.

2 Put the butter and sugar in the bowl of a stand mixer fitted with the paddle attachment. Mix on high speed for a few minutes, until butter and sugar are whipped together and become lighter in color. Scrape down the sides of the bowl. Add the tahini and vanilla and beat again until the tahini is completely incorporated.

3 In another bowl, whisk together the flour, baking powder, and salt. Add the dry ingredients to the wet ingredients, mixing on medium speed until well combined. Don't be afraid of overmixing.

4 Using a small scoop or spoon, scoop out about a tablespoon of dough. Form it into a ball and place on a baking sheet, leaving 2 to 3 inches between cookies. Use a spoon or your fingers to gently flatten the tops of the cookies. Sprinkle the cookies with sesame seeds.

5 Bake for 11 to 14 minutes, rotating the baking sheets halfway through baking. Remove them from the oven when the edges are just starting to brown.

6 Let the cookies cool for 5 minutes on the baking sheets before moving them to a wire rack to cool completely. The cookies will keep in an airtight container at room temperature for a few days.

chocolate chocolate cookies

7 ounces 80% bittersweet chocolate, chopped (1¼ cup)

8 tablespoons (1 stick) unsalted butter

¾ cup coconut sugar

2 large eggs, at room temperature

⅓ cup cocoa powder

¼ teaspoon sea salt

Flaky salt (optional)

When we have people over for dinner, I'll often just serve squares of good dark chocolate as a sweet bite at the end of the meal. I find that most of the time, friends just want a little something to go with coffee, tea, or those last few sips of wine. This cookie is perfect in that same bitter-sweet way. Theo and I like these topped with a little flaky salt, but Elie prefers them plain. You really can't go wrong.
MAKES 16 COOKIES

1 Preheat the oven to 350 degrees F. Line two large baking sheets with parchment paper.

2 Place 5 ounces of the chocolate (about 1 cup) and all the butter in a medium pot set over low heat. Gently melt the chocolate and butter, whisking until smooth and glossy. Let cool slightly.

3 Using a stand mixer fitted with the whisk attachment, on medium speed whisk the sugar and eggs together until very fluffy, about 3 minutes. Pour a couple of tablespoons of the warm chocolate mixture into the egg mixture to warm the batter, whisking until combined. Pour in the rest of the choco-late mixture and whisk on medium speed until combined. Add the cocoa and salt, and whisk until you get a smooth batter. It will be very thin. Stir in the remaining 2 ounces chocolate.

4 Chill the batter in the refrigerator for 15 minutes. Use a cookie scoop to portion out 2 tablespoons of the batter for each cookie, leaving at least 1½ inches between the cookies, as they will spread out slightly during baking. You should get 16 cookies, 8 on each baking sheet. Top the cookies with a little flaky salt, if desired.

5 Bake for 11 to 13 minutes, until the cookies have puffed up and the edges are set. (They will settle as they cool.) Let the cookies cool on the baking sheets for at least 10 minutes before transferring them to a wire rack to cool completely to room temperature. The cookies will keep in an airtight con-tainer for up to 4 days—if they last that long.

elie's pecan toffee

1 pound (4 sticks) unsalted butter, plus more for the baking dish

2 cups cane sugar

¼ cup water

Pinch of sea salt

2 cups toasted pecans, chopped

1 cup chopped 70% bittersweet chocolate (about 5 ounces)

Flaky salt, for sprinkling

Elie doesn't cook. But every now and then, he gets the urge to make something sweet, like homemade chocolate ice cream or buttery caramels. One year, he decided to make Pecan Toffee for our annual Christmas Eve party. Everyone raved. The next year, friends asked if he was making it again—and the tradition began. Friends will time their holiday visits based on whether or not Elie has made his famous toffee. Everyone wants to go home with a bag of this buttery burnt caramel, chocolate, and pecan treat. · MAKES ABOUT 2 POUNDS

1 Butter a 9 by 13-inch baking dish.

2 Combine the butter, sugar, water, and sea salt in a large, heavy-bottomed pot. Turn on the heat to medium-high. Cook, stirring continuously. The mixture will first look grainy, and then like bubbling cheese. Keep stirring until the mixture is smooth and has turned a light caramel color. Remove from heat and immediately stir in the pecans. Pour the mixture into the baking dish and using a silicone spatula, spread it into an even layer. (It will be very hot, so be careful.) Sprinkle the chocolate evenly across the top. Let the chocolate melt slightly, and then spread it in an even layer over the candy. Sprinkle the salt over the chocolate.

3 Leave the baking dish on the counter for the candy to harden completely This will take at least an hour and might take several hours. Once it is hardened, break it into rustic pieces. Store in an airtight container at room temperature for up to 4 or 5 days.

pastry crust

½ pound (2 sticks) unsalted butter

2 large egg yolks

⅓ cup ice water

¾ cup (105 grams) sorghum flour, plus more for rolling the dough

½ cup (45 grams) almond flour

½ cup (84 grams) potato starch

½ cup (68 grams) tapioca starch

¼ cup (30 grams) buckwheat flour

½ teaspoon sea salt

Grated zest of 1 lemon

MAKE AHEAD

You can make the dough ahead of time and store the disk, tightly wrapped, in the refrigerator overnight or in the freezer for up to 3 months. Thaw overnight in the refrigerator before rolling.

MAKE IT YOUR OWN

I love the slightly earthy flavor of buckwheat flour, but you can use all sorghum flour.

OF NOTE FOR SPECIAL DIETS

The egg yolks make the dough easier to work with, but if you don't eat eggs, omit the egg yolks and add 2 to 3 tablespoons more ice water.

This recipe will also work with a plant-based butter substitute.

I am much more of a savory cook than a baker, and pies used to intimidate me. I was always afraid of adding too much liquid, of overworking the dough, of making it bland or tough. But then I realized: It's just pie! If you're afraid of pastry, please don't be. We fail at 100 percent of the things we never try. MAKES ENOUGH DOUGH FOR ONE 10-INCH GALETTE OR ONE 8- OR 9-INCH SINGLE-CRUST PIE

1 Cut the butter into 1-inch cubes and place in the freezer. Whisk together the egg yolks and water in a glass measuring cup with a spout and place in the refrigerator.

2 Place the sorghum flour, almond flour, potato starch, tapioca starch, buckwheat flour, salt, and lemon zest in a food processor. Pulse a few times to combine.

3 Add the butter to the dry ingredients in the food processor. Pulse a few times to incorporate the butter into the dry ingredients, with fairly large pieces of butter remaining.

4 Pour in the egg yolk mixture and pulse again until the dough starts to come together into a ball. Sprinkle the counter lightly with sorghum flour. Pour out the dough onto the counter and using your hands, bring it together into a ball and then flatten into a disk. Wrap the disk in plastic wrap and place in the refrigerator. Let the disk rest and chill for at least 30 minutes.

5 To roll the dough, dust the countertop with a little sorghum flour. Unwrap the disk and place it on the floured surface. Start rolling the dough from the center and work outward, turning the dough every few rolls to prevent it from sticking. Roll it into an even circle. If the dough cracks, just pinch it together with your fingers and roll again. If it's too sticky, dust with more sorghum flour. Continue to roll the dough until it is about ⅛ inch thick. Use the dough for a galette or pie.

TIPS FOR PERFECT PASTRY CRUSTS

Make sure all your ingredients stay cold.

Keep the pieces of the butter on the larger size. As the butter melts, it creates steam, which results in a flaky crust.

If the dough doesn't seem to be coming together, add a little more water.

While you don't want to overwork the dough, don't be afraid to knead it until it comes together.

The more you make pastry, the better you'll get. But if you never try, you'll never enjoy the taste of your own pie.

apple galette WITH VANILLA BEAN WHIPPED CREAM

4 crisp red apples (such as Cosmic Crisp or other crisp, sweet-tart variety)

⅓ cup coconut sugar, plus more for sprinkling

½ teaspoon ground cinnamon

¼ teaspoon ground ginger

¼ teaspoon ground allspice

¼ teaspoon sea salt

Grated zest of 1 lemon

1 teaspoon fresh lemon juice

2 tablespoons unsalted butter, melted

1 prepared Pastry Crust (page 242)

1 large egg, beaten

Vanilla Bean Whipped Cream (recipe on page 275), for serving

MAKE IT YOUR OWN

You can use this same method to make a galette with any seasonal fruit—pears, plums, peaches, raspberries. Just vary the amount of sugar and spices to pair with the fruit.

NUTRITION NOTE

I like to leave the skin on the apples, because the nutritionist in me just can't cut away the fiber and nutrients in the skin. But if you prefer, you can peel the apples first.

The smell of apple pie always reminds me of my Mom. When I was little, she was always in the kitchen baking. Homemade cookies, fresh sandwich bread, dinner rolls, and pie. We often came home from school to the aroma of apples and cinnamon bubbling under a buttery crust. We'd top it with Breyers vanilla ice cream, letting the warm pie melt the ice cream to a creamy pool that mixed with the juice from the spiced apples. This simple apple galette served with vanilla whipped cream brings back that memory. • MAKES ONE 9- TO 10-INCH GALETTE; SERVES 8

1 Preheat the oven to 400 degrees F. Line a baking sheet with parchment paper.

2 Thinly slice the apples. Transfer the apple slices to a large bowl.

3 Whisk together the sugar, cinnamon, ginger, allspice, and salt in a small bowl. Pour the sugar mixture over the apples. Gently toss the apples, distributing the sugar and spices evenly. Add the lemon zest, lemon juice, and butter and toss again.

4 Roll out the dough according to the directions in the recipe until it is about 12 inches across. Once the dough is rolled out, place it in the center of the prepared baking sheet. (I find it easiest to hold the baking sheet next to the counter and slide the dough onto the sheet.)

5 Either pile the apple slices onto the center of the crust, or take time to place the slices on the crust in a decorative manner. (You can make a spiral or overlapping rows, starting in the center.) Leave 2 to 3 inches of dough around the outer edge. Once the apples are arranged, fold the dough up and over the apples. (It doesn't have to be perfect. You want to have uncovered apples in the middle.) Brush the crust with the egg, then sprinkle a little sugar over the crust.

6 Bake for 35 to 40 minutes, until the apples are bubbling and the crust is a deep golden brown. Serve warm or at room temperature, with the whipped cream.

chocolate pecan pie

1 prepared Pastry Crust (page 242)

3 large eggs

¼ cup bourbon or water (if you don't drink alcohol)

1 ¾ cups dark brown sugar

½ teaspoon sea salt

4 tablespoons (½ stick) unsalted butter, melted

2 teaspoons pure vanilla extract

1½ cups pecan halves, toasted

6 ounces 80% bittersweet chocolate, chopped (1 heaping cup)

Flaky salt, for sprinkling on top

I can't remember a Christmas growing up without Chocolate Pecan Pie, a Kentucky classic (commonly referred to as Derby Pie). It was my Dad's favorite. The recipe from my childhood was sticky sweet, made with corn syrup and milk chocolate chips. This is still sweet, but a bit more reserved. The bittersweet chocolate, extra pecans, and flaky salt balance everything out. It's rich and decadent in the best possible way. · MAKES ONE 8- OR 9-INCH PIE; SERVES 8

1 Preheat the oven to 400 degrees F.

2 Roll out the pastry dough according to the directions in the recipe until it is about 12 inches across. Transfer the dough to an 8- or 9-inch pie plate. Press the dough into the pie plate and crimp the edges. Place in the refrigerator to chill while you make the filling.

3 Place the eggs and bourbon in a large bowl and whisk until very well blended. Whisk in the sugar and sea salt. Add the butter and vanilla and whisk again.

4 Sprinkle the chocolate and pecans over the bottom of the pie shell. Pour in the filling. The pecans will automatically float to the surface. (That's what you want.) Sprinkle with a little flaky salt.

5 Bake for 10 minutes. Reduce the temperature to 325 degrees F and bake until the center of the pie is set, about 1 hour. Remove from the oven and let cool completely. Serve the pie at room temperature. The pie will keep, tightly covered at room temperature, for 4 or 5 days.

chocolate hazelnut banana bread

½ cup extra virgin olive oil, plus more for greasing the pan

3 ripe bananas

¾ cup coconut sugar

3 large eggs

1 teaspoon pure vanilla extract

1 cup hazelnut flour or almond flour

¾ cup sorghum flour

½ teaspoon sea salt

½ teaspoon baking soda

½ teaspoon baking powder

½ cup chopped 80% bittersweet chocolate (about 3 ounces)

¼ cup blanched hazelnuts, chopped

MIXING TIP

When making gluten-free quick breads like this, don't be afraid of overmixing. Aerating the batter will ensure it rises properly and will prevent the bread from being too dense.

Hazelnuts are local to the Pacific Northwest, and we're lucky to have a hazelnut orchard a few miles from us, Holmquist Hazelnuts. I buy their hazelnut flour at our farmers' market, but you can purchase it online. It's a delicious addition to cookies and quick breads in place of almond flour. Chocolate and hazelnuts are a classic combination, one that gives a new life to banana bread. If I give Theo a slice of this for breakfast, I'm met with squeals of delight. · MAKES ONE LOAF

1 Preheat the oven to 350 degrees F. Grease the bottom and sides of a 8 ½ by 4 ½-inch loaf pan with oil.

2 Put the bananas in a medium bowl and mash with a fork until fairly smooth. Add the oil, sugar, eggs, and vanilla and whisk until smooth. Add the hazelnut flour, sorghum flour, salt, baking soda and baking powder. Whisk again until very smooth, about 1 minute. Stir in the chocolate.

3 Pour the batter into the prepared loaf pan and sprinkle the hazelnuts on top. Place the pan on the upper-middle rack of the oven and bake for 55 to 65 minutes, until golden brown on top, and a wooden skewer inserted in the middle comes out clean.

4 Place the pan on a wire rack to cool. After 15 minutes, slide the edge of a knife around the sides of the pan to loosen the bread. Gently turn the bread out of the pan and place it directly on the rack to cool completely before slicing. Store at room temperature, well covered, for up to 3 or 4 days.

maple-pumpkin bread

1 cup extra virgin olive oil, plus more for greasing the pan

4 large eggs

One 15-ounce can pure pumpkin puree (not pumpkin pie mix)

1 cup maple syrup

1 teaspoon sea salt

1¼ teaspoons ground cinnamon

1 teaspoon ground ginger

¼ teaspoon freshly grated nutmeg

1 teaspoon pure vanilla extract

1 cup almond flour

1 cup sorghum flour

½ cup teff flour

2 teaspoons baking soda

Gluten-free powdered sugar, for dusting (optional)

When the cool, dark evenings of fall set in, this bread always makes its way to the table. It's decidedly not very sweet, which makes it a perfect pairing for coffee. In addition to almond flour, I use a mix of sorghum and teff flours, because I like the higher protein and nutrition content of these grains. It's a one-bowl recipe, which makes for easy cleanup. I love baking it in a Bundt pan, because it makes it feel more special and elegant. · SERVES 12

1 Preheat the oven to 350 degrees F. Coat the inside of a 12-cup Bundt pan with a thin layer of oil.

2 Beat the eggs lightly in a large bowl, until combined. Add the pumpkin, oil, maple syrup, salt, cinnamon, ginger, nutmeg, and vanilla. Whisk together well. Add the almond flour, sorghum and teff flours and baking soda. Whisk again until the batter is smooth. (You don't have to worry about overmixing, since there is no gluten in the batter.) Pour the batter into the prepared pan and smooth the top.

3 Bake for about 40 minutes, until the top is golden brown and a skewer inserted in the cake comes out clean. Let the bread cool in the pan for about 5 minutes, then turn it out onto a wire rack and let it cool for another 10 minutes. Transfer the bread to a serving plate and dust it with powdered sugar, if desired. The bread will keep at room temperature, tightly wrapped, for about 3 days.

lemon olive oil cake

1¼ cups extra virgin olive oil, plus more for greasing the pan

1 cup almond flour, plus more for dusting the pan

1 cup sorghum flour

1 cup millet flour

1 tablespoon baking powder

1 teaspoon sea salt

1 cup maple syrup

4 large eggs

1 cup whole milk Greek yogurt

½ cup lemon juice, divided

Grated zest of two lemons, divided

¼ cup coconut sugar

Gluten-free powdered sugar, for garnish

Theo helped me develop many of the dessert recipes in this book, including this one. I was going to put an orange glaze on this cake, but he asked for lemon. He was right—the puckery sweetness of the lemon glaze makes the cake. I love serving this cake for brunch, a coffee date or afternoon tea. Sweetened only with maple syrup, it can pass for breakfast. Dusting the pan with almond flour helps the cake to release from the pan easily. • SERVES 12

1 Adjust an oven rack to the lower-middle position and pre-heat the oven to 350 degrees F. Grease a 12-cup Bundt pan with oil and lightly dust it with almond flour.

2 Whisk together the almond flour, sorghum flour, millet flour, baking powder, and salt in a large bowl. Add the maple syrup, eggs, oil, yogurt, ¼ cup lemon juice and zest from one lemon. Whisk well, until everything is combined. Do not worry about overmixing.

3 Pour the batter into the prepared pan. Gently tap the pan on the counter to settle the batter. Bake until the cake is golden brown on top and a wooden skewer inserted into the center comes out clean, 45 to 50 minutes. Check the cake right at 45 minutes, as overbaking will cause the cake to be dry.

4 Let the cake cool for 5 minutes. Turn the cake out onto a wire rack set over a rimmed baking sheet.

5 While the cake is baking, place the remaining lemon juice and zest and the coconut sugar in a small saucepan. Bring to a boil. Stir until the sugar has dissolved. Remove from the heat.

6 As soon as you've placed the cake on the rack, brush it with the glaze, making sure all the syrup soaks in. Let the cake cool completely. Dust with powdered sugar. The cake will keep at room temperature, well covered, for up to 3 days.

DAIRY-FREE LEMON OLIVE OIL CAKE • The yogurt helps with the texture and keeps this cake moist. If you don't eat dairy, substitute coconut yogurt. Everything else remains the same.

flourless dark chocolate cake

1 cup (2 sticks) unsalted butter, plus more for the pan

½ cup unsweetened cocoa powder, plus more for the pan and dusting the top

¼ cup heavy whipping cream

8 ounces 85% bittersweet chocolate, chopped (about 1 ¼ cups)

5 large eggs, at room temperature

1 cup coconut sugar

1 tablespoon instant espresso powder

1 teaspoon pure vanilla extract

½ teaspoon sea salt

Vanilla Bean Whipped Cream (page 275; optional)

Chocolate is almost considered a food group in our home, it's enjoyed so often. This cake, inspired by the Flourless Chocolate Brownie Cake in Sarah Copeland's *Everyday is Saturday*, is one of our favorites. Many years ago, I remember watching Ina Garten on Barefoot Contessa making chocolate brownies with espresso and saying, "Adding coffee makes chocolate taste more like chocolate." She was right, of course. The addition of the espresso powder adds extra depth and richness to this dense chocolate cake. · MAKES ONE 9-INCH CAKE; SERVES ABOUT 10

1 Preheat the oven to 350 degrees F. Position a rack to the center of the oven. Butter the bottom and sides of a 9-inch springform pan. Dust the inside of the pan lightly with cocoa powder, tapping out any excess.

2 Heat the butter and cream in a medium pot over low heat. When the butter is melted, add the chocolate and stir until the chocolate is melted.

3 Whisk together the eggs, sugar, cocoa powder, espresso powder, vanilla, and salt in a medium bowl. Stir in about ¼ cup of the melted chocolate mixture to warm the batter slightly and prevent the eggs from scrambling. Whisk in the rest of the chocolate mixture until the batter is smooth. Pour the batter into the prepared pan

4 Bake for 35 to 40 minutes, until the cake has just cooked through.

5 Remove from the oven and let cool completely. Run a knife around the edge of the cake and then carefully release the sides of the pan. Transfer the bottom of the pan with the cake to a cake plate. When ready to serve, sift more cocoa powder over it and serve with whipped cream, if desired. Store the cake, well wrapped in plastic wrap, in the refrigerator for up to 3 or 4 days. Let come to room temperature before serving.

SUSTAINABLE KITCHEN TIPS

(WITHOUT BEING PERFECT)

I try to make environmentally responsible choices in my kitchen as much as possible, while also giving myself grace. Here is what works for me.

I am a member of the Clean Counter Club. I don't like a lot of "stuff" on the counter, not even my compost bin. I struggled to compost regularly until I put a full-sized trash can under the sink with a biodegradable liner. Now I just pull out the can when I'm cooking and toss all the scraps in the bag. The bag gets full every few days and then I take it to the green bin. It's an easy win. A separate full-sized trash can for plastic, metal and glass, and paper makes recycling easy, too.

For the most part, I have a plastic-free kitchen. For food storage, I use freezer-safe glass containers with plastic lids, quart- and pint-sized canning jars, reusable silicone food storage bags, reusable cloth produce bags, and beeswax food wrap. See the Resources section for some of my favorite brands. Investing in these products up front ends up saving money in the long run—and keeps plastics out of landfills and waterways.

For cooking, invest in a few good cast-iron, stainless-steel, and/or carbon steel pans. They will last a lifetime and are naturally nonstick without the chemicals. Cast-iron pans are inexpensive and can often be found at thrift stores. I have my great-grandmother's skillet, which is probably close to 100 years old. I use it every day.

For cleaning, I make my own kitchen cleaner using a little Dr. Bronner's soap and water, mixed in a reusable spray bottle. It's cheap and effective. If something needs a scrub, a little baking soda and a scrub brush do the trick. I also buy biodegradable plant-based dishwashing soap and dishwasher tablets. I find the Ecover brand works best.

Instead of reaching for a paper towel to wipe up the counter, I grab a reusable rag or towel. I buy inexpensive flour sack towels in bulk, and use them for doing dishes, wiping up spills, and (clean, of course!) to wrap around freshly washed produce to store it in the refrigerator.

The type of food you purchase has a big environmental impact. I realize making sustainability-driven choices is a privilege, though. For the most part, I buy whole foods—food not already in a package. As much as possible, I shop at the local farmers' market and food co-op, buying food produced close to home. I use the Environmental Working Group's guide to the produce with the highest and lowest levels of pesticides (called the "Dirty Dozen" and the "Clean Fifteen") to decide which fruits and vegetables to purchase organic. When it comes to animal products, I mostly purchase from local farms and from farms that use humane and environmentally friendly practices. I know these choices can be expensive, and are not even available in every community.

All of these tips are given with love, knowing they can't and won't work for every home. Take what feels useful, and leave the rest.

CHAPTER NINE

THE BASICS

almond milk

I make almond milk every four to five days. It's always in my morning latte, and it's what I pour over granola. If you don't consume cow's milk, make this almond milk to use in the pancake recipe on page 52 and in other baked goods. · MAKES ABOUT 1 QUART

2 cups raw almonds

Filtered water

2 pitted dates

¼ teaspoon sea salt

1 Place the almonds in a jar and cover with filtered water. Soak at room temperature for at least 8 hours, or overnight.

2 Drain and rinse the almonds. Place them in a high-speed blender. Add 4 cups filtered water, the dates, and the salt. Blend until totally smooth.

3 Place a nut milk bag or clean kitchen towel over a large bowl or 1-quart glass measuring cup. Pour half of the almond puree into the bag. Twist the top of the bag closed or bring the corners of the towel together, then squeeze, forcing the milk through. Discard the almond pulp. Repeat with the remaining puree.

4 Almond milk can be refrigerated for up to 5 days or frozen for up to 3 months. If I'm going out of town, I pour it into single-serving jars and store them in the freezer. Thaw overnight in the refrigerator before using.

WALNUT MILK · Use the same method to make walnut milk, substituting walnuts for the almonds. I like adding a little cinnamon to the finished milk, to help balance the bitterness of the walnuts. It's delicious in coffee.

toasted sunflower seeds and toasted pumpkin seeds

These two seeds are toasted exactly the same way. Make a batch of each and store in your refrigerator to top everything from salads to soups to roasted vegetables. They also make a great snack. · MAKES ABOUT 2 CUPS

2 cups shelled sunflower or pumpkin seeds

1 tablespoon extra virgin olive oil or avocado oil

Sea salt

1 Place the seeds in a heavy-bottomed skillet. Drizzle with the oil and stir. Place the skillet over medium-low heat. Cook, stirring often, until the seeds are toasted, brown, and fragrant. (This can take up to 20 minutes. Don't be tempted to turn up the heat. That will cause the seeds to toast unevenly, and some will burn.)

2 Sprinkle with ¼ teaspoon sea salt or more, depending on how salty you like them. Stir. Let the seeds cool completely. Store in an airtight container in the refrigerator for up to 6 months.

PICTURED ON PAGES 258-259: (1) Golden Almond Butter; (2) Toasted Sunflower Seeds; (3) Chili Oil; (4) Aleppo-Style Pepper; (5) Zhug; (6) Fresh Chili Harissa; (7) My Spice Blend; (8) Toasted Pumpkin Seeds; (9) Toasted Buckwheat; (10) Labneh

salted almonds
(OR ANY OTHER NUT)

Deeply roasted nuts are great for snacking or adding crunch (and extra protein) to salads or vegetable dishes. I roast big batches of nuts and then store them in the refrigerator in glass jars. Use this same method for almonds, pecans, walnuts, cashews or blanched hazelnuts. Pecans and walnuts will roast more quickly, so start checking them at 6 minutes. · MAKES 2 CUPS

2 cups raw, unblanched almonds

1 tablespoon extra virgin olive oil

Sea salt

1 Preheat the oven to 350 degrees F. Line a rimmed baking sheet with parchment paper.

2 Place the almonds on the baking sheet. Drizzle with the oil and ⅛ to ¼ teaspoon sea salt, depending on how salty you want them. Using your hands, rub the oil and salt into the almonds Spread out the almonds in a single layer.

3 Bake for 8 to 10 minutes, until the almonds start to brown and smell toasty. They will continue to cook slightly after you take them out of the oven, so take them out when they are a shade lighter that you like them. Let cool completely. Store in an airtight container in the refrigerator for up to 6 months.

toasted buckwheat or millet

Toasted buckwheat and toasted millet add great crunch and flavor anywhere you would use toasted breadcrumbs or croutons. · MAKES 1 CUP

1 cup buckwheat groats or whole millet

Spread the buckwheat in a dry heavy-bottomed skillet and place over low heat. Toast, stirring frequently, for 3 to 4 minutes, until it has begun to pop and smells toasty. Transfer to a plate and let cool completely. Store in an airtight container in the refrigerator for up to 6 months.

nut butter

It's hard to eat purchased nut butter once you start making your own—the flavor of homemade is so much better. You can use this method to make almond butter, hazelnut butter, walnut butter, or peanut butter. Be sure to let the nuts cool completely before blending. Adding MCT oil will thin the nut butter to a more spoonable consistency, but it's optional. Note: You do need a high-speed blender, such as a Vitamix; a regular blender will not be powerful enough. •
MAKES ABOUT 2 CUPS

2 cups raw nuts (almonds, hazelnuts, or walnuts)

MCT oil (optional)

Sea salt (optional)

1 Preheat the oven to 350 degrees F. Line a rimmed baking sheet with parchment paper.

2 Spread the nuts in a single layer on the baking sheet. Bake for 8 to 10 minutes, until toasted and fragrant. Let cool completely.

3 Transfer the nuts to a high-speed blender. Blend on high speed until smooth. Use the plunger to help move the nuts around. If you like, you can add a few tablespoons of MCT oil to thin the nut butter and help make it more smooth. You can also add ⅛ to ¼ teaspoon sea salt and blend again. Spoon or pour into a glass jar and store in the refrigerator for up to 3 months.

PEANUT BUTTER • Start with 2 cups unsalted roasted peanuts and follow the instructions for blending.

GOLDEN ALMOND BUTTER • Follow the recipe, adding 1 tablespoons ground turmeric and 1 tablespoon ground ginger after blending; blend again until evenly mixed through. (Adding the spices at the beginning will prevent the nut butter from getting smooth and creamy.)

my spice blend

I add my signature spice blend to everything from shakshuka to zhug to roasted meats to the chicken-zucchini meatballs on page 196. I make it every week or two and store it at room temperature to have it handy whenever I need it. If you can't find whole spices, substitute ground spices using the same measures. •
MAKES ABOUT ¼ CUP

2 tablespoons cumin seeds

2 tablespoons coriander seeds

1 tablespoon fennel seeds

1 teaspoon cardamom seeds (from green cardamom pods)

1 Combine all the spices in a dry skillet set over low heat. Slowly toast the spices, stirring frequently, for 3 to 4 minutes, until they become fragrant. Transfer to a bowl and let cool.

2 Put the spices in a mortar and crush with a pestle until finely ground. Alternatively, grind the spices in a spice mill or clean coffee grinder. Pour the spice blend into a glass jar, cover tightly, and store at room temperature. Toasted spices are best used within a week or so.

spicy dukkah

Dukkah is a Middle Eastern spice mix made from toasted nuts and spices. You can find recipes for versions featuring different nuts and combinations of spices. I prefer pistachios, but you can experiment with hazelnuts or almonds. Sometimes I like to add a little cardamom. Dukkah is delicious on salads, avocado toast, eggs, and roasted meats. •
MAKES ABOUT ¾ CUP

½ cup unsalted raw pistachios	1 tablespoon fennel seeds
1 tablespoon coriander seeds	¼ teaspoon red pepper flakes
1 tablespoon cumin seeds	1 teaspoon Maldon salt or other flaky salt

1 Put pistachios in a small dry skillet set over medium-low heat. Toast, stirring occasionally, until they're are golden, about 5 minutes. Transfer the pistachios to a bowl and let them cool. Alternatively, roast them in the oven at 350 degrees F for 5 to 7 minutes, then cool.

2 Sprinkle the coriander, cumin, and fennel seeds in the same skillet over low heat. Slowly toast the spices, stirring frequently, for 3 to 4 minutes, until they become fragrant. Add the spices to the bowl with the pistachios and let them cool.

3 Transfer the nuts and spices to a food processor or a mortar and coarsely grind. Pour into an airtight container and stir in the pepper flakes and salt. Dukkah can be stored in the refrigerator indefinitely.

baharat spice mix

Baharat is an aromatic Middle Eastern spice blend that can be used in soups and stews, or as a dry rub for chicken, fish, or meat. •
MAKES ABOUT ¼ CUP

1 tablespoon cumin seeds, toasted and ground	1 teaspoon ground cloves
1 tablespoon coriander seeds, toasted and ground	1 tablespoon Aleppo-style pepper
¼ teaspoon cardamom seeds, toasted and ground	1 teaspoon ground cinnamon
1 teaspoon freshly cracked black pepper	¼ teaspoon freshly grated nutmeg

Mix all of the spices together. Store in an airtight container and use within 3 months.

charred peppers

Charred peppers give a subtle smoky flavor to the Stacked Chicken Enchiladas (page 207), Chicken Poblano Soup (page 128), and other dishes. Use the same method for red bell peppers, poblano peppers, or a mixture of both.

1 Preheat the broiler to high.

2 Arrange peppers on a rimmed baking sheet pan and place under the broiler. Let the peppers blister and blacken on one side. Using tongs, turn the peppers. Repeat until the peppers are charred on all sides.

3 Place the peppers in a glass or metal bowl and cover tightly with plastic wrap. Let them steam for about 20 minutes, until cool enough to handle.

4 Peel off the charred skin. It's okay if some of it doesn't come off. (Note: poblanos vary in spiciness. If your skin is sensitive, you might want to wear gloves.) Remove and discard the stem and seeds, Cut the peppers lengthwise into slices. Use as desired. Store in an airtight container in the refrigerator for up to 5 days or in the freezer for up to 3 months.

honey-chili butter

This butter is made for the fried chicken and waffles on page 56, but it can be used anywhere you'd like a sweet heat. Adjust the heat by using different varieties of chiles. • MAKES ABOUT 1 CUP

1 dried ancho chile

1 dried guajillo chile

1 dried pasilla chile

1 dried ghost chile (a.k.a. bhut jolokia)

8 tablespoons (1 stick) unsalted butter

2 cloves garlic, peeled

1 teaspoon fennel seeds

1 bay leaf

1 teaspoon sea salt

½ cup honey

1 Rinse the chiles to remove any dust. Let them dry completely.

2 Place the butter in a small saucepan over low heat. Once it has melted, add the garlic, fennel seeds, and bay leaf. Let the garlic and spices infuse the butter for about an hour. The heat should be very low, with the butter barely bubbling around the garlic.

3 While the butter is infusing, prepare the chiles. Remove the stems from the chiles and discard. Using kitchen shears, cut the chiles into smallish pieces. Place the pieces, including any seeds, in a high-speed blender. Pulse until the chiles are chopped but not turned into powder.

4 Strain the butter through a sieve into a glass measuring cup. (Discard the garlic and spices.) Add the chiles, salt, and honey and stir until thoroughly mixed. Serve warm.

5 The butter will keep, tightly covered, in the refrigerator for up to 3 months. Rewarm before serving.

chili oil

Chili oil is another signature ingredient in a lot of my cooking—you'll see it used over and over again in this cookbook. It ends up on the table at most meals as a spicy condiment, adding deep flavor and subtle heat. Make your chili oil as mild or spicy as you like, depending on which dried chiles you choose. Using a variety of chiles gives the oil a more complex flavor. If you like a smoky flavor, substitute a dried chipotle for one of the other chiles. The total weight of the dried chiles should be about 3 ounces. Each batch of chili oil tastes a little different, because even the same variety of chiles varies in heat and flavor from bag to bag. · MAKES 1½ TO 2 CUPS

2 dried ancho chiles

3 dried guajillo chiles

3 dried pasilla chiles

1 dried ghost chile (a.k.a. bhut jolokia)

1 cup avocado oil or extra virgin olive oil

2 cloves garlic, peeled

1 teaspoon cumin seeds

1 teaspoon coriander seeds

1 teaspoon fennel seeds

1 bay leaf

1 teaspoon sea salt

1 teaspoon coconut sugar

1 Rinse the chiles to remove any dust. Let them dry completely.

2 Place the avocado oil in a small saucepan over low heat. Add the garlic, cumin, coriander, and fennel seeds, and the bay leaf. Let the garlic and spices infuse the oil for about an hour. The heat should be very low, with the oil barely bubbling around the garlic.

3 While the oil is infusing, prepare the chiles. Remove the stems from the chiles and discard. Using kitchen shears, cut the chiles into smallish pieces. Place the pieces, including any seeds, in a high-speed blender. Pulse until the chiles are chopped but not turned into powder.

4 Strain the oil through a sieve into a glass measuring cup. (Discard the garlic and spices.) Add the chiles, salt, and sugar and stir until the salt and sugar have dissolved. Let the oil cool completely. Pour into a jar, cover tightly, and store in the refrigerator for up to 3 months.

A FEW TIPS

If you have trouble finding dried chiles in your grocery store, check the Resources section for where to buy online.

When grinding the chiles, stop before they're ground to a powder. Let there be some small pieces of chiles remaining. They add a nice texture to the oil.

Sometimes the oil will solidify in the refrigerator. If it does, let it come to room temperature before using.

oven-dried tomatoes

If you have a garden with an overabundance of tomatoes in the summer, try this method for preserving them. Use these wherever you would use tomato paste, or blend them into a rich sauce for pasta. They are delicious layered in a sandwich for a winter BLT, or added to a chopped salad. · MAKES 24 PIECES

12 Roma (plum) tomatoes

⅛ teaspoon sea salt

2 tablespoons extra virgin olive oil

1 Preheat the oven to 350 degrees F. Line a baking sheet with parchment paper.

2 Cut the tomatoes in half lengthwise. Squeeze each half to remove the seeds; discard the seeds. Place the tomatoes in a bowl and toss with the salt and oil. Arrange the tomatoes cut side down on the baking sheet. Roast for about an hour, until the tomatoes are soft and starting to caramelize.

3 Let cool to room temperature. Store in an airtight container in the refrigerator, for up to 4 days. Alternatively, freeze for up to 4 months.

olive oil–roasted tomatoes

These simply roasted tomatoes work in so many dishes—as a simple pasta sauce or a topping for pizza, on noodle bowls, with eggs. Add some to a snack board or serve with bread. The roasted lemons are delicious—eat them skin and all. · MAKES 1½ CUPS

2 cups cherry or grape tomatoes

1 or 2 cloves garlic, peeled

1 lemon, cut into 6 wedges

⅛ teaspoon sea salt

⅛ teaspoon red pepper flakes

3 tablespoons extra virgin olive oil

1 Preheat the oven to 425 degrees F.

2 Combine all the ingredients in a small baking dish. Roast for 20 to 25 minutes, until the tomatoes are blistered and split and have released their juices, and the lemons are starting to char. Use warm, or let cool to room temperature. Store in an airtight container in the refrigerator for up to 5 days. (If storing, you might want to remove the lemons. As they sit, their flavor gets strong.)

fresh tomato salsa or sauce

When it comes to a fresh salsa, I like a very simple, clean-tasting version without onion or garlic. With cilantro, this is the perfect topping for tacos. But switch out the herbs and it becomes something else. Add fresh basil for a summer addition to a cheese board; add parsley or tarragon and it becomes a sauce for fish. · **MAKES ABOUT 1 CUP**

2 cups cherry or grape tomatoes, halved or quartered

Grated zest of 1 lemon

Juice of ½ lemon

¼ cup loosely packed fresh cilantro leaves, finely chopped

1 tablespoon extra virgin olive oil

Sea salt

1 Place the tomatoes, lemon zest and juice, cilantro, oil, and ⅛ teaspoon salt in a medium bowl and toss together. Taste and add more salt if necessary. Serve at room temperature.

2 This is best served the same day it's made. If you want to make it ahead, store it in an airtight container in the refrigerator. After 2 days, it will start to lose texture and flavor.

roasted tomato salsa

If I want a salsa with more complex flavors, this is the one. Use this salsa any way you would use a regular salsa, or as an alternative to the other enchilada sauce on page 207. It also makes a delicious topping for fish or chicken. Double, triple, or quadruple the recipe and freeze the extra for later. You can also think about this ingredient list only as a guide, and vary the salsa depending on what you have on hand. · **MAKES ABOUT 1½ CUPS**

1 medium onion (about 6 ounces), cut in large pieces

2 cups cherry or grape tomatoes, or 2 large tomatoes, cored and quartered

4 tomatillos, husks removed, quartered

2 poblano peppers, stemmed

1 or 2 cloves garlic, peeled

2 tablespoons avocado oil or extra virgin olive oil

Sea salt

¼ teaspoon red pepper flakes

1 cup loosely packed fresh cilantro leaves and stems

1 Preheat the oven to 425 degrees F.

2 Place the onion, tomatoes, tomatillos, peppers, and garlic in a baking dish. Add the oil and ¼ teaspoon salt and toss to coat. Roast for 25 to 30 minutes, until the vegetables are very soft and starting to char.

3 Transfer the vegetables to a blender. Add the pepper flakes and cilantro and blend to the desired consistency. (For a salsa for tacos, I usually leave it with a little texture. For enchilada sauce, I blend until smooth.) Taste and adjust salt, if necessary. Store it in an airtight container in the refrigerator for up to 5 days or in the freezer for up to 3 months.

zhug SPICY GREEN SAUCE

If you like spicy food, you will like this sauce. Zhug (you can just pronounce it "zoog") is a Yemenite hot sauce that gives a bright burst of flavor and heat to any dish. It's a must swirled into hummus or drizzled on falafel, but don't relegate it to only Middle Eastern meals. We serve it on eggs, with roasted chicken, braised meat, and roasted vegetables. You can also use it as an alternative to salsa on tacos. · MAKES ABOUT 1 CUP

3 jalapeño chiles, stemmed and coarsely chopped

1 tablespoon My Spice Blend (page 262)

½ bunch fresh cilantro, coarsely chopped

½ bunch fresh parsley, coarsely chopped

Grated zest of 1 lemon

1 teaspoon sea salt

¼ cup extra virgin olive oil

1 Place all the ingredients in a food processor or high-speed blender. Pulse several times, until everything is blended but it's not a smooth paste. Pour into a jar, cap tightly, and store in the refrigerator.

2 Zhug will keep in the refrigerator for 5 days or in the freezer for up to 3 months. If you're using it from the freezer, let it thaw overnight in the refrigerator.

MAKE IT YOUR OWN

The heat of this zhug will depend on the heat of your jalapeños. If you like things very spicy, substitute serrano chiles.

gremolata

This simple and bright parsley sauce could also be labeled as a salsa verde or chimichurri and is a delicious accompaniment to almost anything. Spoon it over a seared steak, drizzle it on roasted vegetables, or use it as a sauce for fish. To keep the bright green color, only add the lemon juice right before serving. The acid in the lemon will turn the parsley a dull green. It will still taste good, but it won't look as pretty. MAKES ABOUT ¼ CUP

½ bunch flat-leaf parsley, leaves only (about 1 cup, loosely packed)

¼ teaspoon Aleppo-style pepper

¼ cup extra virgin olive oil

Grated zest and juice of 2 lemons

Sea salt

Finely chop the parsley. Combine the parsley, pepper, oil, lemon zest and juice, and ¼ teaspoon salt in a small bowl. Stir together. Taste and adjust salt as needed. Serve immediately. Without the lemon juice, the gremolata will keep in the refrigerator, covered, for up to 3 days.

MAKE IT YOUR OWN

You can vary the flavor of the gremolata by adding other ingredients: chopped olives or capers for a briny punch, sumac, or grated Parmigiano-Reggiano. You could also substitute basil or tarragon for some of the parsley, which is especially delicious on fish.

crispy shiitake chips

We go through weeks where we make these shiitake chips every single night. They are delicious as a snack, right off the pan. We also use them to top noodle bowls, on pasta, or add into any dish that could use that umami flavor. Either discard the stems or freeze them to use in chicken or vegetable stock. · MAKES ABOUT 1 CUP

8 ounces shiitake mushrooms, stemmed

2 to 3 tablespoons extra virgin olive oil

⅛ to ¼ teaspoon sea salt

⅛ teaspoon Aleppo-style pepper or red pepper flakes

1 Preheat the oven to 425 degrees F. Line a baking sheet with parchment paper.

2 Tear the mushroom caps into halves or quarters, depending on their size. Place the pieces on the baking sheet. Drizzle with the olive oil and sprinkle with salt to taste and the pepper. Using your hands, toss to coat the mushrooms. Spread out the mushroom in a single layer. (Make sure they are distributed evenly over the sheet pan and none are overlapping.)

3 Place the baking sheet on the bottom rack of the oven and bake for about 20 minutes, until the mushrooms are browned and crispy to the touch. You may have to remove some of the mushrooms as they get done, as they tend to dehydrate and crisp at different rates.

4 Transfer the mushrooms to a bowl and snack immediately. As they sit, they will lose their crispness, but they are still delicious as a snack or added to other dishes. Store any leftovers in an airtight container in the refrigerator for up to 5 days.

fresh chile harissa

Elie and I went on a day date to Seattle and had lunch at The London Plane, one of our favorites. I ordered baked eggs, which came with a fresh chile harissa. I immediately went home and tried to recreate that fiery, flavorful sauce in my kitchen. This harissa is brighter and more spoonable than a harissa made with dried chiles. It's delicious with eggs, as part of a mezze platter, over roasted vegetables or meats, and as an ingredient in dips. It's lovely stirred into Shakshuka (page 63), or as a topping on pizza. · MAKES ABOUT 2 CUPS

2 red bell peppers

1 poblano pepper

4 Fresno chiles

2 serrano chiles

1 tablespoon My Spice Blend (page 262)

1 teaspoon sweet paprika

2 teaspoons sea salt

Grated zest and juice of 1 lemon (about 3 tablespoons juice)

3 tablespoons extra virgin olive oil

1 Preheat the broiler to high.

2 Arrange the bell peppers, poblano, Fresnos, and serranos on a rimmed baking sheet and place under the broiler. Char the peppers and chiles, turning occasionally, until all sides are evenly blackened, about 5 minutes for the smaller peppers and 8 minutes for the bell peppers.

3 Transfer the peppers and chiles to a large glass or metal bowl. Cover the bowl with plastic wrap to allow them to steam and cool for about 20 minutes.

4 Peel off and discard the charred skin. It's okay if some of it doesn't come off. Remove and discard the stems and seeds. (You may want to wear gloves to protect your hands.) Place the flesh in a high-speed blender. Add the spice mix, paprika, salt, lemon zest and juice, and olive oil. Blend until smooth. Transfer the harissa to a glass jar and store in the refrigerator for up to 1 week or in the freezer for up to 3 months.

labneh

A thick yogurt cheese, labneh is delicious spread on bread or as a creamy base for roasted vegetables. I will often fill a shallow bowl with labneh, drizzle the top with olive oil, add either za'atar or sumac, and serve it with Sourdough Flatbread (page 34) as a snack before dinner. · MAKES ABOUT 2 CUPS

One 32-ounce container whole milk Greek yogurt

Grated zest of 1 lemon

1 teaspoon fresh lemon juice

½ teaspoon sea salt

1 Whisk together all the ingredients in a medium bowl.

2 Line a large sieve with three or four layers of cheesecloth and place over a bowl. The bowl should be a size so that the sieve can sit comfortably on the top without tipping, but the bottom of the sieve should not touch the bottom of the bowl.

3 Scrape the yogurt mixture into the sieve and cover with another layer of cheesecloth. Place the bowl in the refrigerator and let the labneh drain for 12 to 24 hours. It should be very thick. Transfer the labneh to an airtight container and store in the refrigerator for up to a week.

homemade mayonnaise

Honestly, I don't always make my own mayonnaise. But sometimes it's worth the extra effort, like when I'm making the Pimiento Cheese on page 81 or the Deviled Eggs on page 82. While many recipes call for using a food processor to make mayonnaise, I find whipping by hand makes the mayonnaise less likely to separate. The Dijon mustard also helps to emulsify the mayonnaise. · MAKES ABOUT 1 CUP

1 large egg yolk, at room temperature

1 teaspoon Dijon mustard

¼ teaspoon sea salt

2 tablespoons fresh lemon juice

1 tablespoon apple cider vinegar

1 teaspoon cold water

¾ cup avocado oil or mild-flavored extra virgin olive oil

Put the egg yolk, mustard, salt, lemon juice, vinegar, and water in a medium bowl. Whisk until very frothy. Whisking constantly, slowly add the oil, drop by drop, until the mixture starts to thicken. Once the mayonnaise starts to emulsify, finish adding the oil in a slow, steady stream, whisking constantly. Transfer the mayonnaise to a jar, cover tightly, and store in the refrigerator. Use within 1 week.

compote of any berry

We live in berry country. Abundant blackberry brambles invade every hillside and roadside, providing ample snacking opportunities in the peak of summer. We're surrounded by blueberry, strawberry, and raspberry farms, and annual trips to the farms reward us with buckets of fresh local berries. There are only so many berries you can eat before they spoil, so I end up turning them into a simple fruit sauce and storing it in small jars in the refrigerator or freezer. A berry compote is delicious spooned over ice cream, added to oatmeal, as a topping for yogurt and granola, or with pancakes or waffles. I love the vanilla bean in this compote, but you don't have to use it. Vary this recipe by adding other spices (cinnamon, cardamom, or star anise) or different sweeteners (maple syrup, honey). If you like your compote sweeter, just add more sugar. PHOTOGRAPH ON PAGE 50 · MAKES ABOUT 2 CUPS

4 cups berries

¼ cup coconut sugar

Grated zest and juice of 1 lemon

⅛ teaspoon sea salt

1 small vanilla bean

1 Combine the berries, sugar, lemon zest and juice, and salt in a medium pot. Using the tip of a knife, split the vanilla bean in half lengthwise. Using the flat blade of the knife, scrape out the vanilla bean seeds and add them to the pot. (Tuck the used vanilla bean into a small jar of sugar and store. The vanilla will perfume the sugar.)

2 Turn the heat to medium. Using the back of a wooden spoon, begin to mash the fruit. As the mixture comes to a simmer, the sugar will begin to melt. Stir the berries and sugar together. Let the berries simmer for about 10 minutes, adding a little water if the compote is too dry and sticks. Continue to stir and mash the berries until you get the desired consistency.

3 Let the compote cool, then transfer to a jar. Cover and store in the refrigerator for up to 5 days or in the freezer for up to 3 months.

vanilla bean whipped cream

There's something remarkably special about the flavor and perfume of real vanilla beans. It can't be replicated. However, whipped cream is delicious any way you make it, so if you don't have vanilla beans, substitute vanilla extract. PHOTOGRAPH ON PAGE 255 · MAKES ABOUT 4 CUPS

2 cups heavy whipping cream, cold

1 to 2 tablespoons gluten-free powdered sugar, depending on how sweet you want it

Seeds scraped from 1 vanilla bean or 1 teaspoon pure vanilla extract

Pour the cream into a chilled bowl. Add the sugar and vanilla. Whip with a whisk just until soft peaks form, but the cream still slides off a spoon. (You want the cream to be able to softly drape over the cake or pie you're serving it on.) Place in an airtight container and store in the refrigerator for up to 8 hours.

vegetable stock

I use vegetable stock when I'm cooking for my plant-based friends or family members, or when I want a lighter, more delicate flavor than chicken stock. I also make this when I don't have chicken stock on hand, as vegetable stock can be ready in an hour. This stock calls for fresh vegetables, but I often supplement them with vegetable scraps from the freezer. Any time I'm chopping vegetables, I put all the bits and scraps in a reusable food storage bag in the freezer. My freezer is always full of bits of onion, mushroom stems, and fennel fronds. It's also a great place to stash herbs that are getting ready to turn. All perfect for stock. I also add spices to my stock, which are optional. The cumin, coriander and fennel seeds provide flavor, and they also aid in digestion. ▪ MAKES 4 TO 5 QUARTS

1 Put the onion, garlic, carrots, celery, fennel, mushroom stems, if using, the parsley, thyme, bay leaves, peppercorns, and cumin, coriander, and fennel seeds in a large stockpot or Dutch oven. Add the water, enough to completely cover all the vegetables. Bring to a boil, then reduce to a simmer. Simmer the stock for about an hour, until flavorful.

2 Strain the stock through a fine-mesh sieve into a clean container. (Discard the solids.) Let the stock cool to room temperature.

3 Pour or ladle the stock into quart-sized glass jars. Cover tightly and store in the refrigerator for up to 1 week or in the freezer for up to 3 months.

1 large onion, unpeeled, halved

3 or 4 cloves garlic, peeled

2 carrots

4 stalks celery

Stalks and fronds of 1 head fennel

Up to 1 cup shiitake mushroom stems (optional)

½ bunch fresh parsley

5 or 6 sprigs fresh thyme

2 bay leaves

6 to 8 black peppercorns

1 tablespoon cumin seeds

1 tablespoon coriander seeds

1 tablespoon fennel seeds

1½ tablespoons sea salt

6 quarts filtered water, plus more if needed

chicken stock

A.K.A. CHICKEN BONE BROTH

Bone broth has become quite trendy in the past few years, but it's nothing more than a stock cooked long enough to extract all the nourishing collagen from the bones of the chicken. Bone broth is a good source of protein, is easy to digest, and can be very healing for those with gut issues. You can absolutely make this stock with the leftovers from a purchased rotisserie chicken. To get the most flavorful bone broth, make sure there is still some meat left on the bones. · MAKES 4 TO 5 QUARTS

Meat scraps and bones from 1 roasted chicken (such as Slow-Roasted Chicken, page 195)

1 large onion, unpeeled, halved

3 or 4 cloves garlic, peeled

2 carrots

1 parsnip

4 stalks celery

Stalks and fronds of 1 head fennel

½ bunch fresh parsley

5 or 6 sprigs fresh thyme

2 bay leaves

6 to 8 black peppercorns

1 tablespoon cumin seed

1 tablespoon coriander seeds

1 tablespoon fennel seeds

1 ½ tablespoons sea salt

6 quarts filtered water, plus more if needed

1 Put the chicken meat and bones, onion, garlic, carrots, parsnip, celery, fennel, parsley, thyme, bay leaves, peppercorns, cumin, coriander, and fennel seeds, and the salt in a large stockpot or Dutch oven. Add the water, enough to completely cover all the bones and vegetables. Bring to a boil, then reduce to a simmer. Skim off any foam or impurities that rise to the surface.

2 Simmer the stock, uncovered, for at least 2 hours and up to 24 hours. The longer you simmer it, the more gelatin will be extracted from the cartilage and the more nutritious the stock. If you are going to cook the stock for 24 hours, I suggest covering the pot and transferring it to a 275 degree F oven.

3 Strain the stock through a fine-mesh sieve into a clean container. (Discard the solids.) Let the stock cool to room temperature.

4 Pour or ladle the stock into quart-sized glass jars. Cover tightly and store in the refrigerator for up to 1 week or in the freezer for up to 3 months.

gluten-free sourdough starter

Don't be afraid of sourdough! Maintaining a gluten-free sourdough starter is quite easy. Once you have a sourdough starter in your refrigerator, you can experiment with so many different recipes—making breads, and adding the sourdough discard to muffins, cakes, cookies, and crackers. For the most part, I keep a sourdough starter made with brown rice flour. Brown rice flour has a neutral flavor and is easy to find in most supermarkets (or online). However, sometimes I want a heartier flavor, and I transition the starter to buckwheat (explained below). If you want to create a gluten-free sourdough culture from scratch, I give you simple instructions here. Alternatively, I have used the sourdough culture from Cultures for Health with great success. Ordering information is in the Resources section.

Building a Sourdough Starter

Day 1: Whisk together **1 cup (140 grams) brown rice flour** and **¾ cup (170 grams) filtered water** in a glass bowl. Cover with a clean kitchen towel and let sit at room temperature for 24 hours.

Day 2: Add another **⅓ cup (45 grams) brown rice flour** and **¼ cup (40 grams) filtered water** to the mixture in the bowl and whisk to combine. Cover with the towel and let sit at room temperature for another 24 hours.

Day 3: Repeat Day 2. The mixture should be starting to bubble and smell yeasty.

Day 4: Repeat Day 2 again. Cover and leave at room temperature for the final 24 hours.

Day 5: After leaving it for another 24 hours, the starter should be bubbly and puffy and ready to use. Transfer the starter to a clean 1-quart glass jar. Cover and keep in the refrigerator until ready to use.

Storing the Starter

I like to keep my sourdough starter in the refrigerator. Keeping the starter cold slows down the fermentation process, letting you go longer between feedings. As long as you feed your starter once a week or so, it should stay healthy and vibrant. If you're away from home for longer, just feed it a few times upon your return before using it in a recipe. Sourdough starters are remarkably resilient.

Feeding the Starter

To feed the starter, measure a heaping ¾ cup (250 grams) of the sourdough starter into a bowl. Add 1 cup (140 grams) superfine brown rice flour and 3/4 cup (170 grams) water and whisk well. (This maintains a sourdough starter with about 120 percent hydration, meaning for every 100 grams of flour there is 120 grams of water. This hydration level gives a more pronounced sour flavor in the baked goods.) Transfer to a clean glass jar and cover with cheesecloth. Leave the jar on the counter for 6 to 8 hours, until the starter has doubled in height. Cover and transfer to the refrigerator.

Transition the Starter to Buckwheat

Once the starter has been established, you can easily transition the starter to buckwheat. Just start feeding the starter with buckwheat flour, using the same volume or weights as for brown rice flour. After a few feedings, the starter will be almost completely buckwheat.

Using the Starter

For baking bread, flatbread, or pizza, use active starter, or a starter that was fed the day before you are going to bake. For cookies, cakes, pancakes, and other recipes, the starter does not need to be active. In a lot of cookbooks (including this one), you will see this referred to as the "discard"—what you remove before feeding the starter. However, I seldom throw away starter. Once a week, I make pancakes (page 52), waffles (page 53) or another recipe using the discard.

Troubleshooting

If you see a layer of clear liquid on the top, that is alcohol that was formed by the hungry starter. Just stir it back in or pour it off and feed your starter normally.

If you see mold growing on your starter, throw it away and build another starter. To prevent mold, store your starter in the refrigerator, feed it regularly, and always use clean jars and utensils.

acknowledgments

It takes a village to produce a cookbook, and I am so very grateful for mine. I have such gratitude for the people in my life who gave their hearts and time to make this dream come true.

First, to Matt Land, my photographer and friend, thank you for the hundreds of cheerful hours spent in my kitchen taking photographs and drinking wine, and hundreds more in the editing room. Your eternal quest for the sun made all the difference.

Steve Moore, thank you for believing in me enough to introduce me to Christine Chitnis. Christine, I could not have made this book without you. Thank you for holding my hand and thinking through every step of this process. Your wisdom, insights and honesty were such a gift.

To my copyeditor, Suzanne Fass, I am in awe of your talent. Your attention to detail is unmatched.

Jan Derevjanik, thank you for answering all my questions, rearranging photos, and generously giving your advice as I stumbled through this creative process. Thank you for designing such a beautiful book. It is exactly how I dreamed it would be.

To my recipe testers, Adan and Rosin Baez, Alison Teng, Alissa Lawton, Anne-Marie Faiola, Annie Sorich, Bonnie Kaemingk, Cerise Noah, Christie McMillan, Daniel Ziv, Emily Ruzzamenti, Hannah and Nova Atkins, Heather Ouilette, Jean Martheleur, Jenelle Johansson and Daniel Zyvitski, Jennifer Morena, Kari Leonard, Kat Stiger, Kathleen Haynes, Kyle Fuller VonFeldt, Lael Dayton, Megan Trout, Michele Dotson, Missy Crovetti, Molly Daniels, Morgan Gaunt, Nancy Grayson, Sarah Formica, Sarah Murphy-Kangas, Tanya

Comerford and Theresa Mertens—thank you! I cannot adequately express how much your time in the kitchen—and your feedback—meant to me.

McKenzie Jones, you have been such an important part of my journey. I love you. And to so many dear friends and family, your support and encouragement makes me feel seen and loved.

Mom, you have always been my greatest cheerleader. Thank you for playing with Theo while I cooked, for always staying late to wash the dishes, enthusiastically accepting all the leftovers, and telling every person you know about this book. I appreciate you. Dad, thank you for instilling in me a love of good food, for feeding me oysters and caviar instead of 'kid food.' I always wanted to eat whatever you were eating.

Theo, spending time in the kitchen with you is a dream come true. Thank you for always giving an enthusiastic "yes!" when I ask if you want to cook with me. As you read this years from now, I want you to know that you truly helped! You have great taste, and you made recipes better. The gift of being your Mom is my greatest joy.

Elie, my love. I don't know how I got so lucky. Thank you for believing in me—for encouraging and supporting this monumental project. Because of you, I feel confident sending this book into the world. But mostly, thank you for that sparkle in your eyes when you look at me. For our ridiculous love. I love you so much.

Lastly, thank you, dear reader. However this book made its way into your hands, I hope you find inspiration here, that this book helps you nourish the people you love.

resources

SUSTAINABILITY

Environmental Working Group
www.ewg.org

Monterey Bay Aquarium
Seafood Watch
www.seafoodwatch.org

CHILI PEPPERS, SPICES and TAHINI

Burlap & Barrel
Aleppo-style pepper, sumac,
za'atar, turmeric and other
spices
www.burlapandbarrel.com

Diaspora Co.
www.diasporaco.com

GIT USA Imports
Al Arz Tahini (Whole Sesame)
www.gitfood.com/al-arz

World Spice Merchants
chili peppers
www.worldspice.com

SALT

Jacobsen Salt
www.jacobsensalt.com

San Juan Island Sea Salt
www.sanjuanislandseasalt.com

GRAINS and FLOURS

Amazon
Jiva Organics Psyllium Husk
Powder
www.amazon.com

Anson Mills
heirloom cornmeal,
grits and polenta
www.ansonmills.com

Authentic Foods
superfine brown rice flour,
sorghum and millet flours
www.glutenfree-supermarket.
com

Bob's Red Mill
www.bobsredmill.com

Cultures for Health
sourdough starter
shop.culturesfor-
health.com/products/
gluten-free-sourdough-starter

Holmquist Hazelnuts
hazelnut flour
www.holmquisthazelnuts.com

Masienda
heirloom masa, tortilla press
www.masienda.com

PANTRY ITEMS

Hyperion Herbs
herbs and teas
www.hyperionherbs.com

Thrive Market
spray ghee, coconut oil
and other pantry items
www.thrivemarket.com

KNIVES, POTS and PANS

Blu Skillet Ironware
carbon steel skillets
made in Seattle
www.bluskilletironware.com

Knifewear on Main
www.knifewear.com

Le Creuset
enameled cast iron
www.lecreuset.com

Lodge
cast iron and enameled cast
iron
www.lodgecastiron.com

Smithey
carbon steel skillets
www.smithey.com

FOOD STORAGE

Stasher Bags
www.stasherbag.com

Bee's Wrap
www.beeswrap.com

LINENS, TABLEWARE and VINTAGE FINDS

Chairish
www.chairish.com

Creative Women
www.creativewomen.net

First Dibs
www.1stdibs.com

Hedgerow
www.hedgerowedison.com

Workshop
www.workshoppnw.com

INTUITIVE EATING and BODY NEUTRALITY

*How to Raise an Intuitive
Eater: Raising the Next
Generation with Food and Body
Confidence* by Sumner Brooks
and Amee Severson.

*More Than A Body: Your Body Is
an Instrument, Not an Ornament*
by Lexie Kite and Lindsay Kite.

about the author

Lisa Samuel is a wife, mother, nutritionist, cookbook author and creative. She designs (and cooks for!) dinners, workshops and retreats. Her cooking is deeply influenced by her childhood in Kentucky, her husband's Israeli heritage and their travels.

The road to her current career was long. But, the common thread throughout her professional life—from community health strategist to lifestyle consultant and personal chef to registered dietitian nutritionist— is her passion for food, community, and the life-changing conversations that come from gathering for a meal.

Early in her professional life, she worked at Good Morning America. She has been a regular guest contributor to Your Morning Saturday on WTOL-TV, and was the host of a local television talk show, Partnerships for Success. At Wright State University Center for Urban and Public Affairs, she became a highly sought-after expert on the design of healthy communities. In 2010, she went back to school to become a registered dietitian nutritionist. With her business partner, she launched a nutrition marketing and consulting company, providing social media strategy and management, spokesperson and media outreach, recipe development, public speaking, and workshops.

She holds a degree in biology from Columbia University, an MBA in marketing from Wright State University, and a completed certification as a registered dietitian nutritionist (RDN) from Bastyr University.

She resides in beautiful northwest Washington with her husband, Elie, and young son, Theo.

index

Published in the United States in
2022 by Lisa Samuel, Bellingham, WA.

Printed in Italy by Graphicom.

Library of Congress Control Number: 2022912865

ISBN: 979-8-218-03581-5

First Edition

Photography: Matthew Land
Design: Jan Derevjanik
Copyeditor and Index: Suzanne Fass

Thank you to Sarah Williamson
for capturing us at work.